A Multisensory Philosophy
of Perception

Casey O'Callaghan is Professor of Philosophy at Washington University in St. Louis.

T0355258

A Multisensory Philosophy of Perception

CASEY O'CALLAGHAN

OXFORD
UNIVERSITY PRESS

OXFORD
UNIVERSITY PRESS

Great Clarendon Street, Oxford, OX2 6DP,
United Kingdom

Oxford University Press is a department of the University of Oxford.
It furthers the University's objective of excellence in research, scholarship,
and education by publishing worldwide. Oxford is a registered trade mark of
Oxford University Press in the UK and in certain other countries

Published in the United States of America by Oxford University Press
198 Madison Avenue, New York, NY 10016, United States of America

British Library Cataloguing in Publication Data
Data available

Library of Congress Cataloging in Publication Data
Data available

ISBN 978-0-19-883370-3 (Hbk.)
ISBN 978-0-19-285963-1 (Pbk.)

For Frances

Preface

Sense perception is the most vivid form of lived human consciousness. You may see the flash of a cardinal taking flight, hear the thumping of a hammer, or detect a faint citrusy smell. Through our senses, we encounter the world. We believe what we see, and our senses guide what we do. The senses are central to distinctively human aesthetic experience. Reflecting on perceptual impairments reveals how much each of our senses matters.

Understanding the interface between the mind and the world has animated a philosophical tradition stemming from Plato's *Theaetetus* and Aristotle's *De Anima*. From the early modern era to the present, philosophical thinking about perception and its significance has been shaped to a remarkable extent by attention to vision. However, vision does not stand alone. At most waking moments, people perceive using their other senses. We hear, smell, taste, and touch our surroundings. Nothing guarantees that what we say about vision extends neatly to the other senses.

Recently, philosophers have challenged claims about perception and perceptual consciousness founded on vision alone. For instance, I have argued that the temporal nature of sounds and the ways sounds occupy pitch space confound "visuocentric" thinking about the objects of perception. Attention exclusively to vision blinds us to the scope and nature of what we perceive. This has implications not just for philosophy but also for art and aesthetics, sound studies, and music theory.

Other philosophers have looked beyond vision to touch, bodily perception, olfaction, and taste for insights about how our senses acquaint us with the world. This has reoriented the philosophy of perception, enriching how we understand spatial awareness, what it is for an experience to represent, and whether brain processes could fully explain sensory consciousness. What goes for vision does not always go for our other senses.

Still, no sense is an island. Each sense operates against the background of others, and people typically perceive using multiple senses. Indeed, the most striking discovery in the cognitive sciences of perception during the past two decades is that sensory systems interact extensively with each other.

Sensory interactions sometimes lead to surprising perceptual illusions. Some people hear sounds as colored, feel touch from sounds, or taste shapes. Synesthesia has inspired artists from Kandinsky and Hockney to Pharrell Williams (*Seeing Sounds*). Some say it helps explain metaphor, creativity, and the origins of language itself. However, synesthesia is rare, affecting just 5 percent of the population.

Perceptual science has shown that sensory interactions are far more widespread. Seeing a talking face can change how speech sounds—for instance, you may seem to hear /da/ rather than /ba/ just because you see someone articulate /ga/. In the sound-induced flash effect, hearing two clicks makes one flash look like two. In ventriloquism, you hear the sound's location differently because you see the dummy. Crossmodal illusions are pervasive. They occur in typical perceiving subjects across a wide range of domains with numerous sensory pairings. Just as visual illusions illuminate how vision functions, crossmodal illusions show how the senses work together.

Crossmodal illusions are surprising. One sense can reshape what you perceive with another. This conflicts with common sense, which presupposes that our senses are separate. What remains unclear—what the science does not settle—is how sensory interactions are reflected in the conscious lives of perceiving subjects, and why they matter. Answering these questions requires confronting philosophical questions about perception and perceptual consciousness.

This book addresses these questions. It explores the multisensory nature of perception and its theoretical and philosophical significance. Against philosophical orthodoxy, which treats perceptual consciousness as a collection of experiences associated with vision, hearing, touch, taste, and smell, this book contends that human perceptual consciousness is constitutively and irreducibly multisensory. It develops an account of multisensory perception in which coordination and cooperation among the senses improves and augments human perceptual capacities. The normal and optimal functioning of each sense requires the support of multiple senses.

According to this account, the coordinated use of multiple senses enhances and extends human perceptual capacities in three critical ways. First, crossmodal perceptual illusions reveal hidden sensory interactions that perform multisensory functions. But such interactions are far more widespread. Typically, they make each sense more reliable and thus a better source of evidence about the environment. The cost is predictable illusions. Multisensory interactions serve an important purpose by improving perception's coherence, accuracy, and reliability. Spatial hearing improves when it listens to vision, and lipreading supports speech comprehension as much as a good hearing aid. Such perceptual improvements can reverberate as epistemic advantages. Believing your senses works better when your senses work together. More reliable perception means more reliable cognition. Multisensory epistemology thus reaches beyond what meets the eyes and the ears. What is puzzling is that crossmodal recalibrations and illusions typically go unnoticed—you may not realize that what you see affects what you hear.

Second, the joint use of multiple senses discloses more of the world, giving us conscious access in perception to novel features and qualities. New aspects of the world are perceptible only thanks to the coordinated use of multiple senses. Umpires in baseball are trained to tell whether a baserunner is safe or out by watching the foot touch the bag while listening for the sound of the ball striking the glove. Umpires are sensitive to perceptible intermodal temporal order. At the movies, images on screen appear to make the sounds you hear—a misaligned soundtrack is grating. Something visible can perceptibly bear audible features. Or, thanks to the way smell, taste, and somatosensation work together, novel qualities, such as flavors—the *mintiness* of mint, the *spiciness* of capsaicin—are experienced only multisensorily.

Multisensory perception therefore does more than improve the testimony of the senses. Sometimes one's multisensory capabilities are evident. The joint use of our senses enables new forms of perceptual awareness. As a consequence, perceptual consciousness is not always specific to one sense or another. Contrary to the received view, this book argues that the phenomenal character of sensory consciousness itself is irreducibly multisensory. This contravenes a central assumption in the empiricist philosophical tradition, according to which each experience has a distinctive sense-specific character. Sometimes, perceptual consciousness itself is ineliminably multisensory.

Third, each sense depends on the influence of others. Multisensory perception even reshapes unisensory perception. Perceptual capacities associated with one sense depend on other senses. Perceptual learning can enable us auditorily to detect features that otherwise are accessible only through sight. Crossmodal parasitism can infuse an auditory experience with characteristics inherited from vision. So, one sense can change over time thanks to another. This means the auditory experience of a congenitally blind person may differ from someone who sees. A surprising conclusion follows. While a deficit in one sense can enhance another sense, deficits in one sense also can ramify as deficits elsewhere. Famously, spatial hearing improves with blindness, but by my account blindness also yields hearing deficits. Appreciating crossmodal plasticity makes room for a novel account of sensory enhancement using prosthetics, such as cochlear implants, and substitution devices.

Sensory plasticity and crossmodal dependence present a dilemma for the sense-by-sense approach. Either it ignores what other senses contribute to sight and hearing, or it excises each sense from the others, thereby throttling back its capabilities and altering its character.

The implication is that no one sense—not even vision itself—can be understood entirely in isolation from the others. This overturns a prevailing unisensory approach to sense perception and perceptual consciousness, which assumes that each sense can be theorized in isolation or in abstraction from the others. Perceiving is not just seeing, hearing, touching, tasting, and smelling at the same time. No complete account of perceptual consciousness or its role can be formulated without confronting the multisensory nature and character of perception. This sets the stage for a revisionary, multisensory philosophy of perception.

Contents

Acknowledgments

Immeasurable thanks to all of the philosophers, scientists, and friends who thought through the ideas in this book with me. I am grateful for your time, your patience, and your insights. Several of you read with care the full draft manuscript and offered extensive feedback. I owe you my sincere thanks for your detailed comments and challenging questions, which were invaluable.

The Institute of Philosophy, in University of London's School of Advanced Study, hosted me for a summer visiting fellowship during which I began work on this book. A National Endowment for the Humanities Fellowship and corresponding research leave from Washington University in St. Louis enabled me to finish it. I gratefully acknowledge this generous support.

1

Introduction

A core tension animates this book. Most times, typical human subjects perceive using multiple senses. Out walking, I see people, trees, colors, and motion. I hear chatter, footsteps, and rustling leaves; smell coffee, and petrichor after rain; feel a breeze, the brush of a shoulder, or mud on the ground. I taste my coffee's acidity, its earthiness. We use our senses together to navigate and learn about the world.

Most theorizing about perception, however, is unisensory. Philosophy and science have focused on one sense at a time. Researchers take pains to secure a quiet setting, isolate a tactual stimulus, or tease out visual experiences from a subject's conscious life. This sense-by-sense approach respects an analytic, dissective approach to sense perception.

This book is about multisensory perception. It is about how our senses work together, in contrast with how they work separately and independently. In particular, it is about how one sense can impact another and about how the joint use of multiple senses enables novel forms of perception and experience. And it is about why this matters. It describes the most critical respects in which perception is multisensory. And it addresses the consequences.

My thesis is that the coordinated use of multiple senses enhances and extends human perceptual capacities. This makes possible novel varieties of perceptual consciousness. These forms of perception illuminate perception's nature and purpose but escape unisensory theorizing.

Perceiving is not just a matter of our several senses working on their own, in parallel. This has both negative and positive consequences. On the negative side, it makes trouble for unisensory approaches. Even if one's focus is a single sense, such as vision alone, investigating one sense at a time risks either an incomplete or a distorted understanding of perception and perceptual consciousness. Since nearly every philosophical account of perception until recently has focused on one sense or another, this consequence is far-reaching.

A Multisensory Philosophy of Perception. Casey O'Callaghan, Oxford University Press (2019).
© Casey O'Callaghan. DOI: 10.1093/oso/9780198833703.001.0001

On the positive side, coordination among senses can improve our ability to negotiate the environment. Even though it causes predictable crossmodal illusions, it nevertheless can make perception more coherent and more reliable. It thereby affects one's epistemic position. Moreover, it enriches perceptual consciousness, both at a time and over time, when compared with parallel unisensory perception. It reveals more of the world. Accordingly, multisensory perception has practical, epistemic, and aesthetic benefits.

Appreciating how our senses work together—how they impact, influence, and cooperate with each other—brings into focus a more accurate, more nuanced understanding of perception and perceptual consciousness. This reveals new puzzles, and it illuminates old ones. It ought to shape any future philosophy of perception.

This chapter sets the stage. It presents the book's plan of attack and its central themes. First, it describes unisensory paradigms for investigating perception in science and in philosophy, and it presents the evidence. Next, it introduces the critical respects in which perception is multisensory and explains why this is a problem for sense-by-sense theorizing. Finally, it raises the central questions any multisensory philosophy of perception must face, and it outlines the answers and arguments that follow.

1.1 Unisensory Approaches

Theorizing about perception in science and in philosophy until recently has been overwhelmingly unisensory. By this I mean that it has proceeded one sense at a time. It has adopted a sense-by-sense approach to perceptual capacities, processes, and consciousness. This means investigating perception in unisensory contexts and abstracting phenomena associated with one sense from what occurs in other senses. This treatment reflects two implicit assumptions. The first is that each sense is explanatorily independent from the others. The second is that the sum of theorizing about individual senses yields a complete account of sensory perception.

These claims require explanation and defense. In what follows, I'll present a case that paradigms of theorizing about perception in science and in philosophy have been unisensory. Then, I'll describe what makes this is a problem.

1.1.1 Science

The empirical problem of perception is how stimulation of sensory receptors leads to perception of the world. Perception science answers by describing processes in which information is extracted from sensory stimulation in a way that enables its use in recognizing, acting, attending, remembering, thinking, and imagining. Its aim is to account for human performance.

This task has two sides. The first is to determine which perceptual capacities typical human beings possess. Which sorts of things and features can we detect and differentiate, and in what conditions? Psychophysics measures our capacity to discern and make use of features in the environment.

The other is to describe and to characterize the nature of the processes that are responsible. What grounds the capacity to perceive? Perceptual psychology and neuroscience each aim to specify which processes extract information from a stimulus and make it available for use in cognition and action. Cognitive psychology describes abstract functions that can be realized in differing physical systems, while neuroscience favors neural mechanisms.

One celebrated paradigm is Marr's computational theory of vision. According to Marr (1982), the solution to the empirical problem of human vision has three components. The first articulates the computational problem vision solves. What are its inputs and outputs? This amounts to characterizing visual capacities. The second is an algorithm. How do things function inside the black box? This is a picture of how vision solves the computational problem. The third is its implementation in the brain. Which hidden processes occur to make human visual capacities manifest? This is a description of neural activity that realizes vision.

This approach to perception is analytical, in two respects. One is vertical. A capacity to perceive is broken down into stages, analyzed as a series of subcapacities, exercised step by step to perform a perceptual task. Motivated by the observation that Gibson (1966) underestimates the difficulty of direct information pickup (29–30; see also Fodor and Pylyshyn 1981), Marr says seeing objects first relies on extracting information about edges from illumination gradients, followed by discerning boundaries, surfaces, and three-dimensional shapes of solids. A scientific account of perception requires describing each step in the process by which the empirical problem of perception is solved.

The other is horizontal. Perception science carves perception at distinct senses, and it dissects each sense according to its constituent capacities. Marr offers a theory of vision alone, not perception overall. One part of this is an account of how vision makes extended objects available for cognition. Color perception is another part of vision (see, for instance, Maloney and Wandell 1986). Other senses mirror this approach. Marr's target, Gibson (1966), a champion of haptic touch, devotes two chapters delineating its capacities and components. Bregman (1990)—the Marr of hearing—describes the means by which audition carves acoustical scenes into distinct audible objects and features. Bregman articulates how individuating sound streams relies on both simultaneous grouping and discerning good continuity in frequency, timbre, and timing.

In these respects, Marr's paradigm is representative. And, in each respect, perception science at large until recently has remained predominantly unisensory. Typical practice in experimentation and explanation has treated perception using one sense rather than multiple senses. It has aimed to discover which capacities belong to a particular sense, such as vision, audition, or touch. And it has focused on specifying the details of capacities deployed using one sense at a time. Moreover, while it has often considered influences on perception from cognition, perception science typically has not considered at each stage of the perceptual process outside influences from other senses. Until the start of the twenty-first century, it has rarely addressed coordination within perception taking place between senses.

Consider the methodology. Experimental paradigms tend to investigate sense perception in unisensory contexts. In practice, this means presenting and varying a stimulus to one sense while holding fixed or trying to eliminate stimulation to other senses. For example, an audition researcher may measure responsiveness to a tone, rather than to a tone and flash combination, or to a tone presented with a busy visual scene. Or, an experimenter may just forget about the blindfold and ignore or abstract from any contributions vision makes to audition, assuming they are insignificant or irrelevant. Until recently—the past decade or two— little systematic attention has been devoted to perceptual contexts involving more than one sense, to the ways in which one sense influences another, and to coordination among senses.

Accordingly, inventories of perceptual capacities and accounts of perceptual processing have remained sense specific. By this I mean that they consider capacities only insofar as they do not rely on and remain uninformed by other senses, and they describe processes fixed by factors stemming only from within a given sensory pathway. In these respects, the science of perception has been chiefly unisensory.

As a consequence, the paradigms in perception science are unisensory. They fail to consider outside influences from other senses, or they ignore and abstract away from such influences. With a few noteworthy exceptions, including early work on speech perception, object perception, and ventriloquism, they do not address collaboration between senses or capacities that require senses to cooperate. Even contemporary Bayesian accounts first focused almost exclusively on vision, before turning to multisensory perception (see, for example, Mamassian et al. 2002).[1]

Unisensory approaches to perception science reveal two assumptions. The first is that the senses are explanatorily independent from each other. In particular, unisensory theorizing presumes that what a sense does in isolation matches what it does in a multisensory context. Any differences affect neither the principles according to which it functions nor its stock of capacities. Each sense is causally or functionally discrete.

---

[1] In vision science, some influential examples of unisensory theorizing from the past four decades include Gibson (1979); Marr (1982); Rock (1983); Treisman (1988); Milner and Goodale (1995); Rock (1997); Mack and Rock (1998); Palmer (1999); Pylyshyn (1999); O'Regan and Noë (2001). In audition science, noteworthy recent paradigms are Bregman (1990); Handel (1993); Blauert (1997).

Contemporary exceptions prior to 2000 include groundbreaking work on speech perception by McGurk and MacDonald (1976) and Fowler (1986), stemming from insights of Liberman et al. (1967); work on object perception and core cognition by Spelke (1990); and Bertelson (1999) on ventriloquism. Fodor's (1983) theoretical understanding of modular input systems as domain specific but not sense specific is trailblazing. Spence and Driver (2004) marks the watershed.

While not focused on perception science alone, Google's n-gram data is revealing. Prior to 1932, the n-gram viewer registers no occurrence in books of the term "multisensory." However, following a steady first trickle of uses, the share of occurrences of "multisensory" spikes roughly fivefold from 1964 to 1976 (during this time, "audition" roughly doubled its share, and "vision" was flat), before leveling and then roughly doubling from the mid 1990s through 2008 (during this period, "audition" increased its share roughly 20 percent, and "vision" was roughly flat). Nonetheless, in 2008, "vision" still had a share 271 times greater than "multisensory," and "audition" had six times the share of "multisensory" ("vision" thus was forty-five times more frequent than "audition" in 2008). (https://books.google.com/ngrams, accessed February 22, 2018)

The second is that the sense-by-sense approach is explanatorily complete. Perceptual capacities include just those associated with each of the respective senses. Perceptual processes involve only functions and mechanisms belonging to discrete modalities. Taken together, sense-specific accounts of perceiving with each of the respective senses exhaust the science of perception. What remains is for cognition. Put simply, Marr, Bregman, and their ilk suffice.

Recent approaches in perception science break from this tradition. For instance, predictive theories treat perception as a hierarchy of distinct states that probabilistically model incoming stimulation and detect errors in order to guide revisions and updates (Hohwy 2013; Clark 2016). Such accounts, like other Bayesian approaches, may treat senses separately or jointly. Accordingly, they provide an attractive framework in which to address multisensory phenomena (see Chapter 2). Researchers during the twenty-first century increasingly have devoted attention to explaining perception in multisensory contexts.

1.1.2 Philosophy

The philosophical puzzle of perception is how to reconcile the possibility of illusions and hallucinations with the character of perceptual consciousness. Perception is a human subject's most intimate form of acquaintance with the environment. From a subject's perspective, things appear just set out in one's surroundings, accessible by means of the senses. But, appearances can be misleading, and things are not always as they seem. Nothing in principle rules out the possibility of a radical, wholesale hallucination that a subject could not tell apart from a typical, veridical perception.

The puzzle has metaphysical and epistemic facets. What is the relationship in which we stand to things and features during perceptual consciousness? Are we ever acquainted with things and features that do not depend on our own consciousness? How do we know? Can experiences enable and justify beliefs about things that are mind independent?

Answers concern the nature and role of experience. One main aim in philosophy of perception is to characterize the nature of perceptual consciousness. For instance, relationalist accounts hold that experience is a conscious sensory relation between a subject and a particular object or feature, requiring the presence of each. In representational accounts, experiences have satisfaction conditions that may be met or unmet. In some accounts, experiences are marked by a subject's consciously instantiating inherently qualitative properties, or qualia.[2]

Another aim in philosophy of perception is to describe the role of experiences. This includes the relationships between experiences and other sorts of mental phenomena. For instance, experiences cause memories, learning, and beliefs. It also is natural to think that experiences must be capable of rationally supporting beliefs. In one type of account, experiences do so just by presenting things to be a particular way. Others say experience itself is neutral, or that it relies on further assumptions to support empirical beliefs.

A related debate about the role of experiences concerns whether information from cognition ever directly affects perceptual consciousness. This bears on whether or not perception is an unbiased source of evidence. If preconceptions shape experiences, that may undermine the support any such "hijacked" experience provides (Siegel 2017).

Thus, the fundamental nature of perceptual consciousness, and the role of perception, especially in relation to sensation, thought, and action, are of particular concern to philosophers investigating perception.

Philosophy of perception deals with two aspects of perceptual consciousness. The first is awareness. By this, I mean the conscious grasp on an object or situation that perception affords. Perceiving makes things available to a subject in a way that enables that subject to recognize, conceptualize, demonstrate, imagine, remember, act, and otherwise cognize them. That conscious grasp is diagnosed in part by the psychological role it plays. Awareness figures critically in addressing epistemic questions about perceptual consciousness.

The other is phenomenality. Experiences are conscious episodes with phenomenal character. Phenomenal character comprises "what it is like" for a subject to undergo a conscious episode (Nagel 1974). How things

---

[2] While in this book I aim as far as possible to be neutral among such approaches—indeed, the book is designed to address concerns distinctive to each—my point in this section is that such accounts have been shaped by attempts to accommodate unisensory rather than multisensory phenomena.

are in consciousness from a subject's perspective is fixed by its phenomenal features. Experience, from a subject's perspective, is part of the philosophical puzzle of perception. Accurately specifying perceptual phenomenal character is a key part of evaluating solutions to the puzzle. Phenomenality also figures critically in addressing metaphysical questions about perceptual consciousness.

One can discern two respects in which philosophy of perception has been starkly unisensory in confronting each of these aspects of perceptual consciousness. The first is that it has focused predominantly on vision. Despite a pronounced recent turn to non-visual forms of perception, such as hearing, touch, and smell, most philosophical work addresses vision and visual consciousness. It is difficult to overstate the influence of thinking about sight and seeing in understanding perceptual awareness, perceptual phenomenality, and their causal and rational roles.

Focusing on vision alone risks overgeneralizing. Visuocentrism ignores counterexamples, novel phenomena, and salient features of awareness and phenomenal character drawn from other senses. Moreover, some good reasons suggest that vision is exceptional. A theory of vision thus should not pass for a general theory of perception. The philosophy of perception is more than the philosophy of seeing.

Nevertheless, I want to set aside visuocentrism. There is a second way in which philosophical work on perception is unisensory. Until recently, it has almost exclusively reflected a sense-by-sense approach. By this I mean that philosophers who investigate perception by and large address one sense at a time. Unisensory methodology treats vision, hearing, touch, taste, or smell in isolation or in abstraction from other senses.

A unisensory approach in philosophy of perception may involve examining what a sense does in a unisensory context or in response to varying a stimulus to just one sense. More frequently, it means attempting to extract from a multisensory episode what belongs to a target sense. The bulk of philosophical work on metaphysical and epistemic dimensions of perceptual awareness and phenomenology manifests this type of unisensory take.

Mostly, the sense-by-sense approach is unstated. The philosophy of perception subsists on examples of perceiving with one sense or another: seeing speckled hens, hearing speech sounds in familiar or foreign languages, smelling scents of roses, tasting Vegemite, or touching spheres and cubes. Even noteworthy works that do not focus on vision alone have taken perception one sense at a time (see, for instance, Matthen 2005).

Some philosophers are more explicit in adopting a sense-by-sense approach. Susanna Siegel's book, *The Contents of Visual Experience*, targets visual experiences this way:

> When you waterski you are in a conscious state with many facets. We can call your overall conscious state during the stretch of time that you are waterskiing your *overall experience*. Your overall experience includes seeing the boat and its surroundings, hearing its motor, feeling preoccupied, keeping your balance, and so on.... From the many facets of waterskiing, we can zoom in on the visual ones.... we can consider the overall experience as a collection of phenomenally conscious states and then ignore the non-visual ones.   (Siegel 2010, 19–21)

Siegel offers an account of isolable visual phenomenal states that can be carved out and theorized separately from other senses. This abstracts from the multisensory whole to treat visual experiences on their own.

In some cases, the unisensory approach is marked as an idealization. Nico Orlandi acknowledges this:

> There are also general questions concerning the independence of visual processing from the processing of other modalities. The issues pertaining to these questions are not always addressed by inferentialists. They are also neglected in this book where I operate under the idealization that the reconstruction of visual objects occurs somewhat independently of the influence of other sensory modalities.
>
> (Orlandi 2014, 28)

These examples illustrate a general trend. Philosophical questions about perception and perceptual consciousness are addressed by considering and describing forms of perception involving one sense at a time.

This is a unisensory approach to the philosophy of perception. Unisensory theorizing begins with the truism that we have multiple senses—multiple ways of perceiving the world. It then treats varieties of perceptual consciousness associated with each sense separately. It abstracts to isolate independent senses, or it analyzes the whole as a co-conscious sum of sense-specific parts. It considers the role of each sense on its own rather than among the senses working jointly. This sort of unisensory theorizing is my main target.[3]

The unisensory approach is reflected in philosophical accounts of awareness and phenomenality. For example, intentionalists generally treat experiences as relations to contents in a specific sensory mode, each of which is understood as akin to a distinctive propositional attitude. Intentionalists hold that an experience's phenomenal features are a subset of its intentional features. Thus, phenomenal features depend on a given sense modality. Some intentionalists maintain that content fixes phenomenal character only within a sensory modality. Intentionalists only recently have considered the consequences of forms of perception that rely on the joint use of multiple senses (for instance, Speaks 2015; Tye 2003).

Relationalists say experiences involve a subject's standing in a specific sensory relation to what is perceived (Brewer 2011). Seeing, hearing, touching, smelling, and tasting are distinctive sensory relations—distinct ways of perceiving corresponding to each of the various senses. Martin

---

[3] In philosophy, some influential examples of unisensory theorizing from the past four decades include Snowdon (1981); Peacocke (1983); Perkins (1983); Harman (1990); Crane (1992); Valberg (1992); McDowell (1994); Lycan (1996); Tye (2000); Byrne (2001); O'Regan and Noë (2001); Campbell (2002); Noë (2004); Matthen (2005); Pylyshyn (2007); Hill (2009); Burge (2010); Siegel (2010); Orlandi (2014); Dickie (2015); Siegel (2017); Schellenberg (2018). Recent examples of unisensory theorizing beyond vision include O'Callaghan (2007); Nudds and O'Callaghan (2009); Lycan (2000); Batty (2011); Richardson (2013); Fulkerson (2014). Some exceptions to unisensory theorizing since 2000 include Nudds (2001); O'Callaghan (2008); de Vignemont (2014), and essays in Bennett and Hill (2014); Stokes et al. (2015); Deroy (2017). Fodor (1983) was avant-garde.

Unisensory theorizing is clearest in the analytic tradition, and it traces to early modern empiricists, such as Locke and Hume. Notably, Carnap's phenomenalistic reconstruction in his *Aufbau* (1928) treats subjects' overall experiences as basic and unanalyzable, but abstracts to characterize classes of experiences corresponding to each sense, including vision (sections 61–94; see, especially, sections 67–8 and 85–6). Goodman's critical response in *The Structure of Appearance* (1951) instead begins with basic qualitative parts of experiences, or sensory atoms. "Qualia," for Goodman, "are to be such qualities as single phenomenal colors, sounds, degrees of warmth, moments, and visual locations" (156), which stand in a primitive relation of "togetherness" to form concrete particulars (158). Where Carnap abstracts to treat senses individually, Goodman constructs each sense from sense-specific qualia. According to Goodman, "Qualia [such as colors and sounds] that do not belong to the same sense realm never occur together" (159).

Among twentieth-century continental philosophers, Merleau-Ponty's *Phenomenology of Perception* (1945) is the most noteworthy exception to unisensory theorizing. Aristotle's *De Anima* (1984), which addresses the common sense, stands out in ancient philosophy.

(1992) is skeptical whether any unifying account exists for sight and touch because each differs fundamentally in how it presents subjects with objects and space.

Qualia theorists invariably treat each phenomenal quality associated with a conscious perceptual episode as distinctive to one specific sense or another. Jackson's (1982) classic essay points to epiphenomenal qualia associated with smelling a rose, tasting a lemon, hearing a loud noise, seeing the sky, seeing ripe tomatoes, and bat sonar. Lewis's (1988) reply adds smelling a skunk, feeling hot fire and cold drafts, and tasting Vegemite. Multisensory qualia are unmentioned.

Even theorists who endorse conscious perception of "high-level" features, such as natural kind and semantic properties, focus on their perception by means of a specific sensory modality. Discussions concern seeing pine trees, tigers, and faces, hearing persons and the meanings of spoken utterances, smelling roses, and tasting vintages. Perception of higher-level features using more than one sense at a time typically is absent from such accounts (cf. Nudds 2001).

Accordingly, perception's rational role most often is restricted to that which stems from singular sensory sources. For instance, thoughts about things and features anchored in multisensory demonstrations go unaddressed. And, in general, epistemology of perception fails to consider incremental support stemming from the coordinated workings of several senses (cf. Matthen 2014).

Paradigms in philosophy of perception thus reveal two assumptions that parallel an earlier perception science. The first is that each sense is explanatorily independent from the others. In particular, it is possible to explain perceptual consciousness in each sense on its own terms. This assumes that the properties of perceptual consciousness associated with one sense are not relevant to explaining the properties of perceptual consciousness associated with another sense.

The second assumption is that the sense-by-sense approach is explanatorily complete. Perceptual awareness includes just the forms associated with each of the respective senses, and perceptual phenomenality reduces to what is specific to one sense or another. Perception's role in supporting thought and action amounts to the role played by each individual sense. Taken together, accounts of perceptual consciousness in each of the respective senses, along with the unity of consciousness, exhaust the philosophy of perception. Perceptual consciousness just is the co-conscious sum of its sense-specific parts.

1.2 Sensory Interactions

Some of the most dramatic developments in the cognitive sciences of perception during the past two decades stem from appreciating the extent to which human senses interact with each other. First, one sense can impact another sense, at a time or over time, thereby affecting perceptual consciousness. This undermines the assumption of explanatory independence. Second, multiple senses work in coordination, sometimes revealing features that are not otherwise perceptible. This undermines the assumption of explanatory completeness.

Synesthesia provides a glimpse. In synesthetes, stimulating one sense can trigger sensations associated with another sense. A synesthete might visualize colors in response to sounds or seem to experience tastes in response to shapes. But synesthesia is quirky, and it is rare. It is hard to see what purpose it serves.

However, one sense can affect another in a way that reshapes experience in just about anyone. Crossmodal perceptual illusions are cases in which one sense changes your experience with another sense. For example, seeing a puppet or an event on screen can affect the apparent location from which you hear a sound. This is the basis for ventriloquism. It is an auditory illusion produced by vision. Seeing a speaker's mouth movements also can change which speech sounds you seem to hear. This is known as the McGurk effect.

The examples multiply, and vision does not always win. Playing a flash along with two beeps can make it look like two flashes. This is the sound-induced flash, a visual illusion induced by sound. A tap on your skin with two beeps also can feel like two taps. Smelling vanilla makes food taste sweeter (sweetness enhancement). The timing of a sound affects when a light seems to illuminate (temporal ventriloquism). In the rubber hand effect, stroking a visible artificial hand with a feather can make it feel like your own hand.

Crossmodal effects in multisensory contexts demonstrate that stimulation to one sensory system can alter perceptual consciousness that is associated with another sense in a way that leads to perceptual illusions. Such illusions are widespread and systematic, and the impact can occur very early in perceptual processing (see Chapter 2).

Crossmodal illusions show that one sense can alter another during a short time span. One sense also can affect another over a longer time span. For example, vision helps calibrate middle-distance locational hearing, and it enables perceivers auditorily to discern relative spatial locations between audible items. As a result, congenitally blind perceivers tend to have spatial hearing deficits and distortions in auditory space. Nonetheless, skilled echolocation can sharpen spatial hearing. For instance, it improves the capacity auditorily to discern locations and shapes of extended bodies. As a consequence, due to differing crossmodal influences and perceptual learning, the auditory experience of a congenitally blind perceiver in a given acoustical setting typically differs from that of a sighted perceiver. Thus, over the long term, one sense can affect perceptual consciousness associated with another sense. The change can be evident even when perceiving with just one sense.

The impact of one sense on another, at a time and over time, demonstrates that features of perception and consciousness involving one sense can depend on another sense. In particular, on a given occasion, both perceptual processes and perceptual consciousness associated with one sense may depend on current or past activity involving another sensory system. In these respects, perception involving one sense is not wholly independent from the other senses.

Senses also work together in coordination, undermining the assumption of explanatory completeness. Psychophysicists and neuroscientists recently have focused on how information from different sensory systems is shared and integrated between senses. Some ways of integrating information are distinctively multisensory. For example, there exist processes in which the response to a certain combination of signals differs from the sum of the responses to the same signals taken individually (it may be greater or lesser). These responses are called *superadditive*. Superadditive processes perform differently in combining multiple cues from how they perform in registering cues separately. Their behavior is non-linear in the face of distinct cues. What is noteworthy here is that some superadditive responses occur exclusively during multisensory stimulation. For instance, a neuron may fire at a rate above its baseline only when it receives both auditory and visual stimulation. Such a response is selectively sensitive to joint auditory and visual stimulation. This response bears information about the joint presence of audible and visible features. Perception even implicates regions of the brain that respond selectively to multisensory stimulation. For instance, the superior temporal sulcus is heteromodal. It is thought to be critical in processing information about speech from different senses, and it is most active with multisensory input.

Coordination goes beyond integration. Perception science provides evidence that typical human subjects in multisensory contexts can detect features that are not perceptible using any single sense and that could not be perceived using several senses independently and merely in parallel. For instance, subjects can be differentially sensitive to the identity of an object or attribute that is perceived using distinct senses. This is not just a matter of responding to the same item or feature using different senses at the same time. It requires a coordinated, distinctively multisensory response. Empirical evidence informed by theoretical considerations also supports the claim that subjects are able to perceive novel intermodal instances of certain relational features, such as simultaneity, rhythm, motion, or causality. For example, a subject may perceive something visible's causing something audible, or a rhythm comprising sounds and touches. I argue in later chapters that the joint use of multiple senses also can reveal novel feature types and qualities that otherwise are not perceptible.

In each of these examples, the joint use of multiple senses makes possible a distinctive form of perception. This does not just amount to using several senses at once, in parallel. Instead, the senses work together to do something new that could not be done separately. Each involves a novel, multisensory way of perceiving.

The coordinated use of multiple senses demonstrates that multisensory perception and consciousness is not exhausted by what is associated with each of the respective senses. By this, I mean that multisensory perception involves more than what each sense could do on its own, independently from other senses. Multisensory perceptual consciousness is not a simple fusion of that which belongs to each of the senses, along with the simple unity of consciousness. In these respects, theorizing about each sense on its own does not suffice for a complete account of multisensory perception.

Sensory interactions thus make trouble for the two assumptions that underwrite unisensory approaches to the science and the philosophy of perception. They challenge the assumption of explanatory independence, according to which each sense can be theorized fully in isolation or in abstraction from the others. And they challenge the assumption of explanatory completeness, according to which assembling accounts of perceiving with each of the respective senses yields a comprehensive understanding of perception.

1.3 Thesis

This book's thesis is that the coordinated use of multiple senses enhances human sense perception by improving it in key respects and augmenting it in others. In particular, it increases coherence and reliability, and it extends the reach of our perceptual capacities. Sensory interactions thus make possible new forms of perceptual consciousness.

Claims about sense perception may concern perceptual processes or perceptual consciousness. My approach in this book is to address each on its own terms, answering considerations relevant to establishing conclusions in each domain.

The first part takes on perceptual processes. In particular, it deals with perceptual functions and capacities. Chapter 2 concerns crossmodal interactions. It argues that crossmodal illusions result from principled interactions between senses that are part of typical multisensory perceptual functioning. Such effects are widespread, and usually do not cause illusions. In fact, they tend to minimize conflict, and they enable us to get things right more often. Sensory interactions thus improve the overall coherence and reliability of perception. Multisensory functioning therefore enhances perceptual capacities we already possess.

Chapter 3 concerns coordination among senses. It argues that typical human perceivers are differentially sensitive to the presence of novel features that could only be perceived thanks to the joint use of multiple senses. This chapter argues, on empirical and theoretical grounds, that perceivers can detect and differentiate the identity of an object perceived with distinct senses, intermodal instances of relational features, such as simultaneity, motion, causality, and rhythm, and novel feature types, including complex flavors. Therefore, when compared with several senses working independently or merely in parallel, the joint use of several senses extends the reach of our perceptual capacities. More of the world can be perceived thanks to collaboration between senses.

The second part turns to perceptual consciousness. In particular, it deals with perceptual awareness and experience. Chapter 4 concerns awareness. Perceptual awareness involves how things seem or appear to be to a consciously perceiving subject. This chapter argues that some forms of perceptual awareness in typical human subjects are constitutively and irreducibly multisensory. For instance, in consciously perceiving a novel intermodal feature, perceptual awareness comprises more than what belongs to each of the various senses taken separately. As a consequence, multisensory perception enables new varieties of perceptual consciousness.

Chapter 5 concerns experience and phenomenal consciousness. Some may contend that multisensory awareness does not guarantee that any perceptual episode has multisensory phenomenal character. This chapter argues that not all perceptual experience is modality specific. In particular, it argues that the phenomenal features of a conscious multisensory episode need not be exhausted by those associated with each of the respective senses along with those that accrue thanks to mere co-consciousness. Thus, multisensory consciousness is marked by phenomenal character that no mere collection of co-conscious unisensory episodes could have. In this respect, multisensory perception makes possible new varieties of phenomenal consciousness.

As a result, the assumption of independence and the assumption of completeness fall short. Each fails as a claim about the subject matter targeted in addressing empirical and philosophical questions about perception. Whether taken as claims about perceptual processes and capacities, or as claims about perceptual awareness and phenomenal character, the claim that each sense is explanatorily independent from the others and the claim that the sense-by-sense approach is explanatorily complete must be revised in the face of multisensory perception and consciousness.

Multisensory perception raises two pressing questions of psychological taxonomy. In the face of multisensory phenomena, what differentiates our senses, and what distinguishes perception from cognition? Chapter 6 concerns the senses. Scientists and philosophers recently have used multisensory phenomena to challenge the distinctness of our senses. Some argue that multisensory mechanisms and functions show that the senses are not distinct, modular information processing systems. Others say multisensory experience shows that the senses are not different phenomenal ways of being related to objects, features, or contents.

Chapter 6 distinguishes the project of individuating the senses from that of attributing experiences to distinct sense modalities. It argues that senses are collections of perceptual capacities unified and distinguished by the manner in which they are exercised. Sensory manners are distinct kinds of information-gathering activity, individuated by their functions. Experiences, on the other hand, are ascribed modalities in accordance with the ways in which perceptual capacities are deployed on an occasion. According to this account, belonging to one sensory modality does not preclude belonging to another, and phenomenology is only an imperfect guide to sensory modality. This proposal is tailored to handle multisensory perception and experience. It preserves the distinctness of the senses, but it rejects their independence.

Finally, this book aims to establish that multisensory phenomena belong to perception rather than to extraperceptual cognition.[4] Its arguments therefore rely on a conception of what distinguishes perception from cognition. This, however, is a controversial topic, and no consensus exists around any given candidate. Moreover, my arguments treat a variety of multisensory phenomena. These include early perceptual processes as well as sophisticated aspects of perceptual consciousness, which differ in important respects from paradigm cases like seeing red or hearing a tone. What guarantees that each falls on the side of perception?

Rather than picking a favorite criterion, I take another approach. Chapters 2 through 5 consider differing explanatory purposes for a distinction between perception and cognition. In particular, distinguishing perception from cognition matters in empirical psychology, rational psychology, and phenomenology. But each project has differing aims and success criteria. This constrains the distinction in distinct ways for

---

[4] The expression, "extraperceptual cognition," avoids confusion between "cognition" in the broad sense, as in, "cognitive science," which includes perception, and "cognition" in the narrow sense, which is opposed to perception. Further uses treat cognition in the narrow sense.

differing explanatory projects. Here, there is no shortcut forward, and we need to focus on details. These chapters argue that each multisensory phenomenon being considered meets the constraints that are relevant for a given domain. Therefore, in the respects described in this book, empirical, rational, and phenomenological considerations support the claim that perception in typical human subjects is multisensory.[5]

This book is my contribution to reimagining the philosophy of perception from a multisensory perspective. This perspective does not presuppose that the senses are explanatorily independent from each other, and it does not treat the sense-by-sense approach as explanatorily complete. Instead, it takes seriously how senses interact and how they cooperate, and it considers the upshots. Rather than tackle it all, this book aims to present a clear case for some of the key pieces and their consequences. It addresses features of perceptual processes and perceptual consciousness. It offers a new way to approach the distinction between perception and cognition. And it proposes an account of the senses that respects perception's multisensory nature and character.[6]

---

[5] Sections 2.2, 3.3, 4.2, 5.6, 5.7, and 7.3 form a contained unit about the perception–cognition distinction.

[6] Readers wishing for a detailed synopsis (or a quick read) can skip now to Chapter 7 for a précis-like review of the framework, arguments, conclusions, and implications of Chapters 2 through 6.

2

Processes

What you perceive using one sensory modality can affect what you perceive through another. This is uncontroversial. If you see a volume knob, you might reach out and touch it. When you hear a whine, you might turn and see its source. One sense thus can have an effect on another sense.

What is surprising is that one sense can impact another sense far more directly. Experimental work demonstrates that sensory systems interact causally with each other in relatively immediate ways. Without a change in how it is stimulated, the activity of one sense can be altered by another sense. Such interactions can impact and reshape perceptual experience. Sometimes, this leads to crossmodal illusions.

This chapter argues that some perceptual processes are multisensory. By this, I do not just mean that sensory systems interact causally or accidentally. Instead, I mean that such interactions are part of perceptual functioning. Multisensory processes thus are fit to play a key explanatory role in perceptual psychology.

I begin with a central empirical finding that any multisensory philosophy of perception must address: crossmodal illusions. Appealing to a combination of behavioral and neural evidence, I argue that crossmodal illusions demonstrate that causal interactions take place between processes associated with stimulation to distinct senses. Next, I argue that these interactions hold among processes belonging to perception rather than to extraperceptual cognition. More specifically, they satisfy criteria that for the purposes of empirical psychology diagnose being perceptual.

Causal interactions, however, do not suffice for multisensory perceptual functioning. Thus, I argue, third, that the types of sensory interactions that sometimes generate crossmodal illusions are not just accidental or merely causal. Sensory interactions are aspects of perceptual functioning. They stem from principled perceptual strategies that in fact help to deal

A Multisensory Philosophy of Perception. Casey O'Callaghan, Oxford University Press (2019).
© Casey O'Callaghan. DOI: 10.1093/oso/9780198833703.001.0001

with noisy, fallible stimulation from multiple sensory sources. Despite sometimes causing illusions, sensory interactions typically enhance the coherence and reliability of perception in multisensory contexts. It follows that some perceptual processes are multisensory in respects that matter in empirical psychological explanation.

This chapter's conclusion concerns the organization of perceptual processes. Crossmodal sensory interactions demonstrate that multisensory processes must figure in any complete empirical understanding of perception and its role in our psychology. This challenges the sense-by-sense approach that until recently dominated empirical psychology and philosophy of perception. And it sets the stage for philosophical arguments establishing that human perceptual capacities, awareness, and experience each are multisensory.

Nevertheless, my argument here is limited in two ways. First, while it demonstrates that some processes are multisensory, it does not establish that any perceptual capacity that belongs to a subject is irreducibly multisensory. Second, while it demonstrates coordination among the senses, it does not establish that perceptual consciousness is constitutively multisensory. I tackle these limitations in subsequent chapters.

2.1 Crossmodal Illusions

The first premise of my argument is that causal interactions take place between processes associated with stimulation to distinct sensory modalities. The evidence stems from behavioral psychology and neuroscience.

Crossmodal illusions are cases in which one sense triggers an illusion associated with another sense. Seeing can make you have illusory tactile impressions, and hearing can cause visual illusions. Activity in one sensory system leads to perceptual illusion in a second sense. Thus, stimulation to one sense can impact and alter experience that is typically associated with another. Because a process responsible for sensory experience of a sort that could have occurred independently is affected by another sensory system, causal interactions take place between processes associated with stimulation to distinct senses.

Experimental psychology proves generous with examples of crossmodal illusion. Crossmodal interactions are not isolated exceptions, but reflect general facts about how perceptual processes are organized. Let me describe some exemplars and their significance.

Vision affects spatial aspects of perception in other modalities. This readily leads to illusions. For instance, vision can cause an illusory experience of spatial location in another sense. Ventriloquism is best known from hearing a puppeteer "throw" a voice. But ventriloquism does not involve throwing sound. It is an auditory spatial illusion caused by something visible. It involves illusorily hearing a voice to come from the place where a dummy is seen. The ventriloquist effect does not require speech. Even a flashing dot can affect where you hear a concurrent beep to come from. As I'll argue, the effect is not the result of a judgment or inference from a visual appearance, but instead results from crossmodal perceptual processes. Ventriloquism is an illusory auditory experience of spatial location that is caused by the visible location of an apparent sound source (Bertelson 1999).

Vision also captures proprioception. In the rubber hand illusion, you feel a visible touch to a rubber hand as a touch to your own hand (Botvinick and Cohen 1998). However, the rubber hand illusion also involves a proprioceptive location illusion induced by vision. Seeing a rubber hand or even a displaced image of your hand through a prism can illusorily shift where you feel your hand to be (Hay et al. 1965; Pick et al. 1969). Moreover, vision causes spatial illusions of size, shape, and orientation in other senses. For instance, seeing an object that is larger than one placed in your palm may affect the apparent felt size of the object you are holding (Rock and Victor 1964).

Each of these cases is compatible with the principle that vision wins. That is, vision dominates another sense whenever a discrepancy exists. Such deference reinforces the impression that vision is the preeminent modality, and it has been used to vindicate visuocentric theorizing about perception (Stokes and Biggs 2015). However, other senses do affect vision. Audition can recalibrate vision and cause visual illusions. Due to temporal ventriloquism, the start of a sound can alter when a light seems to switch on so that the light's onset seems synchronous with the sound's. A sound's duration also can alter the apparent duration of a visual stimulus. A quick beep can make a moving visible target appear to freeze momentarily. Sound also can alter visually apparent rate and temporal order (see Vroomen and de Gelder 2000).

At this point, one might think crossmodal illusions are relatively limited. Some concern spatial features, and some concern temporal features. And they are predictable. Vision impacts other senses when it comes to space, and audition impacts other senses when it comes to time. However, crossmodal illusions are far more widespead. Other pairs of senses can interact in the perception of spatial and temporal features. Audition and proprioception interact for spatial features—proprioception tends to win, but not always. Touch can impact the visual experience of temporal attributes.

Moreover, typical patterns of dominance sometimes are reversed. Under certain conditions, audition dominates visual spatial experience. When illumination is dim and visual reliability is low, audition affects vision. When visual spatial information is ambiguous, audition can resolve the ambiguity. Even smell can modulate vision under conditions of binocular rivalry (Zhou et al. 2010, 2012).

Furthermore, a variety of other perceptible features can drive interactions and illusions across modalities. Qualitative characteristics sometimes generate crossmodal illusions. In the parchment skin illusion, hearing a crinkling sound alters the apparent felt texture of a surface (Jousmäki and Hari 1998; Guest et al. 2002). Crunching sounds reportedly affect the apparent flavor of potato chips (Zampini and Spence 2004). Smell can alter taste. Odors, like vanilla, strawberry, almond, lemon, caramel, and lychee, affect the apparent sweetness of a tastant. And these effects are odorant-specific and tastant-specific. So, strawberry odor enhances sweetness but suppresses saltiness; odors such as ham, peanut butter, and chocolate do not enhance sweetness, but may enhance and suppress other tastes.[1] Such effects illustrate that unexpected crossmodal interactions are widespread.

The examples multiply. Some of the strongest multisensory effects concern speech. Speech perception presents particularly compelling crossmodal illusions, including the McGurk effect (McGurk and MacDonald 1976). When presented with the sound of the bilabial /ba/, which is pronounced with the lips together, along with incongruent video of a speaker articulating the velar /ga/, pronounced with the tongue

---

[1] Djordjevic et al. (2004) is a fascinating review and discussion of the effects of perceived and imagined odors on perceived taste.

at the back of the palate, many listeners report experiencing clearly the sound of the alveolar /da/, pronounced with the tongue near the front of the palate. The McGurk effect is a compromise between the articulatory gestures used to utter /ba/ and /ga/. The effect quickly stops when you look away from the mouth. Gick and Derrick (2009) show that even a puff of air on your neck can make you mishear an unaspirated /b/ as an aspirated /p/. The McGurk effect originally was used to support the Motor Theory of speech perception, which holds that speech is a special case, unlike typical environmental sounds in how it is handled perceptually (see Liberman 1996). Its true significance as a representative crossmodal illusion only more recently has been appreciated. Speech perception is robustly multisensory.

One modality can influence causal impressions associated with another. Consider the motion–bounce effect (Sekuler et al. 1997). Two disks on a screen that start from adjacent corners and then travel diagonally, crossing in the middle, most frequently look to subjects to stream past one another. But a sound played when the disks intersect makes the disks most frequently appear visibly to bounce and rebound from each other. The presence of an auditory stimulus resolves the visually ambiguous display to look like the motion resulting from a collision. Meyerhoff and Scholl (2018) show that a sound can even affect illusory visual crescents detected in cases of visual causal launching. When a green disk appears causally to "launch" a red disk it in fact completely occludes, it illusorily appears to many subjects that a crescent of the red disk remains uncovered. A sound measurably increases the apparent size of this illusory visual crescent.

As a final example, consider a fascinating crossmodal illusion discovered by Shams et al. (2000, 2002). In this effect, audition impacts vision even though stimulation to each sense is unambiguous and there is no obvious conflict. In the critical experiment, a single circular black disk is quickly flashed along with two brief beeps. This stimulus causes many subjects to report not just two beeps but also *two* flashes. This is the sound-induced flash illusion. Sounds can impact the number of events you seem visually to experience.

The illusion is strongest when presented extrafoveally, but otherwise it persists through changes to stimulus characteristics and to setting. The effect continues for three and sometimes four beeps, at a variety of beep intervals and disk sizes. One sound also can make two flashes seem like one flash. But a visual stimulus is required. The sound alone does not generate a visual experience. And the illusion is asymmetric. Vision does not impact audition in this way. However, other senses can trigger the illusion. Violentyev et al. (2005) reports a similar touch-induced flash illusion.

Shams et al. describe the sound-induced flash effect as a phenomenological change to the conscious character of visual experience that is produced by audition. They argue that it is a visual perceptual illusion caused by a sound and that it results from crossmodal perceptual mechanisms.

A recent extension of the paradigm shows that a sound–flash pairing can postdictively induce an illusory flash that coincides with an earlier sound or suppress a flash presented in absence of a sound, which Stiles et al. (2018) dub respectively the illusory and the invisible audiovisual rabbit.

This is not just adaptation. Unlike adaptation, which builds and decays, a crossmodal illusion takes place immediately, and it ceases once the stimulus is gone. Adaptation and crossmodal illusions may even compete. An intermodal recalibration might resolve a discrepancy that otherwise would lead to adaptation (Welch and Warren 1980).

Crossmodal illusions also are unlike crossmodal attention cueing (Posner 1980; Spence and Driver 2004). The processes responsible for crossmodal illusions do not just speed one's response, improve accuracy, or increase the salience of a perceptual target in another sense. They change which determinate feature you seem to experience, leading to an error. And, while attention can enhance multisensory processing, especially for spoken language (Talsma et al. 2010), crossmodal illusions need not be mediated by selective attention. Bertelson and de Gelder (2004) claim that crossmodal effects in spatial perception occur pre-attentively: "Cross-modal interaction reorganizes the auditory-visual spatial scene on which selective attention later operates" (165).

The upshot is that a crossmodal perceptual illusion takes place when stimulation to one sensory system impacts perceptual experience associated with another sensory modality in a way that leads to misperception or misleading perception. As with other perceptual effects, subjects differ in whether and to what extent they are susceptible to crossmodal illusions. And some crossmodal effects are stronger than others.

Nevertheless, these results show that sometimes information from one sense can change how another responds. A process connected with one sensory system can impact a process responsible for experience that is associated with another sense.

I have described a selection of effects from an expanding body of experimental research charting interactions among senses. These results support the claim that some illusions are crossmodal. The research trend is robust and so far has not faced formidable replication challenges (Open Science Collaboration 2015). This warrants investigating the theoretical and philosophical consequences (cf. Machery and Doris 2017).

Crossmodal illusions are surprising. That vision is misled by the mere presence of a sound, that seeing a rubber hand can sway bodily awareness, and that vision so clearly alters the speech sounds you seem to hear is hard to believe even after it is demonstrated. Part of what generates the surprise is allegiance to a conception of the senses as discrete, independent modes of perception.

As in the study of perception more generally, crossmodal illusions are a window on perceptual processes. They provide evidence about perceptual mechanisms and thereby shed light on the principles of normal perceptual functioning. They reveal perceptual organization that otherwise is disguised. Crossmodal illusions draw attention to the respects in which perception is multisensory. Explaining them illuminates why it matters.

2.2 Perception

My argument's next premise is that sensory interactions occur among perceptual processes. That is, they implicate the sorts of psychological processes responsible for whether and what one perceives. The reason is that causal interactions responsible for crossmodal illusions satisfy criteria for belonging to perception rather than extraperceptual cognition.

What marks the distinction between perception and extraperceptual cognition? There is no shortage of candidates. No uncontroversial criterion exists, and nothing like consensus exists around any candidate. Rather than pick a favorite, it is fruitful to ask: What are the explanatory purposes for a distinction between perception and cognition, and what constraints do they impose on psychological taxonomy?

Empirical psychology is one explanatory context in which perception is distinguished from extraperceptual cognition. Since experimental results and perceptual processes are in question, empirical psychology is a relevant context. Firestone and Scholl (2016) say:

> Easily, the most natural and robust distinction between types of mental processes is that between perception and cognition. This distinction is woven so deeply into cognitive science as to structure introductory courses and textbooks, differentiate scholarly journals, and organize academic departments. (Firestone and Scholl 2016, 1)

The style of explanation in empirical psychology is a species of functional explanation. It aims to capture actual and potential observable behavior by describing mechanisms that produce it by implementing differing types of capacities or functions, such as extracting information from sound waves, singling out objects, withdrawing from noxious stuff, storing information, minimizing error, and organizing complex actions. For a state or process to be of a given psychological kind, suited to serve in empirical psychological explanation, is for it to implement a certain kind of causal-functional role. Perceptual states and processes are those that occupy a particular sort of role—the perceptual role.

Perception's role is to ground or tether cognition in the world. And one way to unpack this is in causal terms. Perception depends causally on the present state of the world. It furnishes materials for cognition and provides information to guide action. Perception triggers thoughts and beliefs, and it enables demonstrative thought about particulars. Lewis (1980) said perceptual experiences stand in a pattern of double causal dependence. They are caused by stimulation from the environment and lead to beliefs about it. Roughly, they stand between sensation and cognition.

Specifics of the perceptual role are open to dispute. So, we can debate whether perception is penetrable by cognition and whether constancies suffice to distinguish perception from sensation. What is noteworthy is that occupying this role—being situated between stimulation and cognition—is not observable as such. Being perceptual is not an observable property of a state or process. That perception is implicated is a theoretical claim, supported with a model and with evidence from stimulation and responses.

Thus, for the purposes of empirical psychology, the perceptual role must be operationalized in terms of what is observable. Accordingly, experiments in perceptual psychology measure properties such as stimulus detection and discrimination thresholds, response times, accuracy, and verbal reports. And experimentalists use techniques to elicit responses to tasks in a variety of conditions. They introduce contrasts or conflicts, as in Stroop, binocular rivalry (as well as binaural and binaral/binasal rivalry), and intersensory discrepancy paradigms. They vary order and timing, employ masks, and load attention, memory, and cognition. They test trained and untrained subjects, young and old, and track performance over time.

Perceptual paradigms also aim to control for confounds. It is critical to rule out competing explanations of performance relying on extraperceptual inference or judgment; memory or learning, which may speed response through priming; task effects, such as adopting a strategy to deal with an ambiguous stimulus or confusing task; and pitfalls such as the El Greco fallacy (Firestone and Scholl 2016).

Lately, neuropsychological evidence about how performance on distinct tasks dissociates and neurophysiological evidence concerning the locus and character of brain activity have played an increasingly powerful part in establishing claims about the perceptual role. For instance, early activity in response to a stimulus characteristic is evidence that perception is implicated, especially when it resembles accepted paradigms, such as spatial or color vision.

Given these measures, we can regiment a psychological role. As a heuristic, map each factor to a dimension in a complex space. Then, plot performance on various tasks in that space. Perceptual tasks, such as color discrimination or multiple object tracking, ought to be nearer to each other on dimensions such as response time and accuracy than to stereotypical cognitive tasks, such as logical inference and performing long division. Perceptual tasks need not cluster perfectly or neatly. However, in this illustration, types of psychological phenomena correspond to regions of space. So, to determine whether some effect stems from perception, plot it to see if it is consistent with stereotypical perceptual tasks.

Behavioral and neural evidence shows that the processes responsible for crossmodal illusions belong to perception rather than extraperceptual cognition. The sound-induced flash effect is an instructive example. Shams et al. argue that it results from a low-level, direct impact on vision by audition that cannot be explained by extraperceptual cognition, by the resolution of an ambiguous stimulus, or by a conceptual or semantic contribution.

First, the crossmodal effect does not result from reasoning that is accessible to the subject or from an otherwise cognitive process, such as deploying a decision strategy for responding to ambiguous or conflicting experiences. Response times and perceptual reports both tell against this, and the effect occurs when we might expect vision and audition each to be clear and univocal. There is no obvious conflict between seeing one disc and hearing two sounds that should compel us to resolve it through the use of cognition. Second, the illusion does not require a semantic or conceptual contribution. It does not involve a familiar multisensory context in which categorical learning occurs, as with spoken language, musical instruments, or automobiles. Generating the illusion does not require experience within any specific bimodal context. It occurs in naïve subjects in novel situations with simple stimuli. Third, this and other crossmodal effects have been shown to be automatic and to stem from interactions that take place in low-level processing characteristic of perception.

In this context, recent results from Meyerhoff and Scholl (2018) are especially noteworthy. They argue that the motion–bounce effect, in which a sound induces visual bouncing rather than streaming, stems from perception and not cognition. The reason is that decision strategies cannot explain the measured, subjectively salient increase in the size of illusory visual causal crescents induced by the presence of a sound in causal launching experiments. As a baseline, unisensory visual launching generates a spatial illusion in which wholly overlapping disks appear never fully to coincide. This is the illusory visual causal crescent (Scholl and Nakayama 2004). In cases of audiovisual launching, when a sound is present, the illusory causal crescent is even larger. Since causal crescents are visual perceptual illusions, Meyerhoff and Scholl (2018) reason that changes in apparent visible spatial features induced by sound in cases of reported launching also reflect perception rather than decisions reached on the basis of perception.[2]

Recent neural evidence reveals interactions responsible for crossmodal illusions in brain areas associated with early sensory stimulation. For example, Watkins et al. (2006) use functional magnetic resonance imaging (fMRI) to show that, in the sound-induced flash effect, audition impacts V1, the primary visual cortex. Auditory processes therefore affect some of the earliest stages of visual processing. In various other effects, crosstalk has been found to occur among early auditory, visual, somato-sensory, proprioceptive, gustatory, and olfactory areas of the cortex. The upshot is that regions of the brain previously thought to be dedicated to unisensory tasks now are known to be influenced by other senses.

Moreover, some brain regions mediate intersensory recalibrations and themselves respond differentially to multisensory inputs. A number of these regions are located in intermediate cortical areas associated with sensation and perception, rather than in areas farther along the processing pathway that respond much later and are associated with extraperceptual cognition, such as the frontal cortex. For instance, some multisensory areas are in the parietal and temporal lobes, each of which is separated from the frontal lobe by a large sulcus, or fissure (the central and temporal sulci, respectively). What is noteworthy is that these regions respond to stimulation from the primary sensory areas and are implicated in perceptual processing. Very roughly, the parietal lobe is associated strongly with sensory integration and processing information about the body, while the temporal lobe is associated with auditory, emotional, and basic linguistic processing. This contrasts with the frontal lobe, which is associated with motor activity and higher cognition.

Two impressive examples illustrate the application of creative neuroscientific techniques to the study of crossmodal illusions. The first concerns speech perception. The superior temporal sulcus (STS) is an area in the brain's temporal lobe that is implicated especially in processing vocalized speech. It is particularly important for phonological processing, as well as perception of animacy. Beauchamp et al. (2010) used transcranial magnetic stimulation (TMS) guided by fMRI to selectively

---

[2] https://www.iwm-tuebingen.de/public/realistic_depictions_lab/auditory_crescents/

disrupt activity in STS. By doing so, they were able to modulate the McGurk illusion while preserving auditory syllable recognition. Nath and Beauchamp (2012) use fMRI comparisons to show that differences in STS activity explain individual differences in McGurk susceptibility. On these grounds, the authors argue that STS (left, ordinarily) is critical for the McGurk effect and thus in multisensory audiovisual perception of spoken language.

The second concerns perception of one's body. Pasalar et al. (2010) report that the posterior parietal cortex is necessary for integrating visual and tactile spatial information about touches to the hand, suggesting that it contains a multimodal map of the space around the hand. Again, they stimulate this area through fMRI-guided TMS and thereby disrupt multisensory integration and conflict resolution. The TMS eliminates crossmodal illusions involving visible and felt touches to the hand.[3]

Dedicated multisensory functioning is not limited to parietal and temporal areas of the brain. The superior colliculi are mid-brain structures implicated in object-directed orientation and behavior, such as gaze shift. In addition to direct superficial retinal connections, their middle and deep layers have connections to other areas of primary and secondary sensory cortices. Each superior colliculus is thought to contain a topographic map with auditory, visual, and somatosensory layers. This enables coordination and integration of spatial and temporal information from multiple senses and facilitates rapid motor responses (King 2004).

The gold standard for a multisensory mechanism is a superadditive response to unisensory stimuli from distinct senses (Stein et al. 2010). A superadditive response is one that differs from the sum of responses to distinct stimuli taken individually. So, for example, a neuron that fires at rate r_1 in response to stimulus s_1 and at rate r_2 in response to s_2, but which does not fire at rate $r_1 + r_2$ in response to s_1 and s_2 together, is one that responds superadditively. Its response, $r_{1\&2}$, to s_1 and s_2 together may be such that $r_{1\&2} > r_1 + r_2$. However, it could be that $r_{1\&2} < r_1 + r_2$. It may even be that $r_{1\&2}$ is suppressed below its base rate. The important point is that a neuron responding superadditively behaves differently when jointly stimulated by both s_1 and s_2 from how it would respond to

---

[3] Bolognini and Maravita (2011) is an accessible review of such non-invasive techniques in the study of multisensory processing.

either taken individually. A neuron that responds by summing s_1 and s_2 may integrate or combine information from distinct senses, but it need not differentiate unisensory from multisensory stimuli. For instance, it may not distinguish weak s_1 and weak s_2 presented together from strong s_1 or strong s_2 alone. A superadditive response, in contrast, can indicate the joint presence of both s_1 and s_2. If s_1 and s_2 are unisensory stimuli from distinct senses, a superadditive response is selectively sensitive to their joint presence. Rather than merely undergoing parallel, unisensory responses, this is a way of being differentially sensitive to a condition of multisensory stimulation. According to this criterion, even some individual neurons in areas associated with sensation and perception are dedicated to receiving and responding to multisensory input.[4]

Some crossmodal illusions therefore satisfy the relevant criteria for being perceptual. According to behavioral measures, these effects are quick, salient, vivid, and widespread. They are stimulus driven, action guiding, and relatively insensitive to beliefs and desires. Crossmodal illusions are not under subjects' deliberate control. It is a critical concern in this literature to rule out the various confounds, such as memory, extraperceptual cognition, and decision strategies for dealing with difficult tasks. According to neural measures, crossmodal effects involve distinctive brain activity associated with sensory and perceptual processes rather than just extraperceptual cognition.

Therefore, according to behavioral measures and neural evidence, some crossmodal illusions exhibit the symptoms of perceptual phenomena. Sensory interactions occur among processes that satisfy diagnostic criteria for occupying the perceptual role, for the explanatory purposes of empirical psychology. Interactions between senses can cause perceptual illusions.

2.3 Functioning

The third premise in this chapter's argument is that sensory interactions are part of perceptual functioning. This matters because causal processes

---

[4] See Stein and Meredith (1993). The essays in Calvert et al. (2004) and Stein (2012) provide a comprehensive review.

that do not help elucidate characteristic functioning hold little interest in psychological explanation.

In the first instance, having a function contrasts with being an accident. Thus, the competing claim that needs to be rebutted is that interactions between senses that produce crossmodal illusions are mere quirks or accidents. The section ahead argues that crossmodal illusions are not just accidental. Unlike synesthesia, they are widespread across the population, and they occur in numerous domains for each typical subject. Just as visual illusions illuminate visual functioning, crossmodal illusions reveal principles that explain performance in multisensory contexts, even when no illusion occurs.

Sensory interactions of the sort that produce crossmodal illusions conform to principles that help to deal with sensory information from multiple sources that is noisy and fallible. These responses serve to take into account relevant information drawn from distinct senses and to weight it according to its source. Doing so minimizes conflict between senses and makes perceptual processes more reliable.

Conforming to such principles thereby enhances our perceptual capacities. In particular, I argue that it improves the overall coherence and reliability of perception in typical human environments. As a result, sensory interactions are intelligible as advantageous and as adaptive. The cost is predictable crossmodal illusions.

Sensory interactions thus bear the marks of functions in contrast with accidents. They are principled, they help explain our perceptual capacities, and they serve a purpose. This supports the conclusion that causal interactions between processes associated with distinct senses are not merely accidental but are part of perceptual functioning. They are a feature, rather than a bug. The upshot is that multisensory processes earn a place in any complete perceptual psychology.

2.3.1 Crossmodal Illusions vs. Synesthesia

In the first place, having a function contrasts with being an accident. A clock's hands track time, but their color does not matter, and the ticking is a side effect. Crossmodal illusions are not entirely accidental. To establish this, contrast crossmodal illusions with synesthesia.

Synesthesia is a condition in which stimulation of one kind causes an experience associated with another. A synesthete might seem to experience colors in response to sounds or distinctive textures prompted by tastes and flavors. In synesthesia, stimulation to one sensory system can impact and alter experience associated with another sense in a way that leads to illusion or hallucination.

Synesthesia, however, is rare. According to Baron-Cohen et al. (1996), synesthesia involving qualitative sensory phenomenology occurs in roughly one in 2000 persons. Simner et al. (2006) put the rate much higher, at roughly one in twenty. Even at the higher rate, synesthesia is an atypical condition, occurring in a small minority. Within individuals, synesthetic effects are relatively isolated and usually are limited to a small range of specific features. Crossmodal illusions, on the other hand, are common across the population and are widespread across a range of differing domains.

Synesthesia is a quirk stemming from highly contingent facts about sensory wiring. It can stem from failure to prune cross-talk between adjacent brain areas (Ramachandran and Hubbard 2001) or from disinhibition due to drugs or stroke (Beauchamp and Ro 2008). And it is surprisingly common for grapheme–color synesthesia to conform to the colors of popular Fisher-Price toy letters (Witthoft and Winawer 2013). Synesthesia results from atypical causal interaction enabled by mere proximity of otherwise functionally distinct brain regions, accidentally uninhibited pathways, or statistical anomalies in a pattern of stimulation.

Synesthesia is robustly and persistently illusory. The inducing sense causes a concurrent experience of a feature belonging to a type that otherwise need not have appeared. Synesthesia involves experiences conjured from whole cloth. Hearing a sound suffices to generate synesthetic color experience without relevant visual stimulation. There is no reliable connection between the colors of things and the colors a synesthete experiences in hearing sounds. Things usually just lack the determinate qualities a synesthete experiences. Synesthetic experiences thus are inappropriate.

Stimulation to one sense alone does not suffice to generate a crossmodal perceptual illusion. Seeing a talker is not enough to experience a phoneme auditorily, and hearing a beep does not suffice visually to experience a flash. Instead, stimulation to one sense alters how things appear through a different sense. A visual stimulus reshapes your auditory experience of a phoneme, and two beeps affects the apparent number of visible flashes you see.

Crossmodal illusions are not mere aberrations or quirks of processing. They do not stem from accidental interference. The triggering stimulus is of a type that generally provides reliable information about the illusory feature. Vision normally affords good information about the location of your hand. Audition typically is accurate when it comes to the temporal features of happenings in your environment. Visible mouth movements provide informative clues about vocal gestures.

Crossmodal illusions thus are appropriate. They are intelligible responses to extraordinary circumstances. The visible source of a sound does not often diverge from where the sound seems to be. Visible events in time usually do correspond in number to their acoustic signs. And visible mouth movements and audible sounds do not often disagree about the phonemes a speaker utters. Reconciling conflicting information across senses generally is a good strategy. In unusual conditions, it leads to illusion.

Crossmodal recalibrations help deal with simple physical facts. Light from an event arrives earlier than sound waves; a neural signal takes longer to reach your brain from your foot than from your eye; triangulating location from interaural pressure differences is less precise than from binocular retinal arrays. Crossmodal interactions help reconcile temporally offset signals from synchronous sources. Crossmodal processes thus cope with conflicting information. Sensory interactions also resolve ambiguity, improve precision, and correct perceptual errors. Conflict, ambiguity, imprecision, and error can stem from differences across sensory systems in perspective, format, encoding, resolving power, accuracy, or noisiness.

Such interactions thus improve perception by making use of information from multiple senses. Vision's impact on other senses concerning spatial features helps in a variety of ways. Vision's spatial resolution is an order of magnitude greater than audition's, so the fact that vision can override audition enhances our capacity to perceive spatial features. Audition's temporal resolution exceeds vision's, so the fact that audition can override vision improves perception of temporal characteristics.

As a result, crossmodal processes commonly help to avoid illusions, as when vision corrects a front–back confusion that is inherent to auditory localization, or when sound and sight are synchronized. They also improve perceptual accuracy, as when visual information boosts audi-tory phoneme discrimination.

Crossmodal illusions thus are accidentally rather than systematically illusory. They stem from processes that most of the time do not cause illusions. Sensory interactions help compensate for imprecision, ambi-guity, and differences in timing. They help resolve conflicts. This makes sense in dealing with noisy, fallible sensory stimulation from multiple sources. In odd circumstances, as when psychophysicists introduce discrepancies, sensory interactions produce illusions. But these illusions are explicable. They are instances of regularities that generally make perception better in multisensory contexts.

2.3.2 Principles

In contrast with synesthesia, the types of sensory interactions responsible for crossmodal illusions are not accidental. Instead, they manifest inter-modal organizing strategies that help to deal with complex sensory information from distinct sources. They predictably stem from processes that generally improve our capacity to perceive. Crossmodal perceptual illusions thus are intelligible as principled perceptual responses—they conform to principles that regularly enable us to get things right. This is a mark that they are part of perceptual functioning.

What are the principles of crossmodal sensory interaction? What governs how multisensory recalibration unfolds? Why does vision some-times win, while at other times audition or touch affects vision? What determines the strength of an illusion?

Two general principles characterize sensory interactions. The first is *conflict resolution*. This principle governs whether and when sensory recalibration takes place. The second is *deference to the more reliable modality*. This principle governs how recalibration unfolds.

Start with conflict resolution. Different senses sometimes bear conflict-ing information. Central cases of crossmodal interaction reconcile infor-mation from different senses. They do so by recalibrating divergent information in a way that reduces conflict. The intersensory discrepancy paradigm capitalizes on this. Ventriloquism squares the books for spatial location, and temporal ventriloquism deals with asynchrony. The McGurk effect reconciles divergent auditory and visual information about a spoken utterance. The sound-induced flash eliminates a numerosity conflict. The parchment skin illusion sorts out contrary tactual and auditory cues about texture. These crossmodal recalibrations minimize disagreements. Some sensory interactions thus resolve conflicts between senses.

Selectively resolving conflicts between senses requires differentiating sensory signals that belong together from those that do not. Conflict requires disagreement, and disagreement requires a common subject matter. Otherwise, it is merely apparent. Even apparent disagreement requires the presumption of a common subject matter.

Perceptual processes therefore must determine when information from different sensory sources concerns the same thing and when it does not.

> Therefore, to make sense of the surrounding environment, the nervous system has to figure out which sensory signals were caused by the same object and should be combined, and which signals were caused by independent objects and should be kept apart. This is quite a non-trivial causal inference problem because the nervous system typically does not have any clue about the causal structure of specific scenes and events at any given time, and thus has to solve this problem purely based on noisy sensory measurements and prior information about the world. (Shams and Kim 2010, 279)

Patterns of sensory interaction thus embody criteria by which perceptual systems determine whether or not to treat information from distinct senses as belonging together and thus as subject to possible reconciliation. These criteria include factors such as spatiotemporal proximity and correlation between signals. Parise and Ernst (2016) propose a mechanism for spatiotemporal correlation detection as a general way to solve crossmodal correspondence problems.

> To successfully combine signals from different sensory modalities, the brain needs to detect which signals contain related information, that is, solve the correspondence problem, integrate this information and dynamically adapt to spatial or temporal conflicts across the senses as they arise. Spatiotemporal correlation has often been advocated as

the main common factor underlying the sensory signals to be integrated: when signals from different modalities originate from the same physical event, and hence contain related information that should be integrated, they usually cross-correlate in time and space.

(Parise and Ernst 2016, 2)

Explaining patterns of multisensory interaction as conflict resolution means appreciating that perceptual processes selectively treat information drawn from different senses as stemming from a common source. Doing conflict resolution thus demonstrates a perceptual concern for common features or sources of stimulation to multiple senses. Crossmodal illusions trade on this. In ventriloquism, the common feature is a location. In the McGurk effect, it is a vocal feature. In the parchment skin illusion, it is the texture of a surface. In the sound-induced flash, it is an event sequence. Implementing conflict resolution reflects sensitivity to the sameness of objects and attributes across sensory modalities.

Conflict resolution and sensitivity to identity generalize. They explain and predict performance, including crossmodal illusions, in a variety of multisensory contexts. Sensory interactions resolving conflict thus manifest principled perceptual performance.

Next, consider deference to the more reliable modality. In conditions of conflict, one sense can influence another. Start with what determines the direction of influence. Vision tends to dominate audition when the disagreement concerns space. Audition tends to win when it concerns time. In each case, one sense is far more reliable as a source of information about the relevant feature. Sometimes, however, the modality that intuitively is not most appropriate biases one that is. Sound can impact felt texture, as in the parchment skin illusion, and vision biases speech perception in the McGurk effect. Biasing also can be reversed. Blurring vision or adding visual distractors increases auditory dominance for spatial location in ventriloquism (Alais and Burr 2004). Adding visual noise increases reliance on tactual cues for size (Ernst and Banks 2002). In each case, altering the reliability of a modality changes dominance patterns. Crossmodal interactions thus flexibly recalibrate in deference to the more reliable sense.

One sense does not always completely override or "capture" another when conflict exists. Total dominance is not the rule. Complete resolution in favor of one sense is a limit case. Crossmodal recalibration and biasing come in degrees. On one hand, conflict resolution need not be complete. Each sense might have only a subtle influence on the other. Consider ventriloquism. In a case of biasing without convergence, we might seem to see something in one location and hear something in another, while one apparent location is affected by the other.

On the other hand, conflict sometimes is resolved by compromise rather than full deference. Thus, for instance, in low light, we might seem to see and hear something in a common spatial location that splits the difference between what each sense would reveal on its own. But, even averaging is not the rule. The testimony of one sense can weigh more heavily than that of another. Frequently, a compromise involving mutual influence and relative weighting occurs.

An optimal weighting function describes mathematically how cues from different sources ideally should be weighted according to their respective reliability to maximize the likelihood of accuracy. Reliability is the proportion of observed variance that is due to true variance rather than measurement error. (Variance measures dispersion of values, equal to standard deviation squared.) Combining cues in this way maximizes the chance of a correct estimate. Optimal weighting functions make idealized predictions of the degree to which biasing should take place.

In the face of a pattern of stimulation to two different senses, the likelihood of a specific feature depends on the reliability of each sense relative to the other for that feature. So, deferring completely to the modality that is most reliable for a given feature does not always lead to the optimal or most reliable perceptual result. If a less reliable source disagrees, that still should be taken into account. To enhance overall reliability, evidence from distinct sources should be weighted appropriately.

Biasing and recalibration between senses typically conforms to a weighting function that incorporates the relative reliability of multiple senses to determine the strength of a given sensory system's contribution to the perceptual compromise (see, for example, Welch and Warren 1980; Ernst and Banks 2002; Landy et al. 2011; Bennett et al. 2014; Rescorla 2018). When the reliability of two senses matches, the perceptual result in each involves averaging. When recalibration yields agreement, apparent convergence results.

Vision carries more reliable information about spatial location than does audition. That is, source variance accounts for more signal variance—vision's signal-to-noise ratio is higher. Thus, visual cues typically make a big impact on the auditory experience of spatial location, while auditory cues make a significantly smaller contribution than visual cues to the visual experience of spatial location. Visual cues make a greater contribution than tactual cues to size perception, but the two contribute equally to texture discrimination (Ernst and Banks 2002).

Ernst and Banks (2002) apply weighting in a maximum-likelihood estimation (MLE) model to explain observed patterns of visual and tactual dominance for size and for texture with varying amounts of noise in each.

[W]e found that height judgements were remarkably similar to those predicted by the MLE integrator. Thus, the nervous system seems to combine visual and haptic information in a fashion similar to the MLE rule: visual and haptic estimates are weighted according to their reciprocal variances.   (Ernst and Banks 2002, 431)

Weighting functions help explain perceptual errors caused by multi-sensory recalibration. In spatial ventriloquism, weighting visual contributions more than auditory ones explains why vision exerts greater influence on audition (Alais and Burr 2004). In temporal ventriloquism, auditory cues outweigh and dominate visual cues. This also explains why a sound biases an ambiguous visual display from mostly streaming to mostly bouncing percepts—apparent visible motion patterns incorporate auditory information that a collision occurs. And it accounts for why visual cues cause the auditory McGurk illusion even though the auditory stimulus itself is unequivocal. Deference to auditory cues arguably would make more sense given audition's strength at resolving spectral and temporal information about speech sounds; however, the compromise that occurs when a visual cue accompanies the auditory signal enhances the reliability of the resulting percept, given that each modality bears information about spoken phonemes.

Similar explanations have been applied to other crossmodal illusions, including the sound-induced flash effect.

The human observer's performance was highly consistent with that of the ideal observer in all conditions ranging from no interaction, to partial integration, to complete integration, suggesting that the rule used by the nervous system to decide when and how to combine auditory and visual signals is statistically optimal. Our findings show that the sound-induced flash illusion is an epiphenomenon of this general, statistically optimal strategy.   (Shams et al. 2005, 1923)

Weighting functions explain multisensory adjustments across a range of cases (see Handel 2006, chapter 9). Multisensory recalibration thus can be understood as special case of a more general cue integration strategy, which also can apply within senses, as with weighting several depth cues or color cues in vision (see Bennett et al. 2014).

Many studies have supported optimal linear cue integration as a model of human perception for stimuli involving relatively small cue conflicts. By and large, these studies have confirmed the two main predictions of the model: With small cue conflicts, cue weights are proportional to cue reliability, and the reliability for stimuli with multiple cues is equal to the sum of individual cue reliabilities.... Multisensory studies have also been consistent with the model.

(Landy et al. 2011, 18)

The leading hypothesis, therefore, is that crossmodal recalibrations stem from a strategy that enhances the reliability of perception. Landy et al. (2011) say, "In most cases, the organism can make more accurate estimates of environmental properties or more beneficial decisions by integrating these multiple sources of information" (5).

A critical but open question, familiar from debates concerning Bayesian approaches to perception, is just how closely crossmodal recalibrations conform to what is statistically optimal (see Rescorla 2015, especially 699–700, 706). Shams and Kim (2010) report that performance matches predictions:

Altogether these findings suggest that in carrying out basic perceptual tasks, the human perceptual system performs causal inference and multisensory integration, and it does so in a fashion highly consistent with a Bayesian observer. This strategy is statistically optimal as it leads to minimizing the average (squared) error of perceptual estimates; however, it results in errors in some conditions, which manifest themselves as illusions.   (Shams and Kim 2010, 280)

Which determinate weighting hypotheses are true, and to what degree recalibrations are optimal, remain open empirical questions. Nevertheless, sensory interactions conform to principles of deference and weighting in dealing with stimulation to multiple senses. Doing so improves the overall reliability of perception, when compared with parallel unisensory processes. Sometimes, however, it yields a crossmodal illusion.

I have argued that crossmodal interactions typically minimize conflict and generally defer to the more reliable sense. These patterns of interaction conform to weighting functions that help explain and predict performance in a range of circumstances. Being principled is a matter of supporting such generalizations. So, sensory interactions are principled rather than accidental or merely causal processes.

2.3.3 Benefits

I have claimed that sensory interactions that sometimes cause crossmodal illusions in fact enhance perception. Some may find this counterintuitive. But I do not mean that crossmodal illusions themselves are an improvement. Instead, I mean that the sorts of interactions among senses that sometimes lead to perceptual illusions generally are beneficial. When things go well, they make perception better in certain respects than it otherwise would be without any such interactions. Again, the cost is an occasional illusion.

It is worth emphasizing the specific respects in which such sensory interactions improve perception. Consider the principles already discussed. Sensory interactions tend to resolve conflicts and to conform to weighting functions. Start with the first. By minimizing conflicts, sensory interactions improve *coherence.* That is, there is greater consistency and less disagreement about things and features in the world as presented in perception than there would be without recalibration that reduces intersensory conflict. For instance, reconciling information from vision, touch, and audition concerning the location, number, and timing of objects and events improves overall perceptual coherence. Coordinating visible and tactual locations for a common object, or audible and visible onset timing for an event, typically makes one's perceptual take on objects, events, and their spatiotemporal features more consistent. This accrues to perceptual judgments and beliefs formed on perceptual grounds.

Now, consider the second. In conforming to weighting functions, sensory interactions improve the overall *reliability* of perception. In the first place, sensory interactions improve the reliability of perceptual capacities we already possess. Here is an illustration. Imagine sitting in a well-lit room with one person talking. You can discern their location by hearing or by sight. You are more likely to get the location of the talker right when you rely on vision alone than when you rely on hearing alone. In such situations, you will be wrong more often and by a greater margin when you are only listening. If you just trusted hearing, adding vision would not make a difference if vision and audition did not interact. However, hearing does rely on visual information, and it recalibrates accordingly. This tends to make audition more accurate concerning location in space than it would be if it did not rely on visual information. Relying on vision improves auditory spatial localization. In this type of situation, spatial hearing is more reliable thanks to multisensory coordination.

This scenario is not atypical. Audition's spatial resolution differs by an order of magnitude from vision's, and audition is prone to systematic errors, such as front–back confusions and illusions of angle and elevation due to the cone of confusion, in which interaural time or level differences match. Vision typically is more precise and more accurate (though audition works better for locations behind your head). For things you can see, relying on vision typically improves the accuracy and reliability of spatial hearing. Vision compensates for audition's limitations.

Sometimes, however, the result is worse. Experimenters can manipulate visual cues to disagree with the location of a loudspeaker. Relying on visual cues causes illusions that otherwise would not have occurred. You therefore make errors because audition defers to vision. Recalibration is a less reliable strategy in the multisensory research lab. The same holds for other cases in which a sound accidentally coincides with a visible event.

Nonetheless, audition tends to serve you better when it relies on visual information about space. Weighting visual information on the whole enhances auditory spatial perception. This is contingent. If you wore distorting prism goggles, or if we inhabited a world in which unrelated sounds and visible events coincidentally happened to occur at nearly the same time, the same perceptual strategy would lead to systematic errors. We would be worse off than with parallel unisensory perception. Given how our world is organized, and given that spatial audition actually is less reliable on its own than spatial vision, sensory interaction and recalibration makes spatial audition more reliable in natural environments, even if the ubiquity of audiovisual technology shifts the statistics.

What goes for spatial audition also applies to other forms of intersensory recalibration. Vision in very low lighting improves when it relies on spatial hearing. Auditory information enhances visual impressions of temporal features. Auditory information about whether a collision has occurred leads more reliably to accurate visual impressions of causal interaction and rebounding—when the display is ambiguous, the addition of a sound biases vision from streaming towards bouncing. Relying on visual and tactual information about articulatory gestures of the mouth improves auditory phoneme comprehension. Generally, one sense does better by relying on cues from others.

This can impact success in action and belief. Subjects act and form beliefs guided by perception. More reliable perception thus can enable more effective action and more accurate beliefs. Multisensory perception therefore benefits cognition and action. Each is a noteworthy enhancement to perception's capacity to fulfill its psychological function.

I have argued that sensory interactions have benefits. One sort of benefit is that they improve the reliability of perception; the analogous claim holds for perceptual belief. This invites additional questions. For instance, claims about the reliability of a belief-forming process face two important questions that stem from objections to reliabilism about epistemic justification. The first concerns *generality* (Goldman 1979). How we characterize a token process affects verdicts about its reliability. A process qua auditory may be unreliable, but that process qua perceptual may be reliable. Reliability claims do not generalize without bound. How should we characterize token perceptual processes for the purpose of assessing their reliability?

My account avoids reliabilism's generality problem. It compares the relative reliability of two sorts of processes, each of which is characterized in a specific psychological manner. For instance, unisensory spatial audition itself is less reliable than spatial audition augmented by weighted recalibration in light of visual spatial information. This is a principled distinction, and it is not ad hoc to ascribe token perceptual processes to these psychological types (cf. Conee and Feldman 1998).

The second concerns *range*. Which contexts we consider affects verdicts about the reliability of a process. A process may be accurate in one type of context but inaccurate in another. Typically, locating sounds at a speaker's lips is accurate, but in the movie theater it is illusory. Multisensory recalibration may be highly reliable for most humans on Earth. However, it would be systematically misleading on Psychology Lab Earth, where visual and auditory cues are a near match to those on Earth but visible and audible events always are wholly distinct and unrelated. Which contexts are relevant to assessing the relative reliability of unisensory and multisensory processes?

My account avoids reliabilism's range problem. The relevant sorts of contexts are typical, natural, Earthly human environments, in which visual and auditory information is more than accidentally correlated. I am not asserting that this difference in relative reliability grounds a difference in justification. Since I am not defending a reliabilist epistemology, I will not worry whether we are brains in vats (Goldman 1986) or inhabit a virtual world. On Earth, different senses typically yield information about related events. Movies and multimedia technologies affect the numbers, even while the practical benefits of recalibration remain.

Interaction and recalibration between senses therefore improves the coherence and the reliability of perception in typical human environments when compared with a collection of independent unisensory strategies. These are significant enhancements to perception. You are more coherent and more reliable, and your perceptual beliefs are more apt to be consistent and true, when informed by multisensory perception.

In some accounts, this implies that sensory interactions modulate perception's epistemic profile. If either coherence or reliability contributes to justification, beliefs formed on the basis of coordinated multisensory perception can be more justified than corresponding beliefs based on parallel unisensory perception. In each case, this could be so even if a subject were not in a position to appreciate it.

2.3.4 Functions

I have argued that sensory interactions of the type that sometimes cause crossmodal illusions are not accidents. They conform to principles of conflict resolution, deference, and weighting. And they improve the overall coherence and reliability of perception. These are marks that sensory interactions are part of multisensory perceptual functioning.

The notion of *function*, however, is fraught. Claims about functions and functioning are philosophical lightning rods. Entrenched disagreement divides theorists over basic questions about the nature of functions. Nevertheless, whatever one's preferred notion of functions, multisensory processes deserve a place as part of perceptual functioning. In particular, according to each of several distinct conceptions of function relevant to explanatory projects in psychology, sensory interactions are good candidates for being part of perceptual functioning.

First, at its most abstract, the notion of function is formal. A function, such as a weighting function, is a mapping from a domain of inputs to a range of outputs. While it is unlikely that sensory interactions conform to optimal weighting functions, the principles that characterize multisensory recalibration determine complex multisensory functions from unisensory inputs to perceptual outputs. However, conforming to a formal function does not explain how a system computes it or implements it. Marr (1982), for instance, distinguishes vision's input–output function, the algorithm by which vision computes it, and the mechanisms that implement this computation. Formal functions are not the sole relevant notion when discussing perceptual psychology. The others are tied to differing explanatory approaches.

One way to explain the capacities of a system is to say how it works. How does it tell time? What makes it tick? We might describe a clock's workings—its hands, gears, and springs—and how together their activities account for its ability to keep track of time. By analyzing the capacities of a system by the capacities of its components, we account for what it can do. Mechanistic explanations, in turn, aim to capture a phenomenon by describing the parts, organization, and activities responsible for it. This project focuses on providing a detailed account of a mechanism whose workings realize the capacities of a system (Machamer et al. 2000).

A second notion of function stems from this type of approach. It concerns the role a component plays in accounting for the capacities of a complex system. Cummins (1983) says:

> In the context of a science, to ascribe a function to something is to ascribe a capacity to it that is singled out by its role in an analysis of some capacity of a containing system. When a capacity of a containing system is appropriately explained via analysis, the analyzing capacities emerge as functions.   (Cummins 1983, 28)

In empirical psychology, Cummins says that ascribing such functions helps explain our psychological capacities. For example, the capacity to detect edges helps explain the capacity to see objects. Edge detection is part of the analysis of our capacity to see objects. Therefore, edge detection is a function in vision. Functions help explain a system's dispositions. Detecting edges is part of what causes us to see objects. Within the context of mechanistic explanations, Piccinini and Craver (2011) say functional analyses are mechanism sketches (Craver 2007). According to this understanding, a function is a role. In particular, it is a role in a system of capacities or causes.[5]

Human beings can perceive certain features, including space, time, and number, using multiple senses. Perception in multisensory contexts is susceptible to a variety of crossmodal illusions and recalibrations. Capacities such as conflict resolution, deference, and reliability weighting each help to account for such effects. They capture aspects of our capacity to perceive features like space, time, and number using multiple senses. Indeed, each figures in a proposed analysis that models our capacity to perceive such a feature using several senses. Each, therefore, emerges as a function in multisensory perception.

A process is part of psychological functioning when it manifests a psychological function. Interactions between processes associated with distinct senses manifest the capacity to resolve conflict and to weight in

---

[5] This notion therefore is connected to Aristotle's *efficient* causes.

favor of the more reliable sense. Indeed, causal interactions between processes associated with distinct senses are apt mechanisms for multisensory perceptual phenomena. According to this approach, therefore, sensory interactions are part of perceptual functioning.

Another way to explain the capacities of a system is to say what it is for. What is its purpose? What does accomplish? A clock is for keeping time, and marking the hour is the reason for the little hand. The tick has no purpose, but it stems from the escapement, whose steady steps serve to track time.

Characterizing how something works does not guarantee that it serves any purpose. And a process could play a role in manifesting a capacity without any reason or aim in doing so. (The clock can make noise, and it can hypnotize, but neither is its characteristic function.) Because it makes sense to ask what perceptual systems are for, causal and mechanistic analysis and decomposition are not the only sorts of explanation relevant to psychology. Teleology aims to explain a phenomenon by describing the aims, goals, and reasons it serves. A third notion of function stems from this type of approach. It concerns the reasons, goals, or ends served by a complex system, its capacities, and its components.[6]

What purpose do sensory interactions serve? Start with perception. Perception's purposes are to guide action and inform cognition. Those are its functions. Multisensory perception improves our capacity to perceive. Sensory interactions coordinate perception across the senses. They resolve conflicts and weight in deference to the more reliable modality. This minimizes disagreement and enhances perception's reliability. In making it a better source of information about the world, better suited to guide action and thought, multisensory perception furthers perception's purposes. Sensory interactions, which serve to reduce conflict and improve reliability, thus aid in achieving perception's ends. Therefore, they contribute to its functioning.

To understand function teleologically is to understand it in terms of an end. However, contributing to achieving a valuable end does not distinguish a function from an accidental benefit. Wright (1973), for instance, emphasizes the need to differentiate fortuitous benefits from genuine

---

[6] This notion therefore is connected to Aristotle's *final* causes.

adaptations. According to Wright, a function requires that a feature is present because it contributes to achieving a goal. This distinct notion of function is etiological.

> The function of X is Z means
> (a) X is there because it does Z,
> (b) Z is a consequence (or result) of X's being there. (Wright 1973, 81)

Suppose sensory interactions function to resolve conflicts across senses and to weight in favor of the more reliable sense. This enhances the reliability of perceptual capacities. According to an etiological account, this implies that sensory interactions occur because they reconcile discrepant information and help us get things right more frequently.

I will not argue expressly that sensory interactions have etiological functions. This raises thorny theoretical issues not specific to multisensory perception (see, for instance, Schellenberg 2018, chapter 2). Moreover, it is tough for a philosopher to establish that a psychological process occurs *because* it does Z. However, again, the contrast with synesthesia is instructive. What is the function of synesthesia? Synesthetic processes do not occur because they aid in perceiving the world or because they cause nice experiences. Synesthesia does not generally guide action or improve cognition. Any benefits to memory and discrimination are accidental. Synesthesia lacks a good Z.

What about evolution? Evolutionary theory does offer a way to specify the history that etiological functions require. An adaptation entails a history of selection. Evolutionary etiology thus promises a biological foundation for teleological functions. Because it promises to deliver naturalistic proper functions, this style of explanation has been popular in philosophy of psychology (see Wright 1973; Millikan 1989; Neander 1991; cf. Nanay 2010).

Demonstrating adaptiveness is not straightforward. Nevertheless, principled sensory interactions are intelligible as adaptive. Coordinating perception across senses provides a benefit. This benefit plausibly confers an advantage in the multisensory environments we and our ancestors have inhabited. A creature's capacity to coordinate multiple sources of sensory information about the world is the kind of feature that could impact its ability to survive and reproduce. Thus, it is an intuitive candidate for selection. By contrast, synesthesia is an offshoot that occurs because mechanisms of multisensory perception go awry.

In summary, the upshot is that whether functions concern causal roles or teleology, sensory interactions of the sort responsible for crossmodal illusions ought to be viewed as part of perceptual functioning.

2.3.5 Synopsis

I have argued that interactions among senses of the sort demonstrated by crossmodal illusions are not merely accidental. Unlike synesthesia, they are prevalent and systematic. The patterns of interaction conform to principles or rules for dealing with information from distinct senses. In particular, they resolve conflicts between senses and weight in favor of the more reliable modality. Thus, they improve the coherence and the reliability of perceptual processes. In addition, they play an explanatory role in accounting for features of our capacity to perceive space, time, number, and causality using several sensory systems. Moreover, they serve the purpose of enhancing perceptual capacities we already possess, for instance, by improving their coherence and reliability. This, in turn, enables more effective cognition and action. Finally, in light of the benefits they provide, sensory interactions are intelligible as adaptive and advantageous.

This is my case for the claim that causal interactions between processes associated with distinct senses are part of perceptual functioning. These interactions are principled, they figure in analyses of human perceptual capacities, and they serve a purpose. Thus, sensory interactions reflect characteristic perceptual functioning rather than mere causes or accidents.

2.4 Conclusion

Some perceptual processes are multisensory. By this I mean that multisensory processes are part of perceptual functioning. First, crossmodal illusions demonstrate through behavioral and neural evidence that processes associated with stimulation to distinct senses sometimes interact causally. Second, these interactions are perceptual. That is, they meet behavioral and neural criteria that diagnose perception, in contrast with extraperceptual cognition, for the purposes of empirical psychology, which uses a species of functional explanation. Finally, sensory interactions have a function. They are not just accidents or quirks. Therefore, some perceptual functioning is multisensory. Thus, explaining perception in functional terms requires appreciating the respects in which perception is multisensory. Since empirical psychology characterizes perception in functional terms, perceptual processes involving sensory interactions are among its proper targets.

2.5 Limitations

This chapter's argument concerns multisensory perceptual processes. As such, it has two significant limitations. It does not establish that a subject's perceptual capacities are multisensory. And it does not establish that perceptual awareness is irreducibly multisensory.

2.5.1 Capacities

The first limitation concerns a subject's perceptual capacities. Sensory interactions do not guarantee that a subject possesses multisensory perceptual capacities. This matters because critical philosophical disputes concerning perception and its role turn on capacities subjects possess.

You could perceive space, time, or causality through audition, vision, or touch alone. Multisensory processes improve a subject's capacity to perceive space, time, and causality by means of audition, vision, and touch. Sensory interactions thus enhance a subject's perceptual capacities. But, each of these capacities can be deployed unisensorily. So, sensory interactions improve capacities a subject already possesses. Doing so may implicate novel subpersonal capacities that are multisensory. However, multisensory processes need not confer to a subject any novel perceptual capacity—a capacity to perceive things in the world that could not be implemented unisensorily.

Suppose, for instance, that a subject's perceptual capacities are individuated by the features each targets. Sensory coordination and recalibration of the sort responsible for crossmodal illusions need not reveal any novel feature beyond those audition, vision, and touch reveal independently. Thus, coordination among subpersonal processes associated with distinct senses is compatible with a subject's deploying only sense-specific perceptual capacities. By analogy, two sources can share information by testimony without tracking any new objects or attributes. Sensory interactions therefore do not guarantee multisensory perceptual capacities.

To be clear, I am speaking of perceptual capacities of subjects. Subcapacities that figure in the analysis of a subject's perceptual capacities, such as conflict resolution and weighting, are multisensory. However, if a perceptual capacity is a capacity to perceive (rather than a capacity that is part of an account of what it is to perceive or of how a creature perceives), these subcapacities need not be full-fledged perceptual capacities. And they need not be attributed to the subject. After all, subjects typically are not aware that intersensory recalibration has taken place or that a cross-modal illusion has occurred. Sensory interactions of this sort are not revealed by introspection. They are subpersonal.

Thus, multisensory functioning does not guarantee that subjects possess a distinctive multisensory perceptual capacity, where that is understood as a novel capacity to perceive a thing or feature through the joint use of multiple senses. This matters because questions about consciousness, responsibility, and perception's epistemic role concern subjects and the capacities they possess. This chapter's argument does not yet secure a place for multisensory perception in such central philosophical topics.

2.5.2 Consciousness

The second limitation concerns consciousness. Sensory interactions do not guarantee irreducibly multisensory consciousness. This chapter's argument concerns subpersonal perceptual processes. Claims about psychological mechanisms, processes, and functions notoriously do not translate neatly into claims about consciousness. Thus, my arguments do not establish claims about consciousness.

Sensory interactions coordinate consciousness across senses. This is a phenomenological upshot. However, beyond coordinated consciousness, causal interactions need not be reflected in consciousness. From the point of view of the subject, perceptual consciousness might remain sense specific. After all, the sensory interactions I have described in this chapter typically go unnoticed. They are not apparent to a perceiving subject just in having the experience. A subject may be none the wiser. To appreciate this, note that for each such crossmodal illusion, there is a matching experience in which no sensory recalibration occurs.

Crossmodal illusions thus could involve wholly distinct experiences associated with distinct senses. Recalibration and coordination could occur between sense-specific conscious percepts. Systematic causal influence also does not guarantee constitutively multisensory consciousness. Perceptual consciousness therefore may be structured as a co-conscious collection of coordinated but sense-specific experiences.

This chapter's argument therefore does not establish that perceptual consciousness is richly or deeply multisensory. So, it does not challenge a conception according to which perceptual consciousness is a fusion of discrete, sense-specific component experiences, or "snapshots." It remains possible that perceptual consciousness is exhausted by sense-specific ways of perceiving and that each phenomenal feature is sense specific. Sensory interactions are compatible with coordinated but parallel unisensory consciousness.

Consciousness matters. It shapes one's evidence and one's self conception, and it affects aesthetic value. This chapter's argument does not yet secure a role for multisensory perceptual consciousness in lived human experience. So, it is not clear that it matters in the ways consciousness matters.

These limitations inspire the chapters that follow.

3
Capacities

One sense can impact another. But sensory interactions are not accidental or mere causal processes. They help resolve conflicts, enhance reliability, and deal with noisy and fallible sensory stimulation. Sensory interactions and recalibrations are part of perceptual functioning. Thus, some perceptual processes that figure in psychological explanation are multisensory.

Multisensory perceptual processes do not guarantee that subjects possess distinctive multisensory perceptual capacities. By this, I mean that sensory systems could interact and perform multisensory functions while a subject has no novel capacity to perceive multisensorily. Resolving conflicts between vision and audition subpersonally improves coherence but need not affect which objects and properties a subject can perceive. Weighting one sense more than another alters the reliability of a process but need not enable a subject to perceive in a wholly new way. Thus, sensory interactions need not change what a subject is capable of perceiving, so multisensory perception may reveal no more of the world than several independent senses. In that case, it makes little difference to the philosophy of perception.

This chapter argues that human subjects possess multisensory perceptual capacities. By jointly using several senses, we can perceive aspects and features of the environment that are perceptible neither with one sense at a time nor through parallel unisensory perception alone. Multisensory perception thus targets new features in the world. The joint use of multiple senses therefore extends human perceptual capacities.

The first premise of this chapter's argument is that typical human subjects are differentially sensitive to objects and features that are presented multisensorily. Relying on psychophysical evidence, I defend the claim that subjects can detect and differentiate a certain range of objects and features in multisensory contexts.

A Multisensory Philosophy of Perception. Casey O'Callaghan, Oxford University Press (2019).
© Casey O'Callaghan. DOI: 10.1093/oso/9780198833703.001.0001

The second premise is that some such features are novel. They could not be detected with an individual sense working on its own, nor through several senses simply in parallel. These include novel feature instances and novel feature types. It follows that typical human subjects have the capacity to detect and differentiate features that are accessible only through the coordinated use of multiple senses.

The third premise is that such multisensory capacities belong to perception rather than extraperceptual cognition. The reason is that differential sensitivity to novel intermodal features supports thought and guides action in the manner characteristic of perception, not only for the purposes of empirical psychology but also for rational psychological explanation.

Therefore, a typical human subject's capacity to detect and differentiate a novel intermodal feature is a perceptual capacity whose deployment relies on the joint use of multiple senses. It is a multisensory perceptual capacity.

A subject's psychological capacities thus include multisensory perceptual capacities. So, multisensory perception can serve in psychological explanations that deal with subjects and their capacities, in contrast with just subpersonal processes and mechanisms. It also can impact theoretical debates that turn on a subject's perceptual capacities, thereby affecting verdicts to questions about awareness, content, and justification.

Nevertheless, this argument, too, is limited. Multisensory perceptual capacities need not be reflected as such in perceptual consciousness. A subject could be differentially sensitive to a feature by means of the senses without being perceptually aware of it. And exercising a perceptual capacity need not require perceptual experience. Multisensory perceptual capacities thus do not guarantee multisensory perceptual consciousness. Two chapters that follow therefore address awareness and experience.

3.1 Capacities

A capacity is an ability or a capability. It concerns what can be done, and it depends on what would happen in various conditions, whether or not they obtain. So, it is a matter of potential rather than present or actual activity. Capacities ground tendencies and dispositions. Capacities thus are distinct from their exercises or manifestations. An individual can possess a capacity whether or not it is being exercised. The latter are episodes or events, and the former are standing characteristics. Thus, performance on an occasion need not reveal a subject's capacities, nor which among them is being exercised.[1]

Psychological capacities include those involved in memory, reasoning, action, awareness, decision making, language, and perception. More specific capacities include the capacity to speak English, to play chess, to empathize with suffering, to perform long division without a calculator, to remember birthdays and telephone numbers, and to perceive colors. Indeed, if minds comprise faculties, it is plausible to treat those as collections or bundles of capacities. My approach is to individuate such collections of capacities by the distinctive ways or manners in which they are exercised (see Chapter 6).

Psychological capacities help explain and predict subjects' responses—their perceptions, recollections, judgments, and actions. One reason is that a capacity is individuated by what it is to exercise it with success. Possessing the capacity to remember seven-digit numbers thus helps predict phone number recall. Another reason is that capacities accommodate flexibility across differing conditions. Pitch sensitivity, for instance, manifests for sounds with distinct timbre, loudness, and spectral profiles, and in a variety of settings. Capacities thus enable relatively robust hypothetical and future projections. A final reason is that a simpler capacity can figure in an account of one that is more complex. Edge detection, for instance, figures in object perception. Simpler capacities thus help account for sophisticated performance.

Empirical psychology investigates human psychological capacities and their limits. It might be thought to involve testing relevant subjunctives. It measures a subject's capacities by measuring performance across a range of conditions.

In the first instance, a perceptual capacity is a capacity to perceive a thing or feature. You may have the capacity to perceive sounds and their

---

[1] In what follows, the focus is on capacities a subject currently possesses, rather than those a subject could come to possess in time with further effort or development. This corresponds to Aristotle's distinction in *De Anima* between first actuality (capacity) and potentiality. Exercises or manifestations of capacities correspond to Aristotle's second actuality (Aristotle 1984).

pitch, timbre, and loudness. Typical humans can do so when awake and in the presence of compression waves between 20 hertz and 20 kilohertz. Perceptual capacities include the capacity to detect the presence of a sound, to differentiate shades of color, to segment a scene into figure and ground, and to discern objects and attributes in one's surrounding as targets for thought and action.

To possess the capacity to perceive a thing or feature, one must be differentially sensitive to it. This requires that a subject would respond in the appropriate way in a variety of conditions. Moreover, in order to count as perceptual, this responsiveness must play the right sort of role in grounding cognition and guiding action. It ought to enable other capacities, such as demonstrative thought, recognition, categorization, learning, and action.

Differential sensitivity to a thing or feature requires the capacity to detect it and the capacity to differentiate it from other things and features. To detect a thing or feature requires being able to respond to it when it is present. To differentiate it—to register that it differs, or to treat it as distinct from other things and features—requires being able to respond differently to it and other things.

For example, seeing an object typically involves not just detecting its presence but also differentiating it from its surroundings and from other objects. Hearing a pitch involves detecting it and differentiating it from distinct pitches and from loudness. Suppose you have the capacity to smell citrus. You can perceive the scent of citrus in sufficiently uncluttered olfactory scenes. This means being sensitive to instances of citrus scent when conditions are right and differentiating between citrus, other scents, and features such as pitches.

Schellenberg (2014, 2018) explicates the notion of a perceptual capacity in terms of the capacity to single out and to discriminate particulars, individuating such capacities according to which particulars they function to single out.

> The function of a perceptual capacity C_α is to discriminate and single out mind-independent particulars $a_1, a_2, a_3, \ldots a_n$, that is, particulars of a specific type.... A perceptual capacity C_α is individuated by the mind-independent particulars $a_1, a_2, a_3, \ldots a_n$ that the perceptual capacity functions to single out.   (Schellenberg 2018, 31)

My description of perceptual capacities differs from Schellenberg's in at least three minor respects. The first is that in my account perceptual capacities may target particulars or repeatables. Thus, it does not explicitly preclude that properties could individuate perceptual capacities. The second is that my account appeals to the capacity to detect and differentiate rather than the capacity to single out and discriminate. This may be just terminological.[2] Nevertheless, it draws attention to a substantive point worth emphasizing. Differential sensitivity itself does not require that a subject possesses further cognitive capacities to select and to discriminate. A subject could detect a feature without being able to single it out by means of attention or thought, and a subject could differentiate two features without being equipped to perform discrimination, to tell them apart, or to appreciate their difference. Typically, however, perceptual capacities play those enabling roles. The third is that I do not insist that distinct perceptual capacities require distinct objects. Distinct perceptual capacities, such as tracking, attending, and demonstrating, may target just the same particulars or attributes.

However, distinct objects in my account suffice for distinct perceptual capacities. With respect to a specific range of things and features, a difference in what two subjects can detect and differentiate means a difference in that to which subjects are differentially sensitive. If the difference plays the right role in their psychology, it suffices for a difference in what they can perceive. Thus, it entails a difference in their perceptual capacities. If two such subjects differ in what they can detect and differentiate, their perceptual capacities differ.

---

[2] Schellenberg's interchangeable uses of "discriminate" and "differentiate" in the following passage suggests this difference is partly terminological:

> There is good scientific evidence that discriminatory, selective capacities are cognitively the most low-level mental capacities employed in perception, so I will focus on this kind of perceptual capacity. A discriminatory, selective capacity is a low-level mental capacity that functions to differentiate, single out, and in some cases type the kind of particulars that the capacity is of. For example, if we possess the discriminatory, selective capacity that functions to differentiate and single out red, we are in a position to differentiate instances of red from other colors in our environment and to single out instances of red. More generally, to possess a discriminatory, selective capacity is to be in a position to differentiate and single out the type of particulars that the capacity is of, were one related to such a particular.   (Schellenberg 2014, 91)

Questions about what can be perceived are questions about what can be detected and what can be differentiated. Among perceptual capacities, I'll count such capacities, which ground or constitute a capacity to perceive.

3.2 Multisensory Capacities

With this understanding of perceptual capacities, to show that typical human subjects possess multisensory perceptual capacities, it suffices to show two things. The first is that multisensory perception enables us to perceive things we could not otherwise perceive. The second is that multisensory capacities can be attributed to perceiving subjects and not just subpersonal perceptual systems.

This chapter's argument relies on the claim that typical human subjects can detect and differentiate certain things multisensorily that cannot be detected and differentiated either unisensorily or through several senses working merely in parallel. Using several senses in coordination, we sometimes detect the presence of such novel features, and the joint multisensory response differs from any parallel unisensory response. Since a multisensory capacity is one whose deployment sometimes relies on the joint use of multiple senses, some perceptual capacities therefore are multisensory.

This section argues that perceivers are differentially sensitive to the presence of novel features that are perceptible only multisensorily. The evidence stems from three types of cases: intermodal binding and identity, novel intermodal feature instances, and novel intermodal feature types. Before presenting the evidence, I say why coordinating perception across senses by itself does not establish this conclusion.

3.2.1 Coordination

To clarify what is at stake, start with an illustrative case that is not conclusive. Chapter 2 argued that crossmodal illusions are evidence for crossmodal recalibration. Crossmodal recalibration demonstrates coordination between distinct senses. In particular, coordination can minimize conflict between senses and defer to the more reliable sense. But, recalibration is selective. For instance, it typically occurs when distinct senses bear conflicting information about the same feature. Ventriloquism reconciles a spatial conflict between vision and audition. The sound-induced flash reconciles a numerosity conflict.

Resolving conflict between senses suggests that perceptual systems are differentially sensitive to common features presented to multiple senses. First, it provides evidence that perceptual systems can detect when a single feature instance is presented to distinct senses. Second, it is evidence that perceptual systems differentiate a common feature presented to distinct senses from distinct unisensory features. Sensory interactions thus are evidence that perceptual systems are differentially sensitive to the identity of a feature that is perceived with distinct senses. If so, multisensory processes can identify features across sense modalities. For instance, they can fix on common audiovisual locations.[3]

Nonetheless, there are two good replies on behalf of the unimodal theorist. The first is that subpersonal differential sensitivity to the identity of features between senses does not guarantee that subjects possess a corresponding perceptual capacity to identify them multisensorily. Given that distinct senses present spatial features differently, subpersonal processes might serve only to coordinate awareness across senses. Thus, it is plausible that perception itself does not suffice for a subject to be sensitive to the identity of common features presented to distinct senses.

The second, and more pressing, is that recalibration does not require identification. Conflict resolution can occur without differential sensitivity to the identity of features presented to distinct senses. Here is one reason why. Features detected with distinct senses may be correlated yet distinct. Thus, each can provide relevant information about the other. Sensitivity to crossmodal correlations can explain intersensory recalibration and conflict resolution. This does not require special sensitivity to the identity of features presented multisensorily. Recalibration therefore is compatible with coordination among unisensory perceptual processes. It does

---

[3] Austen Clark (2011) develops a related idea. Clark argues that crossmodal cueing of attention requires identifying locations across senses. That is because, in order for a cue presented to one sense at a given location to speed responsiveness using another sense to a target at the same location, the location perceived using each distinct sense must be identified as the same place. This argument is subject to the same two limitations I describe in the main text that follows.

not demonstrate differential sensitivity to identity across senses, in contrast with sensitivity to distinct yet correlated features. Further evidence is needed for identification.

Coordination between senses is a significant multisensory accomplishment. But, it does not establish that subjects possess novel multisensory perceptual capacities. The cases that follow are designed to surmount these obstacles. Each is a case in which subjects are differentially sensitive to features of the world only thanks to the joint use of multiple senses.

3.2.2 Binding and Identity

By means of perception, typical human subjects can identify objects across sensory modalities. This is a critical multisensory capacity.

Human subjects perceive individual things and their features (Cohen 2004). Perceptible individuals include objects and events, and among their perceptible features are attributes and parts. Individuals can be perceived to have several features at once. When you perceive multiple features jointly to belong to the same individual or to be coinstantiated, call that a case of *feature binding*.[4]

The paradigms of feature binding are intramodal. A visible figure may look jointly reddish and round. "E" has a visible part "F" lacks. A developed experimental literature deals with visual feature binding and its relation to visual awareness (see, especially, Treisman and Gelade 1980; Treisman 1996, 2003). But, binding also occurs in other modalities. A piercing alarm sounds high-pitched and loud. Fresh oysters feel cool and clammy to the touch. Fried chicken tastes of salt and oil. After a flood, carpet smells mildewy and pungent.

Feature binding also occurs across senses. Attributes or parts presented to different senses can belong perceptibly to the same thing. So, for example, you might visuotactually perceive a brick's being jointly red and rough. This contrasts with just perceiving something red and something rough, like seeing a stop sign while feeling sandpaper. Or, you might audiovisually perceive an explosion at once to be jointly loud

---

[4] Please note that throughout this book I use the term "feature" to apply generically to properties, qualities, attributes, or parts, following its role in the literature on feature binding.

and bright. This contrasts with just perceiving something loud and something bright, like hearing a trumpet and seeing a camera flash. Each is a case of intermodal feature binding.

In binding, features perceptibly belong together. Thus, we are sensitive to more than just properties or parts. We are sensitive to coinstantiation, joint parthood, or bundling. This relation corresponds to the presence of feature-bearing individuals. Intermodal binding thus involves sensitivity to individuals with features perceived using distinct senses. Since those features perceptibly belong together, it involves sensitivity to the identity of individuals perceived using distinct senses. Thus, we have a capacity that targets multisensory individuals. This is a multisensory perceptual capacity.

What is the evidence? Experimental researchers commonly report that perceptual systems bundle or bind information from different senses to yield unified perceptions of common multimodally accessible objects or events. For instance, Vatakis and Spence (2007) say, "There appear to be specific mechanisms in the human perceptual system involved in the binding of spatially and temporally aligned sensory stimuli" (754).

Crossmodal illusions commonly are cited as evidence. The intersensory discrepancy paradigm generates an illusion and thus establishes sensory interaction. Two senses bear conflicting information, and their responses recalibrate. This is taken as evidence that perceptual systems discern when sensory information concerns something common and treat it as such.

> The bias measured in such experimental situations is a result of the tendency of the perceptual system to perceive in a way that is consonant with the existence of a single, unitary physical event.... Within certain limits, the resolution may be complete, so that the observer perceives a single compromise event.
>
> (Welch and Warren 1980, 661–4)

However, I want to emphasize that crossmodal illusions alone do not establish intermodal binding. Perceiving in a way that is consonant with a single event does not imply perceiving something to be a single event. The senses may agree without identifying common targets as such. Two mutually informed best guesses might just line up. So, conflict resolution guarantees neither integration nor binding. Differential sensitivity to the identity of individuals across senses requires more than coordination.

Here, the study of binding within a sense using experimental methods provides valuable guidance in understanding the multisensory case. If standard measures used to diagnose intramodal feature binding translate to intermodal contexts, that could provide evidence for or against intermodal feature binding. Four such phenomena have been reported to support intermodal binding.

The first is illusory conjunction. Unattended perceptible features sometimes mistakenly appear coinstantiated. An unattended red square and green circle can cause subjects to report seeing a red circle, and an unattended "O" and "R" can lead them to report seeing a "Q." This is evidence for a contrast between bound and unbound features. A merely illusory conjunction—an apparent "Q" when only an "O" and "R" are present—illustrates how distinct features can appear coinstantiated. Illusory feature conjunctions traditionally have been used to diagnose intramodal feature binding (see, for example, Treisman and Schmidt 1982).

Cinel et al. (2002) argue that illusory conjunctions occur between vision and touch. As measured by performance errors, an unattended felt texture can be ascribed incorrectly to a visible shape with another texture. Cinel et al. glued things to cardboard to construct objects with a distinctive surface texture (*carpet*, *Lego*, *fur*, *beans*). They presented distinct objects tactually (hidden beneath a screen) and visually. The tasks involved determining the orientation of the tactual object and the texture and shape of the visual stimuli. In a series of studies, subjects regularly misattributed a felt texture to a visible shape.

Cinel et al. argue that illusory conjunctions of visible and tactual features are "perceptual in nature" (1261) and "preattentive" (1244) rather than memory failures or effects of extraperceptual cognition. Loading memory by prompting both visual and tactual texture reports in fact reduced illusory conjunction errors, even though relying on memory to recall which features belonged to which objects ought to have increased errors in this more demanding task (Experiment 4 vs. Experiment 1, 1251). The effect was enhanced for stimuli in the same hemifield (Experiment 2) and with reduced attention (Experiment 1), consistent with unisensory results. The authors conclude, "These results demonstrate that ICs [illusory conjunctions] are possible not only within the visual modality but also between two different modalities: vision and touch" (1245).

Nonetheless, studies involving illusory conjunction typically rely on perceptual reports rather than direct psychophysical measurements. Indeed, Cinel et al. prompt reports and forced choices to probe feature conjunctions. This methodology is subject to extraperceptual interference and confounds. So, it is valuable to have further evidence.

The second phenomenon is the object-specific preview effect. Kahneman et al. (1992, see, especially, 176) propose that visual object perception involves object files, which are temporary episodic representations of persisting real-world objects. Object files organize information about distinct perceptible features (Kahneman and Treisman 1984).

Previewing a target affects one's capacity to recognize it later, but only if its two appearances are "linked" to the same object. If an object's features match at two times, reviewing it enhances recognition. If its features do not match, reviewing it hampers recognition. Unlinked objects yield no preview effect.

A preview benefit requires matching feature combinations ascribed to a common object. A preview penalty requires mismatching feature combinations ascribed to a common object. No object-specific preview benefit or penalty accrues for perceptible features not attributed to the reviewed object. Object-specific preview effects therefore are a critical diagnostic for intramodal feature binding (Kahneman et al. 1992). Zmigrod et al. (2009) say, "Interactions between stimulus-feature-repetition effects are indicative of the spontaneous binding of features and thus can serve as a measure of integration" (675).

Object-specific preview benefits and penalties occur intermodally. Zmigrod et al. (2009, 674–5) report that patterns of performance that characterize unimodal feature binding occur intermodally between audition and vision, and between audition and touch. For instance, based on a study presenting a sequence of colored circles, each paired with a specific pitch, they argue that color–pitch pairs may be bound (each stimulus was presented for 50 milliseconds, the second separated by 450 milliseconds from response to the first). That is because presenting $color_1$ with $pitch_1$ at t_1 followed by $color_1$ with $pitch_2$ at t_2 impairs responsiveness at t_2 (slows it and degrades its accuracy) both to $color_1$, when compared with repeating $pitch_1$ in the color identification task, and to *pitch*₂, when compared with pairing distinct *color*₂ in the pitch task (Experiment 1). The fact that an auditory pairing incurs object-specific preview effects for vision conflicts with what is predicted by the hypothesis that we harbor only modality-specific object files with intramodal binding.

Zmigrod et al. (2009, 682–3) conclude that feature binding occurs across sense modalities, and posit "episodic multimodal representations." Jordan et al. (2010) also find "a standard, robust OSPB" between vision and audition and conclude that their data "explicitly demonstrate object files can operate *across* visual and auditory modalities" (501).

Unlike illusory conjunctions, object-specific preview effects do not just rely on perceptual reports. Instead, they are measured by reaction time and percent error differences in task performance. Nonetheless, since they use stimuli presented in sequence, object-specific preview effects do rely on memory and recognition, thus providing only indirect support for synchronic binding.

The third phenomenon is attentional spreading. Attention to one feature of an object enhances the salience of its other features, compared with attention to features of a distinct object or to unattended features of the same object. This is not just due to spatial attention. It relies on object-oriented attention. Richard et al. (2008) say:

> An attentional spreading view of object-based attention proposes that the rate and efficiency of perceptual processes are improved by spreading attention through an attended object. This spreading likely enhances the representation of the attended object relative to unattended objects.
>
> (Richard et al. 2008, 843)

Attentional spreading is evidence for binding because the effect occurs only for features that belong to a common attentional object.

Spreading of object-based attention also occurs across sensory modalities (Busse et al. 2005; Talsma et al. 2010, 405–6). As measured by differences in event-related potentials, attention to a visible feature can enhance responsiveness to an audible feature, when compared with responsiveness to an audible feature paired with either an unattended visible feature or with an attended visible feature of a distinct object. When the visible and audible stimuli occur at the same time, the effect holds for features in distinct locations, so it is not just due to focusing in the right place. It holds for distinct stimulus features, so it does not just stem from focusing on a common property. And it occurs for task-irrelevant auditory stimuli, so it is not just a matter of paying attention to whatever will help you complete a task.

Crossmodal attentional spreading is a way of being differentially sensitive to the identity of items presented to distinct senses. It is evidence that some objects of perceptual attention are multisensory, jointly bearing features perceptible with distinct senses. Like object-specific preview effects, this paradigm relies on psychophysical measures rather than perceptual reports. However, unlike preview effects, it can be measured for stimuli presented at one time, so it does not rely on memory or reidentification.

The fourth phenomenon is integration. Integration is combining information to yield a single product. Doing so selectively is evidence of differential sensitivity to a common information source.

Stein et al. (2010) characterize multisensory integration as "the neural process by which unisensory signals are combined to form a new product" (1719). Superadditive effects are evidence of integration. A superadditive effect occurs when the multisensory neural or behavioral response to a stimulus differs measurably from the sum of the modality-specific responses to that stimulus (see Chapter 2). Such effects are reported to be widespread (Stein 2012).

Superadditive effects are significant because they provide evidence that perceptual processes do not just reconcile conflicts between senses. Instead, multisensory processes sometimes integrate information concerning a common source and generate a novel type of response. This outstrips whatever effect recalibration and coordination has on sense-specific processes. Integration as such does not entail feature binding, but intermodal feature binding does require integrating information from distinct senses concerning a common object. Where integration targets a common object, it is evidence for binding. Baumgartner et al. (2013) in fact reimport this criterion as evidence for binding in a unisensory context.[5]

---

[5] Still, in my view, binding is distinct from integration. Binding requires retaining intact information about the respective sources, while integration does not.

So, we have evidence for intermodal feature binding from four paradigms used to establish intramodal feature binding. Comparing unisensory and multisensory experimental work thus supports the claim that we can detect and differentiate common individuals bearing features perceived with distinct senses. These capacities impact performance in selection and discrimination tasks, and they can be used to make perceptual reports. This supports the conclusion that typical human subjects have the capacity perceptually to keep track of individual objects and events presented multisensorily.

Identifying something across senses is not just exercising capacities in parallel using several senses. Instead, it involves keeping track of something from one sense to the next. This is a new sort of exercise of the general capacity to perceive an individual. It targets things presented to multiple senses. Thus, through the joint use of several senses, human subjects are able to detect and differentiate things in a distinctive, multisensory way.

For a given range of things and features, a difference in that to which subjects are differentially sensitive suffices for a difference in perceptual capacities. Since binding affects discriminatory performance concerning a range of individuals, this suffices for a difference in perceptual capacities. Therefore, the capacity perceptually to identify individuals across senses is a multisensory perceptual capacity.

Neverthethess, intermodal binding does not add to our perceptual capacities in the same way that distinct senses do. Each distinct sense reveals objects and features in the world that others do not. Audition reveals individuals (sounds and events), feature instances (locations behind us), and features of types (pitch) to which vision is blind. However, intermodal binding and sensitivity to identity do not require that any such new object or attribute in the world is perceived. In visuotactually perceiving a baseball in your hand, or in audiovisually perceiving a talker uttering a sentence, you perceive just the one object, or the one event, and its visible, tactual, or audible features. And you could perceive all of those things together in absence of binding.

What differs in binding is how you bundle and carve things up, rather than the basic inventory of objects and attributes to which you are perceptually related. In this respect, binding is a structural fact about perception. In contrast, each sense is not just another way to perceive the same things and features. The senses are not just structural variants. If multisensory perception is just a structural variant of parallel unisensory perception, it still matters, but its significance is limited in comparison with the differing varieties of unisensory perception.

3.2.3 Novel Feature Instances

The next type of case shows that some multisensory perception reveals new feature instances. In particular, some feature instances are perceptible only through the joint use of multiple senses. No single sense on its own nor any collection of senses working independently suffices. Human subjects can detect and differentiate such features. Thus, multisensorily, we are differentially sensitive to things that otherwise could not be perceived.

This, too, reflects a multsensory perceptual capacity—one that can be exercised in a way that relies on multiple senses. The examples establish a difference in what subjects can detect and differentiate. Thus, they suffice for distinct perceptual capacities. But, this case differs from intermodal binding in that it is clear subjects are sensitive to new instances of features in the world that could not otherwise be perceived.

Structural properties provide the best examples. Consider temporal, spatial, and causal features. First, temporal relations hold between things perceived with different senses. Most subjects quickly and accurately can judge temporal order across modalities (see, for example, Spence and Squire 2003). Umpires in baseball tell whether a baserunner is safe or out by watching the runner's foot strike the bag and listening for the sound of the ball hitting the fielder's mitt. In close calls, vision alone is unreliable due to the distance between the base and the mitt. My claim is that the umpire does not simply perceive each one and then work out the relation. The umpire multisensorily discerns the temporal relation—the order and interval—between visible and audible events.

Why think we are sensitive to intermodal temporal relations rather than distinct unisensory events in sequence? One reason is that an extensive experimental literature details responsiveness to intermodal temporal relations. Synchrony is especially instructive. Müller et al. (2008, 309) say, "A great amount of recent research on multisensory integration deals with the experience of perceiving synchrony of events between different sensory modalities although the signals frequently arrive at different times" (309). Spence and Squire (2003) describe a temporal ventriloquism effect and a "moveable window" for multisensory integration that contribute to perceptually apparent synchrony. Stone et al. (2001) define the audiovisual *point of subjective simultaneity* as the timing at which a subject is most likely to indicate that a light and a tone begin simultaneously. What is noteworthy is that apparent synchrony typically requires visual stimulation to precede auditory stimulation by an average of about 50 milliseconds. The upshot is that in typical contexts outside the lab we detect synchronous events despite asynchronous sensory responses.

This is a sophisticated achievement. Keetels and Vroomen (2012, 170) describe it as "flexible and adaptive." It requires accommodating timing differences introduced during physical and sensory transmission.

> To perceive the auditory and visual aspects of a physical event as occurring simultaneously, the brain must adjust for differences between the two modalities in both physical transmission time and sensory processing time.... Our findings suggest that the brain attempts to adjust subjective simultaneity across different modalities by detecting and reducing the time lags between inputs that likely arise from the same physical events. (Fujisaki et al. 2004, 773)

Subjective simultaneity is adjusted for synchronous events. Part of the evidence for adjustment is that it can be disrupted, leaving apparent asynchrony. Moreover, it is selective. Signals near in time need not be adjusted if not taken to stem from simultaneous physical events. This means that temporally misaligned signals can be treated in differing ways. Those treated as stemming from synchronous events are adjusted, and those taken as stemming from asynchronous events are not. This can be true for signals with the same timing.

Thus, we respond to synchronous events in a way that differentiates them from asynchronous events. In particular, being near in time can signal synchrony, but it need not. How perceptual systems treat signals near to each other in time differs when they are taken to indicate synchrony and when they are not. Even two events that are represented as occurring at a time need not be represented as synchronous. This can be assessed in terms of whether, if the two events had occurred at slightly different times, they would or would not have been treated as synchronous. Therefore, we are differentially sensitive to intermodal synchrony in contrast with asynchrony. Perceptual systems thus are sensitive to the relative timing of events across senses.

This does not yet establish that subjects, in contrast with subpersonal perceptual systems, are differentially sensitive to simultaneity, rather than just perceiving at the same time. We need evidence that the relevant type of sensitivity can be attributed to a perceiving subject.

Intermodal meter perception provides a compelling case. Meter is the structure of a pattern of rhythmic sounds—its repeating framework of timed stressed and unstressed beats. Meter can be shared by patterns of sound whose rhythms differ. A piece's time signature indicates its meter. Meter is perceptible auditorily and tactually.

Huang et al. (2012) demonstrate that it is possible audiotactually to discriminate a novel musical meter that is discernible neither audibly nor tactually: "We next show in the bimodal experiments that auditory and tactile cues are integrated to produce coherent meter percepts." Appealing to psychophysical measures of detection and discriminability, they assert, "We believe that these results are the first demonstration of crossmodal sensory grouping between any two senses" (Huang et al. 2012, 1).

The experiments present rhythmic sound sequences through a headphone to the left ear and distinct sequences of inaudible vibrations to the left finger. The researchers first measure accuracy in identifying duples and triples presented unisensorily, either to hearing alone or to touch alone. Next, in a distinct unimodal condition, neither sequence independently has any identifiable meter—subjects are at chance whether the sounds alone or touches alone form a duple or triple. Then, in the key bimodal condition (Experiment 2), those same unisensory patterns of sounds and vibrations presented together contain cues for either duples or triples. When presented bimodally, subjects are able to discern with accuracy well above chance whether a duple or triple is present in the bimodal stimulus. In some cases, bimodal performance outstrips unisensory identification of duples and triples presented to touch alone.

To illustrate this phenomenon intuitively, consider a simple case of intermodal meter perception using an audiotactual rhythm pattern.

Suppose you hear a sequence of rhythmic sounds by itself. Next, suppose you feel a different rhythmic sequence of silent vibrating pulses on your hand. Now combine the two. You hear a sequence of sounds while feeling a differing sequence of pulses on your hand. You can attend to the sounds or to the vibrations. But it also is possible to discern and attend to the metrical pattern formed by the audible sounds and the tactual pulses—the audiotactual duples or triples. Perceiving the intermodal meter differs from perceiving either of the unimodal patterns in isolation. It also differs from perceiving two simultaneous but distinct patterns. The intermodal meter pops out.

So, musical meter has novel intermodal instances that subjects reliably detect and differentiate. Doing so is not just discerning distinct unimodal meters. Instead, it requires the coordinated use of multiple senses. Intermodal meter perception thus involves differential sensitivity to a novel feature instance that could not be perceived using one sense alone or through several senses in parallel working wholly independently. Therefore, it involves a perceptual capacity that targets a new feature instance and that is deployed multisensorily. Since perceptual capacities are individuated by their targets, so that differing targets suffice for distinct capacities, this suffices for a distinct, multisensory perceptual capacity. Multisensory meter perception thus extends one's perceptual capacities, when compared with unisensory meter perception.

Intermodal meter perception is enough to demonstrate differential sensitivity to novel feature instances. Other cases are fertile ground for future research. Take spatial features. Matthen (2015a) defends the Kantian thesis that space is premodal on the grounds that modality-specific spatial maps require coordination. Crossmodal recalibrations demonstrate that information about space in fact is coordinated across different senses. Thus, it is possible in principle to detect and differentiate spatial relations that hold between things experienced with different senses.

Plausibly, subjects do perceive intermodal spatial relations. For instance, you can detect the spatial offset between an audible sound coming from just to the left of a visible speaker. And you can discern when a visible feature and a tangible feature are located in the same place. A sound paired with a light oriented vertically grabs your attention when presented following a sequence of sound and light pairs oriented horizontally. A natural explanation for these capacities is that you see a located feature, hear a located feature, and multisensorily detect the novel intermodal spatial relation that holds between those features.

Moreover, intermodal motion may be perceptible. As evidence, a novel intermodal motion pattern suffices. For instance, you could hear a sound on the left and then see a spot to its right and detect intermodal motion. Here is a more complex example. Imagine two beeps repeatedly sounding in turn on the left and right in front of you. Now interleave a sequence of two lights flashing straight ahead above and below them. The beeps audibly move back and forth, and the flashes visibly move up and down. Jointly, their clockwise motion is perceptible.

A skeptic will deny that such novel intermodal motion is perceptible rather than inferred or worked out. As in unimodal cases, merely apparent or illusory intermodal motion is a good test. Some researchers have reported intermodal apparent motion. Harrar et al. (2008), for instance, claim that there is visuotactile apparent motion between lights and touches. Others agree:

> Apparent motion can occur within a particular modality or between modalities, in which a visual or tactile stimulus at one location is perceived as moving towards the location of the subsequent tactile or visual stimulus.... For example, with an appropriate time interval between a visual stimulus at one location and a tactile stimulus at another location, the participants would perceive some kind of motion stream from the first to the second location. In this kind of intermodal apparent motion, the motion stream is composed of stimuli from two different modalities.   (Chen and Zhou 2011, 369–71)

Moreover, Chen and Zhou (2011) and Jiang and Chen (2013) each report that auditory and visuotactile apparent motion influence each other. That merely apparent visuotactile motion affects merely apparent auditory motion is evidence that we are sensitive to some (visuotactile) intermodal motion.

The reports of Allen and Kolers (1981) are intriguing. They find no apparent motion for an integrated, traveling, hybrid audiovisual object (1320). However, in a heteromodal condition involving a light and a sound in different locations, the authors do find evidence of apparent intermodal motion. This recalls the color phi phenomenon.

One of the authors (Allen) once perceived what could be regarded as a sonorous light or a luminous sound in motion between a visual and an auditory stimulus. The following is an account written at the time of the occurrence:

A light breaks away from the location of the visual stimulus at the latter's onset—its trajectory can be followed for perhaps .5 meters, but a sense of its continuing to the ear is strong. The light seems to arrive there at the onset of the tone and then returns to the location of the visual stimulus, arriving there at the offset of the tone. One could ascribe a "sonorous" quality to the light, especially on its return to the location of the visual stimulus during the onset of the tone. The phenomenon repeated perhaps 25–30 times.

(Allen and Kolers 1981, 1320)

Nevertheless, this is a descriptive report. Others have failed to find intermodal apparent motion. Huddleston et al. (2008) test for audiovisual apparent motion. Huddleston et al. use alternating LED lights and white noise bursts at four distinct locations in a vertical plane, corresponding to 12, 3, 6, and 9 on a clock's face. In particular, they present LEDs switching between 12 and 6 o'clock positions in sequence with white noises alternating between 9 and 3 o'clock. They observe, "Although subjects were able to track a trajectory using cues from both modalities, no one spontaneously perceived 'multimodal [apparent] motion' across both visual and auditory cues" (1207). Subjects do not report impressions of apparent clockwise intermodal motion.

However, the results of Huddleston et al. are inconclusive. Even while subjects failed to report spontaneous perceptually apparent audiovisual motion, their psychophysical results show that subjects are able accurately to discern the direction of audiovisual motion. In the multisensory condition, participants were 90 percent accurate reporting the direction of intermodal motion when each stimulus was presented for at least 175 milliseconds (Huddleston et al. 2008, 1214, figure 6). Notably, this matched performance in a comparable unimodal auditory condition that used two *different* types of sounds, including a white noise burst and a "distinctive" complex sound.

Thus, there is an alternative interpretation. Perceiving motion requires identifying something as moving. Lights and noises separated by space may enable motion detection, but they need not meet further conditions for conscious awareness as of a single item apparently traveling from one place to another. An LED and a noise burst may be insufficiently related to appear as a single traveling object. Therefore, they generate no impression of intermodal motion. Stronger identity cues may reveal apparent intermodal motion.

Other features have instances that are discernible multisensorily. Take causal features. Philosophers have described cases in which human subjects perceptually experience intermodal causal relations. Nudds (2001) argues that it is possible multisensorily to perceive a visible event's producing or generating a sound: the colliding vehicles perceptibly make the crashing sound (see also Siegel 2009). There also is good empirical evidence that we are sensitive to intermodal causality (Sekuler et al. 1997; Guski and Troje 2003; Choi and Scholl 2006; Shams and Beierholm 2010). In particular, we detect causal relations between things perceived with distinct senses and differentiate intermodal causality from generic spatial and temporal relations. If so, typical human subjects are differentially sensitive to intermodal causality. Plausibly, this stems from perception.

Where do things stand? Some relational feature instances are perceptible only multisensorily. Examples include meter and simultaneity. Results from psychophysics and neuroscience show that we are differentially sensitive to the presence of such features. We register them, and we treat them differently from unisensory features. This sort of distinctive multisensory response enables subjects to single out and to discriminate features such as intermodal spatial, temporal, and causal relations. Therefore, typical subjects have the capacity perceptually to detect and differentiate novel intermodal feature instances.

It follows that not every feature instance a subject can detect and differentiate is discernible either with one sense at a time or with several independent senses working in parallel. Some feature instances are perceived only through the joint use of several senses. A multisensory perceptual capacity is one whose deployment sometimes involves the joint use of several senses. Thus, the capacity to discern novel feature instances requires a multisensory perceptual capacity. Moreover, it targets new, otherwise imperceptible features in the world. Multisensory perception therefore reveals more of the world than any collection of senses working independently.

Nevertheless, these features are not unfamiliar or alien. Each feature I have described belongs to a type with instances that are perceptible using one sense. You can perceive spatial, temporal, and causal relations through vision, touch, or hearing alone. So, none of these examples shows that multisensory perception reveals a wholly new or distinctive kind of feature in the world.

In contrast, each distinct sense does reveal features of types that are not perceptible with any other sense—these are its proper sensibles. In this respect, therefore, each distinct form of unisensory perception may differ from multisensory perception. For all I have said, multisensory perception reveals no new kind of property.

This, in turn, constrains the degree to which our multisensory capacities are novel. None of the multisensory capacities I have described is unique or wholly distinctive. By this I mean that none targets an unfamiliar type of perceptible feature. Instead, each multisensory capacity corresponds to a unimodal capacity that targets (unimodal instances of) features of the same type, which can be deployed using one sense at a time. By contrast, each distinct sense has its distinctive perceptual capacities.

3.2.4 Novel Feature Types

Some features belong to types whose instances could only be perceived multisensorily. In this respect, they are unlike spatial, temporal, and causal features. You could not discern any instance of the type through a single sense. The capacity to detect and differentiate such a feature requires multiple senses. Perceiving it thus requires a perceptual capacity that can be deployed only through the joint use of several senses. Therefore, it employs a distinctive multisensory perceptual capacity.

Flavor is one candidate for such a novel feature type.[6] Flavor perception involves taste, smell, and trigeminal somatosensation working

---

[6] Balance is another. Being in balance is a perceptible feature of your body or of something you balance, such as a book, serving tray, or funambulist's pole. Its perception relies on vestibular, visual, and proprioceptive information about acceleration and orientation with respect to gravity, which is unavoidably integrated very early in sensory processing. Vestibular or visual disruptions to balance, as in labyrinthitis, in outer space, or when spinning, lead to vertigo. Since balance is not wholly exteroceptive, I set it aside. See Wong (2017).

in concert. But flavor is not fully perceptible through taste, olfaction, touch, or somatosensation independently. The distinctive and recognizable *mintiness* of fresh mint ice cream and the *spiciness* of capsaicin are perceptible only thanks to the joint operation of several sensory systems. Perceiving flavor involves a new, multisensory perceptual capacity.

To perceive flavor fully requires stimulating taste buds, smell receptors, and the trigeminal nerve. The taste system suffices to detect the basic tastes of salty, sweet, bitter, sour, and umami. However, retronasal olfaction is required to discern flavors (see Smith 2015). You could not perceive the flavor of butter, fried chicken, pineapple, vanilla, or cardamom without retronasal olfaction. Odors sensed after traveling up through passages at the back of your mouth, the retropharynx, are referred to the mouth and contribute to apparent flavor. This is why food seems bland when you are stuffed up with a cold.[7]

Flavors are perceptible features attributed to stuff in the mouth. However, flavors are complex features. They have a variety of aspects. Taste is just one aspect of flavor. Sweetness and bitterness are part of the flavor of chocolate. Olfactory attributes also are aspects of flavor. A key part of the distinctive flavor of chocolate is an attribute detected and differentiated through smell (Small et al. 2005). Olfactory characteristics are constituents and not merely dissociable concomitants of flavor.

Somatosensory attributes also are constitutive of flavors. Capsaicin gives chilis their pungency by activating nociceptors; nicotine is bitter at low concentrations but burns at increasing concentrations; tannins give pomegranates and pecans their astringent flavor; even salt is an irritant at high concentrations (Simon et al. 2008). In each case, a feature accessible somatosensorily is part of flavor. Flavor, therefore, is a complex multisensory property.

No sense on its own fully reveals flavor. Flavor is a novel type of feature discernible in the first instance only through multisensory episodes. The capacity to detect and differentiate flavors therefore requires the joint use of several senses. It cannot be deployed unisensorily.

---

[7] To demonstrate this, hold your nose and put a jellybean in your mouth. Chew for a moment. Now let go of your nose. What was first just sugary goo now has the vivid flavor of cherry, root beer, or bubblegum. The retronasal scent enables the experience of flavor. This also works with wine. Thanks to Barry C. Smith, who first taught me this demonstration.

Nevertheless, if flavor is just an agglomeration—an otherwise unstructured mixture—or a collection of gustatory, olfactory, and tactual qualities bound to an individual, then flavors pose no special trouble. Since all of their components are perceptible unisensorily, detecting and differentiating flavors may just stem from unisensory capacities or simple intermodal feature binding.

In reply, first, a flavor is not just a range of sense-specific features. Flavors do have sense-specific attributes among their components. However, a flavor is not just a bunch of features, each of which is discernible with an individual sense. The reason is that it is possible to detect olfactory, somatosensory, and gustatory features alongside but as distinct from a flavor. So, a flavor is not just a mixture.

Second, a flavor is not simply a collection of sense-specific features bound to an individual. A flavor's components do perceptibly belong to a sensible individual located in the mouth. However, a flavor is not identical with coinstantiated sense-specific attributes. The reason is that it is possible to detect olfactory, somatosensory, and gustatory features, to discern that they belong to a common individual, but to fail to differentiate the collection as a unified flavor profile. For instance, sometimes the intense heat of a chili stands apart from its flavor. Simple coinstantiation does not exhaust flavor.

Instead, flavor is a complex but unified feature. It involves a structure, pattern, or relation among its components. It is a configurational property. By analogy, a shape is not just its collected components. The lines and angles must stand in the right relations. A flavor has a novel sort of organization and structure among its sense-specific components. The arrangement matters. For instance, enthusiasts care about the attack and finish of a flavor profile in time.

Even at a time, flavor is an organic unity among sense-specific aspects. The components of flavor are bound up with and infuse each other. Color, with its aspects of hue, lightness, and saturation, provides one way to model flavor. Alternatively, flavor may be a multisensory gestalt. In either case, flavor involves structurally unified rather than merely compresent features perceived with distinct senses.

Flavor presents another intriguing prospect. The case of mint is telling. The distinctive, recognizable flavor of mint is evident only thanks to the joint work of several sensory systems. Perceiving it requires detecting the joint presence of several sense-specific stimuli at once while differentiating them from distinct, sense-specific attributes. However, it may involve something more. A quality that is not revealed through any sense on its own—*mintiness*—may be an additional aspect of mint's flavor. The point is not to deny that sense-specific qualities, like being tingly, bitter, and cool, characterize the full, unified flavor of mint. And the point now is not just that sense-specific attributes need not exhaust its flavor. The point is more specific: perception of flavor could involve sensitivity to a further qualitative component beyond the various sense-specific characteristics. Thus, sense-specific qualities need not exhaust a flavor's qualitative profile.

This prospect is significant. Each sense reveals novel qualities, including, respectively, color, pitch, scent, tastes, and warmth. For all I have said, multisensory perception reveals no novel type of quality—no basic qualitative sensible property. In that respect, multisensory perception may differ from each distinct sense. However, if *mintiness* includes a sui generis quality, then multisensory perception reveals a distinctive, novel type of qualitative feature, beyond those each individual sense discloses. This matters especially in characterizing the basic ingredients of perceptual consciousness. I return to it in Chapter 5, when discussing the character of multisensory experience.

Nevertheless, I have argued that flavors are novel features of a type that cannot fully be perceived unisensorily. Flavors are complex, and they involve characteristics drawn from taste, smell, touch, and somatosensation. Flavors, therefore, are perceptible only multisensorily. However, they are not simple mixtures or coinstantiated sense-specific features. Thus, it is not possible to detect and differentiate flavors with any single sense, and using separate senses independently in parallel does not suffice. Detecting and differentiating flavors requires the joint, coordinated use of several senses. But flavor perception is not just a matter of intermodal binding, and it is not just perceiving a new instance of a familiar type of feature. Therefore, flavor perception involves a novel, distinctively multisensory perceptual capacity. Multisensory flavor perception may even reveal novel qualities.

3.2.5 Synopsis

I have argued that typical human subjects can detect and differentiate things and features that are accessible only multisensorily. We are differentially sensitive to novel intermodal features, including intermodal binding and identity, spatiotemporal attributes, and flavor. This sensitivity stems from the coordinated use of several senses.

Some capacities therefore can be deployed by jointly using multiple senses. From intermodal binding, it follows that a sensible individual can be identified across senses. Thus, the capacity to detect and to differentiate individuals can be exercised in a way that relies on multiple senses. Therefore, it is a multisensory capacity.

Novel feature instances, such as intermodal musical meter, demonstrate that some capacities reveal features in the world that are not perceptible unisensorily nor through several senses working independently in parallel. Therefore, the capacity to detect and differentiate such a feature is a multisensory capacity.

Novel feature types, such as flavors, are perceptible only through the joint use of several senses. Since we are differentially sensitive to flavors, this shows that some capacities are deployed in the first instance only multisensorily. Therefore, some capacities are distinctively multisensory.

3.3 Multisensory Perceptual Capacities

I have argued that subjects can detect and differentiate novel things and features that are accessible only through the coordinated use of multiple senses. Thus, typical human subjects have multisensory capacities. The next premise is that they are perceptual. By this, I mean that they belong to perception and not solely to extraperceptual cognition. My argument is that they satisfy criteria that demarcate the perceptual role. I address empirical and rational aspects of perception's role and challenges stemming from each. This chapter concludes that typical human subjects have multisensory perceptual capacities.

3.3.1 Empirical Psychology

Empirical psychology employs a species of functional explanation. For the purposes of empirical psychology, being perceptual is a matter of occupying a specific sort of causal-functional role. Chapter 2 defended the claim that sensory interactions responsible for crossmodal recalibrations and illusions are processes that belong to perception rather than to extraperceptual cognition. In particular, they satisfy criteria stemming from the explanatory purposes of empirical psychology.

My argument here is similar. Typical human subjects are differentially sensitive to novel features presented multisensorily. I have described experimental research whose aim is to establish that this sensitivity implicates selective processes that belong to perception and not just to extraperceptual cognition. This research appeals to measures used to isolate the perceptual role. For instance, it relies on behavioral evidence of detection and differentiation, such as thresholds, discrimination, matching, classification, and accuracy. It measures response times, and it controls for confounds, such as inference, memory, learning, and task effects. Such sensitivity thus is not limited to subpersonal processes. It is reflected in subjects' behavior and performance.

This evidence supports five theoretical considerations that together reinforce the conclusion that sensitivity to intermodal features occupies the causal-functional role of perception.

First, we are susceptible to multisensory feature illusions. Wholly independent unisensory features may illusorily seem to instantiate an intermodal feature, such as coinstantiation, identity, simultaneity, meter, motion, or causality. Fast, relatively compulsory responses and salient sensory phenomenology in absence of judgment and belief are marks of perceptual processes (see also Meyerhoff and Scholl 2018).

Second, intermodal constancies implicate perception, in contrast with mere sensation (see Burge 2010). An intermodal feature can seem to remain constant or unchanged through differences in sensory stimulation. Consider visuotactile size constancy. When distinct visual and tactual objects with differing sizes are illusorily identified, their apparent sizes often match rather than differ. Or, consider intermodal meter. An intermodal meter can remain a triple through differences in audible or tactual rhythmic detail. Synchronic crossmodal constancy and diachronic intermodal constancy are evidence for processes that occupy the perceptual role.

Third, adaptation supports perception, in contrast with extraperceptual cognition (see Block 2014). Perceptual adaptation transfers across senses. For example, repeatedly viewing left-tilted lines affects not only the apparent visible orientation of a later vertical line, towards tilting right, but also apparent haptic orientiation (Krystallidou and Thompson 2016). Using dynamic multisensory stimuli, Watson et al. (2014) report crossmodal audiovisual adaptation effects. Specifically, they presented subjects with movies of faces, morphed between happy and sad expressions, paired with expressive vocalizations, morphed between happy and sad. Behaviorally, adapting to a happy voice with a happy face makes a later neutral face seem more sad than it would have seemed if you had only adapted visually to faces. They use fMRI to show that multisensory neuron populations in posterior superior temporal sulcus (pSTS) modulate crossmodal adaptation effects independently from unimodal adaptation in visual and auditory areas.

Fourth, such sensitivity plays the right role in relation to thought and action. The joint use of several senses enables us not just to detect and differentiate, but also to recognize, appreciate, and reflexively act in light of features that are accessible only multisensorily. Subjects can single out intermodal features attentively or demonstratively, and they can discriminate them from unimodal features. Sensory coordination thus triggers cognition and guides action in the manner of perception.

Fifth, the capacity to detect and differentiate novel intermodal features is relatively immune to differences in extraperceptual cognition. It is not especially sensitive to background experience. It does not require memories or concepts of the relevant features. And it is not under direct deliberate control. These features are evidence that multisensory capacities belong to perception.[8]

---

[8] Chapter 4 discusses some respects in which multisensory perception is sensitive to further cognitive factors. But that does not conflict with the main point being made here, since the factors to which it is sensitive differ from those that are key in diagnosing perception in contrast with cognition.

Still, when compared with paradigms of unisensory perception, such as seeing red or hearing tones, some multisensory capacities clearly are "higher level." Detecting and differentiating intermodal identity, motion, causality, or rhythm is "downstream" from visual object tracking or pitch perception. It implicates processes that begin later and that are farther along the processing stream following sensory stimulation. It relies on sense-specific capacities. It is more sensitive to attention. It may be influenced by cognition, learning, and skill. And it is less mandatory than seeing a red patch in front of your face. There is more individual variation. So, these effects plot some distance from sensitivity to colors, sounds, and shapes in the multidimensional feature space that delineates perception and extraperceptual cognition.

In principle, this is no problem. Vision research provides clear precedents for early, middle, and later perception. Pylyshyn (1999), defending vision's distinctness from cognition, grants that some perception beyond early vision is penetrable by cognition. It still counts as vision. Even Fodor (1983), a staunch advocate of the perception–cognition divide, holds that perceptual modules perform basic abstract categorizations by inferring from lower-level sensory features such as color, shape, and motion.

Nevertheless, this raises three concerns. The first is that perception is not a unified natural kind with a shared essence. Thus, empirical psychology need not invoke or recognize it. In reply, however, psychological kinds may be more akin to homeostatic property clusters, situated in regions of a multidimensional feature space. If so, perception tolerates variety. Multisensory capacities thus may differ from paradigms of unisensory perception in a range of respects. This does not preclude multisensory and unisensory capacities belonging to a common psychological kind corresponding to perception.

The second concern is that perception fragments into distinct clusters or kinds. This is a real threat. And it is familiar. From the perspective of empirical psychology, attention, memory, concepts, and even the visual system itself each may split into distinct phenomena. Nonetheless, if each cluster or capacity can be distinguished from cognition, and if each plays a similar type of role, or contributes to playing a unified role in relation to cognition, that is enough to secure a distinction between perception and cognition. After all, vision, audition, touch, taste, and smell each are distinct psychological kinds, but each belongs to perception rather than extraperceptual cognition. And each may comprise early, middle, and later capacities. In the context of this discussion, if several distinct kinds correspond to perception, that is a discovery rather than an objection.

The third concern is most pressing. No obvious empirical boundary divides perception from cognition. Most empirical measures are continuous rather than discrete. So, a continuum might stretch between perception and extraperceptual cognition. This is one lesson from empirical psychology. Rather than a sharp cut differentiating wholly distinct types of causal-functional roles, psychological reality might be marked only by proximity or distance from the paradigms. Since some multisensory capacities are more cognition-like than canonical cases of perception, this is a real worry. How can we be confident that sensitivity to novel intermodal features lands on the side of perception?

However, continuity does not rule out a clear distinction. Consider night and day. Day differs starkly from night. We say, "clear as day and night." Nonetheless, night gives way gradually to day, and day bleeds into night. Is twilight day or night? Perception may differ categorically from cognition, even if the boundary is not clearly marked. Distinctness does not require discreteness. A practical way to deal with a vague or continuous boundary is just to draw the line, or to accept the gray areas.

I have characterized multisensory capacities as perceptual. They bear key marks used to diagnose perception in empirical psychology. They are nearer to paradigms of perception than to paradigms of thought. Nonetheless, I am comfortable saying perception can be more like cognition than used to be thought possible. And multisensory perception can shade into cognition. Thus, some multisensory capacities fall in the borderlands. But what is left out once we measure and characterize these phenomena? For the purposes of empirical psychology, any remaining dispute is terminological.

3.3.2 Rational Psychology

This raises a different worry. It concerns perception's rational role. I'll explain what I mean by perception's rational role and then describe the worry.

Notions of perception and cognition originate in folk psychology. *See, hear, judge, infer,* and *believe* are among the stock of concepts we use in making sense of people and what we do. Saying someone has a belief and a desire, or some inference rules, or evidence, does not just causally explain what they do. It conveys something about what they should do if they are practically, theoretically, or epistemically rational. We assess people on these grounds. For example, Trump should not have thought he could fire Comey without consequence. Comey was right to see it coming, but his pleasure at Trump's squirming was unfitting. Sanders's discomfort makes sense of his wincing. Gorsuch ought not be so confident about the use of midazolam in lethal injections.

Accordingly, these concepts are used in rational and normative accounts. Such accounts deal with the reasons for which subjects act, the considerations that support inferences, and better and worse ways to manage a cognitive economy. The explanations they offer trade in norms and ideals for cognition and action.

Characterizing a phenomenon as perceptual thus matters for explanatory purposes beyond empirical psychology. In epistemology and theoretical rationality, perception, belief, credence, memory, and inference have differing justificatory roles. In action theory and practical rationality, what there is reason to do depends in distinct ways on what you want, believe, and perceive. In rational psychology, what it is to be sensitive to reasons and what reasons you possess each differ in perception, inference, and belief.

Allow that we can refine and revise folk conceptions and platitudes. We may split concepts where we need a finer distinction. We may distinguish sensory from affective and motivational aspects of pain, beliefs from credences, and episodic from semantic and procedural memory. We also may merge concepts where there is reason to collapse a distinction, as with *arousal.* We may sharpen or eliminate confused notions, like *intuition.* We may introduce new ones, such as *alief.* These are tasks for philosophical psychology.

Empirical psychology might perform better in the descriptive project of explaining and predicting behavior in causal-functional terms. Moreover, empirical explanation may not need any folk psychological notions. Functional decomposition might suffice for its purposes.

However, it is a datum that other sorts of explanation deploy psychological notions. Rational explanation aims to make sense of, to assess, and to prescribe behavior in terms of these psychological states, along with reasons and norms.

Here, then, is the worry. Suppose multisensory capacities differ by degrees from central exemplars of perception. Their causal-functional profiles could even be similar enough to belong to a common kind for empirical psychological explanation. Nonetheless, the differences could be rationally significant. They could ground a difference in epistemic status or even in basic rational standing. Suppose, for instance, that some multisensory effect is more sensitive to attention, memory, or learning than a paradigm of perception. That could make an epistemic or a rational difference, in degree or in kind.

Therefore, even if multisensory phenomena satisfy criteria for occupying the perceptual role for the purposes of empirical, causal-functional explanation, they might differ from paradigms of sense perception in respects that impact justification or rationality. If so, multisensory capacities need not occupy the role of perception for the purposes of rational or normative explanation. In that case, again, their philosophical interest as perceptual phenomena is severely limited.

Addressing this requires saying more about perception's rational role. What is the rational role of perception in contrast with cognition? Its central feature is that perception grounds access to one's environment. Perception anchors or tethers cognition in the world. Call this perception's grounding role. Here is an attempt to capture it. Through sensitivity and differential responsiveness to things and features of the environment, which is not directly susceptible to deliberative control by the subject, perception enables and supports contentful thoughts, judgments, and actions. Chapter 2 unpacked this in causal terms. However, there are rationally and normatively significant aspects of this grounding role.

Do multisensory capacities play the right rational role? First, I have argued that some multisensory capacities involve differential sensitivity to the presence of novel intermodal features, including identity and binding, simultaneity, motion, meter, and flavor.

Second, this sensitivity is stimulus-dependent in a way that paradigms of cognition need not be (see Beck 2018). The distinctive multisensory response does not persist beyond the stimulus, and it is not directly under a subject's conscious, deliberate, or deliberative control.

Third, it reliably triggers recognition, demonstrative thoughts, judgments, and beliefs with the right content. You recognize the common source of a flash and a bang, and you entertain demonstrative thoughts about *that* multisensory object, *that* intermodal rhythm, and *that* flavor.[9] The default is that you come to believe my voice and my mouth movements belong to a single perceptible utterance. You reflexively reach up to grab the ball you see, or instinctively turn to look for the source of the sound. It takes effort to do otherwise. Multisensory responsiveness thus enables novel thoughts, activities, and awareness.

There are at least three normatively significant features of this role. (i) Things that occupy it are *assessable*, as more or less accurate or reliable. They can be illusory or lead you astray, and they tend to do so more or less commonly. (ii) They provide *evidence* about the world. And (iii) they *rationally support*—they warrant or justify—cognitive states like beliefs and actions, which are not themselves directly sensitive to the world.

Consider each normatively significant feature. (i) Multisensory capacities provide a foothold for *assessability*. Indication can misfire. A capacity can be deployed in absence of or fail to discern its object.[10] Thus, in the face of a stimulus, a distinctive multisensory response can be inappropriate, or less than ideal, from a normative standpoint. (ii) A multisensory response that manifests differential sensitivity to shared objects or intermodal features can provide *evidence*. Schellenberg (2016), for instance, argues that the deployment of a capacity to single out a feature can be evidence of the presence of that feature. And (iii) it could *rationally support* cognition. A coordinated multisensory response manifesting differential sensitivity to an intermodal feature either reveals or makes more likely the presence of the feature it indicates. Thus, it can provide a subject with warrant or justification for making judgments or forming perceptual beliefs with corresponding contents. Multisensory phenomena thus are suited to serve perception's rational role.

Multisensory capacities indeed can affect and modulate the epistemic profile or status of perception. Multisensory processes can provide new

---

[9] Thus, it satisfies·what Speaks (2015) calls the Availability/Difference and Demonstrative Availability principles (see, especially, 122–32).

[10] Schellenberg (2018) thus takes perceptual capacities to ground representational content, in light of their baseless or unsuccessful exercises.

and better evidence, not just about new features, but also about old ones. In Chapter 2, I argued that weighting testimony from different senses according to its relative reliability can enhance (or degrade) overall reliability. Speech perception is dramatically better in audiovisual contexts. Lipreading boosts speech comprehension as much as a good hearing aid. Deferring to vision refines sound localization. Trusting audition improves visual estimates of temporal order and numerosity. Each sense can work better when the senses work together.

Perceptual beliefs founded on one sense therefore tend to be more reliable when that sense is informed by others. Moreover, a perceptual belief about an intermodal feature, such as identity, causality, or flavor, that is founded on multiple senses and that stems from reliable multisensory capacities may be more secure than a corresponding belief that relies on an explicit inference from parallel unisensory features. Inference can be more variable and error-prone with respect to such features. So, perceptual beliefs can be enhanced epistemically thanks to multisensory capacities. In some contexts, they are diminished. Thus, multisensory capacities can make an epistemic difference to perception. They can impact its capacity to support cognition.

The upshot is that multisensory capacities exhibit key features of perception's role for the purposes of epistemic, rational, or normative explanation. Their exercises can be assessed in relation to norms of accuracy, correctness, appropriateness, and reliability; they provide evidence; and they are apt to rationally support cognition. This of course is compatible with making a rationally significant difference when compared with unisensory capacities. Multisensory capacities can modulate perception's specific epistemic contribution. But, this does not require a difference in the kind of rational role multisensory capacities occupy, when compared with unisensory perceptual capacities.

Nevertheless, cognition may influence multisensory effects. Top-down causes can impact multisensory processes. Attention, assumptions of unity, and semantic coherence each have been reported to modulate intermodal binding. For instance, an image of a male face more easily binds the sound of a male voice than a female voice. Vatakis and Spence (2007) suggest this results from cognitive expectations about congruence.

This is rationally significant. If, for instance, assuming that there is one source triggers intermodal binding, then binding should not further warrant or justify your belief in a single utterance (see Siegel 2017). This does threaten to undermine the role of some multisensory phenomena in epistemically supporting cognition. If paradigms of perception are not so affected, it may suffice for a difference in rational role or epistemic standing.

My response is that multisensory effects are just one alleged example of cognitive penetration of perception. Plenty are unisensory. Nothing is special about multisensory examples. They are in good company among unisensory effects that belong to perception. And, like paradigms of unisensory perception, not all forms of multisensory perception must be susceptible to cognition. The results from psychophysics indicate they are not.

However, to accommodate any top-down influences that do undermine perceptual justification, we may need to revise our understanding of how and when perception grounds cognition. For example, we might reject dogmatism, according to which some perceptual justification is immune to etiology (Pryor 2000; Siegel 2012). Even so, the revision need not require recognizing a wholly different kind of rational role or epistemic standing for that which can be "hijacked." And it can leave intact which sorts of things figure in the revised role. The profile I described above still applies. We just need to tailor our account of when and why things stand in particular rational or justificatory relations. Perception thus retains its role in grounding cognition, even if the specific rational or epistemic status of perceptual episodes can vary.

The upshot is that multisensory capacities can causally and epistemically or rationally support cognition and action. Thus, they play a role in grounding cognition that is characteristic of perception, in contrast with extraperceptual judgment, inference, and other forms of cognition. Therefore, for the purposes of rational psychology and normative explanation, some multisensory capacities belong to perception.

3.4 Conclusions

Some perceptual capacities can be deployed in ways that rely on the joint use of multiple senses. And they are reflected in subjects' performance. Therefore, typical human subjects possess multisensory perceptual capacities. My argument makes use of empirical evidence, such as observed performance in neural and behavioral experiments, and theoretical claims about the nature and role of perceptual capacities.

This argument depends on the claim that we are differentially sensitive to things and features presented multisensorily—to individuals, novel feature instances, and novel features types. Such features could not be detected and differentiated using any one specific sense nor through several senses simply working in parallel. Key examples include intermodal binding and identity, intermodal instances of relational features, and complex multisensory attributes such as flavors.

This sensitivity belongs to perception and not just extraperceptual cognition. In particular, it satisfies criteria used to diagnose the perceptual role, both for the purposes of empirical psychology, which employs a species of causal-functional explanation, and for the purposes of rational psychology, which implicates normative explanation. Moreover, such capacities belong to subjects, not just subpersonal systems, in light of the role they play in a subject's psychology. Overt performances manifest differential sensitivity to intermodal features.

Multisensory capacities thus are relevant in answering questions that turn on a subject's perceptual capacities. Their significance is acute in debates that depend on whether or not an aspect of perception is sense specific. So, they matter in settling the truth of concept empiricism, articulating the nature of perceptual content, determining whether perception is rich or thin, and assessing the strength of perceptual justification. Multisensory perception therefore is poised to impact empirical psychology, rational psychology, and debates about the nature of perception.

3.5 Limitation

Perceptual capacities need not be reflected as such in perceptual consciousness. One could possess a capacity without exercising it. More to the point, a capacity may be exercised without corresponding consciousness on the part of a subject.

Focus on conscious awareness. Occurrent responsiveness does not imply awareness. More specifically, occurrent sensitivity to a perceptible feature does not guarantee conscious perceptual awareness of it. A subject could respond differentially to the presence of a feature by means of a perceptual process without being aware of that feature or of doing so. Think of a professional athlete. Athletes are sensitive to the presence of certain features that enable successful performance. Batters react to the angle of a pitcher's throwing arm. But it is not uncommon for an athlete to seem wholly unaware of being sensitive to some critical feature. In mundane, amateur perception, more features shape our thoughts and actions than we are consciously aware. Sensitivity thus can bypass awareness.

To establish this, it is enough that a process responsible for the exercise of a given perceptual capacity can unfold without corresponding awareness. Experiments show, for instance, that a binding process can occur without conscious awareness of binding. In particular, implicit measures of binding, such as object-specific preview effects, can disagree with a subject's overt reports. This has been reported for both intramodal and intermodal binding (Mitroff et al. 2005; Zmigrod and Hommel 2011, respectively).

It follows that one could exercise a multisensory perceptual capacity, such as the capacity to detect and differentiate an intermodal feature, without conscious awareness of that feature and without conscious awareness of doing so. If multisensory capacities were exercised only without awareness, that would limit their philosophical significance.

This matters for three main reasons. The first is that we care about consciousness in itself. Consciousness is the core of how people conceive themselves to be. And it can anchor assessments of value. Thus, its character is of inherent interest. The second concerns the mind–body problem. How to characterize conscious awareness accurately is one key piece in understanding the relationship between the mind and the physical world. The third is more pressing. It concerns the rational significance of awareness. Being consciously accessible does makes a rational difference. And perception typically does provide reasons that are accessible to subjects.

My argument about the rational role of multisensory capacities appealed to facts about perceptual processes, psychological architecture, and performance that need not be accessible to subjects as such. A subject can fail to appreciate possessing the capacity to detect and differentiate a feature, and its cognitive role need not be evident. A process's reliability and stimulus dependence need not be obvious from the first-person perspective. Thus, multisensory processes could have the features I described, and subjects could possess multisensory perceptual capacities, even without this impacting the reasons that are accessible to subjects. If so, multisensory phenomena do not occupy perception's typical rational role.

Awareness matters. According to a weak interpretation, awareness suffices for a rational or epistemic difference. Awareness of a feature makes it possible for a subject to cite and thus appreciate that feature as a reason. The subject can employ it to rationalize belief or action. This redounds to one's rational or epistemic status. But, this is compatible with the claim that capacities exercised without awareness can make a rational or epistemic difference.

However, according to a strong interpretation, awareness is required for such a difference. In particular, without awareness, a relation between thought and perception is not a rational relation. It is not reasons sensitive. This, in turn, threatens to undermine my claim that multisensory capacities play a rational role that is typical of perception. One sort of reply is that the strong interpretation just begs the question. For instance, reliabilists about epistemic justification reject the strong interpretation. But, I want to set this aside.

There is a further concern. Someone might maintain that attributing perceptual capacities to a subject requires that the exercise of such capacities is reflected as such in awareness—performance does not suffice. Thus, multisensory capacities exercised without corresponding consciousness need not be attributed to perceiving subjects. This threatens to undermine my claim that multisensory perceptual capacities belong to typical human subjects.

My view is that the alleged necessary conditions sometimes are satisfied. Showing that some perceptual awareness is multisensory therefore defuses the concerns. By satisfying the sufficient condition, this also shows that multisensory awareness makes a rational or epistemic difference for perceiving subjects. Establishing multisensory perceptual awareness thus is the aim of Chapter 4.

4

Awareness

The previous chapter argued that some perceptual capacities are multisensory. These capacities can be deployed in ways that rely on the joint use of several senses. Thus, they can be used to target novel features that are accessible only multisensorily.

Nonetheless, the capacity to detect and differentiate a feature could be deployed unconsciously. So, exercising a perceptual capacity does not guarantee corresponding consciousness. Exercising multisensory capacities therefore is compatible with unisensory consciousness. Thus, it remains possible that a subject's perceptual consciousness is exhausted by that which is associated with each of the respective senses. If consciousness is unisensory, the philosophical significance of multisensory perception is severely limited.

This chapter and the next address multisensory perceptual consciousness. One facet of consciousness is awareness. Awareness concerns what is accessible or available to a subject. Another facet is phenomenology. Phenomenology concerns what it is like to be a subject. This chapter's focus is awareness. It argues that perceptual awareness is constitutively and irreducibly multisensory. By this, I mean that perceptual awareness involves several senses but is not exhausted by that which is associated with each of the respective senses. Chapter 5 addresses experience and phenomenology.

I begin by characterizing perceptual awareness. Informally, awareness is registering a feature (an individual or attribute) or a condition. In this sense, awareness has objects, and it requires their being present to consciousness.[1] This makes such an object occurrently accessible, or available

---

[1] Here, by "object," I mean, roughly, "intentional object" or "target of awareness," rather than "material object" or "body" (cf. Anscombe 1965). But, I wish to remain neutral on whether such objects must be actual items, events, or attributes in the world or instead are compatible with illusion or pure hallucination.

A Multisensory Philosophy of Perception. Casey O'Callaghan, Oxford University Press (2019).
© Casey O'Callaghan. DOI: 10.1093/oso/9780198833703.001.0001

to a subject for use in reasoning and action. In this respect, awareness is akin to access consciousness, in that it is a matter of occupying a role in a subject's psychology (Block 1995). In this chapter, I set aside any part in awareness for phenomenality. That is the subject of Chapter 5.

Awareness admits hybrids and extraperceptual contributions. It need not belong wholly or fully to perception. Perceptual awareness thus implicates perception as a constituent or required sustaining cause. An aspect of awareness is associated with perception only if perception fixes the corresponding object or attribute that is made available to a subject for use in thinking, reasoning, and acting.

This chapter argues that some awareness is multisensory. The exercise of multisensory perceptual capacities can make a novel intermodal feature accessible, or available to a subject for use in thought, reasoning, and rational action. Moreover, this is a case of perceptual awareness. It is made possible and sustained by perception, which fixes the relevant objects. My argument relies on the previous chapter's conclusions, coupled with further evidence from judgments, actions, appearances, and dissociations. Setting aside phenomenality, such availability suffices for multisensory perceptual awareness.

Therefore, this chapter concludes that perceptual awareness is constitutively multisensory. That is, perceptual consciousness includes forms of awareness that are associated with multiple senses and that cannot fully be captured without mentioning several senses. Just as importantly, such phenomena are irreducibly multisensory. By this, I mean just that the relevant variety of awareness is not exhausted by sense-specific, unisensory forms of awareness. It cannot fully be captured in terms of the contributions of separate senses. It is more than the sum of its sense-specific parts. Thus, not all perceptual consciousness ultimately is specific to one sense or another.

It follows that multisensory perception can make a difference where awareness matters. For instance, multisensory perceptual episodes can make a rationally relevant difference, whether awareness is required or merely suffices for such a difference (see Chapter 3). In particular, if awareness suffices for a rational difference, multisensory perceptual awareness sometimes makes a rationally relevant difference, other things equal. If, on the other hand, awareness is necessary for some perceptual phenomenon to make a rational difference, this chapter establishes that multisensory perception sometimes meets that threshold. Moreover, if attributing a perceptual capacity to a subject requires awareness, that condition is satisfied, deflecting a potential objection to Chapter 3, which concluded that typical human subjects possess multisensory perceptual capacities.

Nonetheless, there remains a limitation. To establish awareness, this chapter demonstrates occurrent availability. Availability, and thus awareness, sometimes accompanies the exercise of multisensory perceptual capacities. However, availability, like access consciousness, need not be reflected as such in perceptual phenomenology. Therefore, multisensory awareness as I have characterized it in this chapter does not show that exercising multisensory perceptual capacities makes a distinctive difference to perceptual experience.

These arguments therefore leave open the possibility that perceptual experience itself is sense specific. Even if awareness is constitutively, irreducibly multisensory, the phenomenal properties of each conscious perceptual episode might be exhausted by those that are associated with some sense or another. So, this chapter's conclusions do not guarantee that perceptual experience itself is richly—constitutively and irreducibly—multisensory. Establishing that is left to Chapter 5.

4.1 Awareness

The first task is to characterize perceptual awareness. Awareness, I maintain, is a form of consciousness. Being aware requires being conscious. It is an occurrent condition of a subject. The type of awareness at stake is not just a background condition, like being awake. Dictionaries say that awareness is knowledge or perception of a situation or fact. It is being apprised. This is not just a matter of feelings. The relevant form of awareness has an object—an item, feature, fact, state of affairs, content, or proposition. But, we can be neutral on whether it is factive. Awareness, in the form relevant here, requires either being directed at something or a relation that could not hold in its object's absence. As such, awareness is a conscious relation to an object (Johnston 2006; Hill 2009).

Awareness is not obviously the same as phenomenal consciousness. Phenomenality concerns "what it is like" for a subject to undergo a conscious episode. Certain differences in what it is like entail differences in phenomenal properties. But, some philosophers think that what it is like for a subject can differ without differences in awareness. For instance, qualia theorists say that differences in what it is like do not require differences in the objects of consciousness or in one's relation to them. Intentionalists and naïve realists can say that awareness and phenomenality involve distinct conscious relations to objects. Accessibility, for instance, may suffice for awareness but not phenomenality. Moreover, differences in that of which a subject is aware need not entail phenomenal differences. Awareness and phenomenality thus may be distinct features of a conscious subject.

What conscious relation to an object is awareness? In this chapter, I am going to set aside any role for phenomenality. The central idea in what follows is that a certain type of accessibility diagnoses awareness. So, bracketing any role for phenomenality, availability suffices for awareness. Roughly, awareness minus phenomenality is access (that is, occurrent accessibility).

By accessibility, I mean that an object is available to a subject for use in thought and action. When something occurrently is accessible to me, it is not hidden to me. It is present to my conscious mind. As such, I can do various things cognitively with it. I can demonstrate it, recognize it, remember it, avoid it, treat it as evidence, try to touch it, judge on its basis, or use it to make inferences. That is the role it plays in my cognitive life. It can be the subject of my thoughts, judgments, or actions. And this need not require mediation by some further act of cognition. For this chapter's purposes, occurrent accessibility secures awareness.

According to Block (1995), access consciousness is "availability for use in reasoning and rationally guiding speech and action" (227). Availability thus secures a sort of access consciousness. This raises delicate issues. If being accessed is being put to use in some determinate form of rational thought or action, availability does not require being accessed. However, it is not enough simply to admit the potential for being accessed while in the present a subject has no occurrent form of mental contact with an object. As envisioned here, awareness requires a vein of information that is presently open to the subject, which may be put to use in thinking, reasoning, and acting. This is what I mean by occurrent availability.

So, awareness is a conscious relation to an object in which a subject stands if it is occurrently cognitively accessible. That is, only if in standing in that relation, the subject occurrently is in a position to think about or act on it.

A human subject may have the capacity to detect and differentiate a feature, even while that feature is not available to the subject for use in thought and action. And a subject could detect and differentiate a feature in the environment without its being available in the right way for thinking, reasoning, and guiding rational action. If so, the subject may remain unaware of it. So, exercising perceptual capacities does not guarantee awareness. And this matters in theorizing about the significance of multisensory perception. For instance, in such conditions, a perceiving subject need not be blameworthy for acts stemming from a lack of actual or potential awareness. Whether it is necessary or sufficient, awareness is one reason it makes sense to hold people accountable.

4.2 Perceptual Awareness

Awareness occurs outside sense perception, in imagination, thought, judgment, emotion, introspection, and action. Awareness is perceptual when it occurs thanks to or in virtue of perception. By this, I mean that the conscious relation of awareness is constituted or causally sustained by sense perception. According to this conception, perception may suffice for awareness.

However, a conscious condition that is constituted or sustained by perception need not be wholly perceptual. Think of being visually perceptually aware of a cloud. It is there, you are conscious, and you see it. You can think about it and act rationally. Your being aware of the cloud—your standing in that conscious relation to it—can include your perceiving, attending, recognizing, demonstrating, conceptualizing, and preparing to act on the cloud. That condition of awareness involves perception and cognition. It relies on a variety of relations to the cloud. Conscious perception of an object unaccompanied by other forms of cognition is not the rule.

Awareness, moreover, admits hybrids. Some forms of awareness, as in perceptually attentive demonstrative thought—*that cloud is racing*—rely on both perceptual and extraperceptual contributions. Indeed, some aspects of your awareness that are perceptual may be inseparable from those involving attention, recognition, judgment, or even action. Thus, in being perceptually aware, it need not be possible to tease out each conscious, exclusively perceptual component. And why bother? Being available to a perceiving subject for thought and action can depend on more than the senses.

So, to make a clear case, I want to focus on those aspects of awareness that do stem from perception rather than from extraperceptual cognition. This is to draw attention to features made occurrently available to a subject by perception. Two things serve to clarify the target. First, such aspects require that a perceptual relation is constitutive of one's awareness of a given feature, or that perception is a required, sustaining cause. Moreover, perception itself must serve to fix the object of awareness. This, for instance, rules out any predicative aspects of awareness whose application conditions differ from those fixed by perception, or those that are constitutively conceptual. Thus, perceptual awareness occurs just in case there is an episode that involves the exercise of perceptual capacities directed at an object or feature in virtue of which that object or feature is accessible, or occurrently available to a subject for use in thinking, reasoning, and acting.

4.3 Multisensory Awareness

Typical human subjects perceptually can detect and differentiate things and features that are accessible only through the coordinated use of several senses. That is the conclusion of Chapter 3. This chapter argues that, in multisensory contexts, exercising such capacities can make novel intermodal features available to subjects for use in thought, reasoning, and rational action. So, subjects meet the conditions for perceptual awareness. Therefore, typical human subjects sometimes are perceptually aware of things and features perceptible only through the joint use of multiple senses. It follows that some forms of perceptual awareness are constitutively and irreducibly multisensory.

Since awareness that involves perception need not be wholly or fully perceptual, and since some perceptual forms of awareness are hybrids, it is tricky to establish that perception itself makes a novel intermodal feature available to the subject for use in thinking and acting. The work is in showing that perception secures the relevant access. My case for this claim appeals to evidence from perceptual judgments and perception-guided actions to demonstrate that novel intermodal features are available to perceiving subjects in thought and in rational action. To show that the exercise of multisensory perceptual capacities is responsible, it appeals to perceptual appearances and to patterns of dissociation. The upshot is that, in the relevant respects, perceptual awareness is multisensory.

4.3.1 Belief

This argument relies on the premise that exercising multisensory perceptual capacities makes novel intermodal features accessible to subjects for use in thinking and acting. The first piece of evidence is that perceiving subjects tend to form beliefs about features that are accessible only multi-sensorily. While instructive, this argument is not conclusive because it leaves open whether some form of extraperceptual cognition makes the critical contribution to fixing the objects of belief.

Consider perceptual judgments. On one hand, perceptual evidence does not always support a judgment that something is both seen and felt, or that a visible event causes a sound. Imagine seeing an airplane and touching a baseball, or touching an elephant and unknowingly seeing it reflected in a mirror. Imagine seeing a cup and hearing a voice.

On the other hand, perceptual evidence can support a judgment that what is seen is what is felt, or that a visible object causes a sound. Imagine holding a pen while looking at it. Normally, it would be silly to judge that the object you see is numerically distinct from the object you feel. Similar claims hold for causal, spatial, and temporal relations. Imagine, in typical circumstances, seeing a dog and hearing its bark but judging the two to be unrelated. Accordingly, perceiving subjects typically do form beliefs about intermodal features.

Forming beliefs about an object or feature on the basis of perception can support the claim that a subject is perceptually aware of that object or feature. A simple explanation for perceptual beliefs about intermodal features that subjects perceptually can detect and differentiate is that intermodal features become available for thought and action thanks to the exercise of multisensory perceptual capacities. Whenever this occurs, a subject is multisensorily perceptually aware.

Any such awareness is constitutively multisensory. It implicates multiple senses. Furthermore, it is irreducibly multisensory. The reason is that being aware of a scene through distinct senses at the same time does not suffice to be aware of an intermodal relational feature. Concurrent unisensory awareness is not enough to make an intermodal relation available for reasoning and action. That requires a further contribution.

The simple explanation allows for differing types of cases, and it leaves room for doubt. In particular, it is reasonable to ask whether perception makes the key contribution. Perhaps no multisensory judgment hinges on perception alone, or is just a matter of endorsing perception. Instead, it may require type recognition, conceptualization, or inference. If so, availability is chalked up to extraperceptual cognition, and multisensory awareness is cognitive, not perceptual.

Take an example. Awareness may involve recognition. Suppose recognition is not wholly perceptual. This by itself is not a problem. If recognizing a feature relies on exercising the perceptual capacity to detect and differentiate that feature, then the cognitive contribution is compatible with perceptual awareness, as I have characterized it. On the other hand, recognition may go beyond perceptual evidence. For instance, you may see the shape of a leaf, check your Audubon guide, and thereby recognize it as a sycamore leaf. This need not involve your being perceptually aware of the property of being a sycamore leaf.

What matters is whether or not perception determines the object of awareness—whether perceiving an object or feature is what makes that object or feature accessible to a subject. If so, which object or feature becomes available is settled by perception and not by extraperceptual cognition. Cognition may contribute to the condition of being aware, but exercising a perceptual capacity in relation to an object or feature nevertheless can account for its being what is available to a subject for use in thinking and reasoning. If so, perception is the source of its availability.

If, however, recognition identifies a feature type that differs from those we detect and differentiate perceptually, or if recognition alone rather than perception is responsible for making that feature accessible, that makes trouble. In either case, perception itself does not settle which feature becomes available to the subject. For instance, it is plausible that in recognizing a visible red octagon as a stop sign (at least for the first time), perception does not settle whether *being a stop sign* is available for thought and action. But that feature is available. So, cognition makes the difference.

Conceptualization is similar. If exercising the capacity to detect and differentiate a given feature partly constitutes or causally sustains awareness that involves conceptualizing that same feature, then that condition may be a case of perceptual awareness. But, suppose conceptualization imposes satisfaction conditions other than the instantiation of the feature to which the perceiving subject is differentially sensitive. For instance, suppose I am perceptually sensitive to something's being blue, but I conceptualize it as being my favorite color. I might think, demonstratively, *that is my favorite color*. Here, I need not be perceptually aware of its being my favorite color. Instead, cognition contributes in a way that rules out perceptual awareness corresponding to *being my favorite color*. That aspect of my awareness does not stem from perception. Many cases of what Dretske (1969) called "epistemic seeing" are in this group.

Cognition, not perception, clearly makes the difference in certain types of inference. In particular, inferences in which a subject "reckons" that a premise supports a conclusion require extraperceptual reasoning (Siegel 2017). Imagine seeing a shadow on the wall. Knowing objects cause shadows, you conclude an object casts it. Perception itself does not settle that an object or a casting is a feature about which you think. Perception enables the thought, but perception does not fix its object. Likewise, seeing a footprint is not being perceptually aware of a footstep. In each case, a further cognitive act, rather than perception, makes the relevant feature accessible.

The concern with multisensory perceptual beliefs, therefore, is that extraperceptual cognition, rather than perception, accounts for the availability of each intermodal feature. If so, then, in the relevant respects, perceptual awareness need not be multisensory. To show clearly that perceptual awareness is irreducibly multisensory, it suffices to show that exercising a distinctively multisensory perceptual capacity, rather than an act of cognition, makes an object or feature available to a subject for use in thinking, reasoning, and acting. This calls for additional evidence that perception fixes the objects of awareness.

4.3.2 Action

We can make progress by recognizing that some actions guided by perception are responsive to intermodal features. Perceptually-guided action does not require cognition that outstrips perception. By this, I mean that it requires neither recognizing, conceptualizing, nor reasoning to the presence of a feature distinct from what is perceived. Action, therefore, is one good indicator of the objects of perceptual awareness (Nanay 2013).

Typical perceptually-guided actions suggest that subjects are sensitive to intermodal features in a way that does not require judgment, conceptualization, or inference. Consider intermodal identity and binding. Imagine crossing a street and hearing something rapidly approaching from your left. You may reflexively jump out of the way, or you may turn quickly to look for it. But it makes no sense to jump from or to look for a sound. Your actions suggest you are aware that sight and hearing share objects. They reveal crossmodal perceptual expectations. Once you have picked up the source by sight, you track and respond to it as a unified perceptible thing or happening, accessible to sight and hearing, rather than as wholly distinct visible and audible individuals.

Another example involves seeing a baseball coming at you and visually "guiding" it into your mitt. Your activities coordinate sight and touch in a way that suggests you implicitly appreciate the ball as a common perceptible target. Or, consider using sight to orient yourself so that you can better listen to the source of a sound. Slightly angling your face away from a source often improves how it sounds, by taking advantage of interaural differences. The ability crossmodally to coordinate actions extends to novel circumstances and new combinations.

As a further example, consider tapping along to an intermodal rhythm. It takes little effort to move in sync to a beat that comprises distinct audible and visible components. You act in response to the intermodal rhythm. You do so because you are sensitive to it by means of perception, not just because you otherwise recognize, conceptualize, or infer its presence.

These activities require responsiveness, orienting, and tracking across modalities. Each is guided by perception rather than just extraperceptual cognition. Their reflexiveness, fluidity, and—in the unspecialized cases—untutored character indicates a tight coupling with perception. These actions trade on and reflect sensitivity to novel intermodal features and configurations of the sort to which we are perceptually sensitive.

If not every such case involves performing a rapid, implicit, extraperceptual inference, or recognizing something that perception does not itself reveal, then some such action requires the exercise of a perceptual capacity that targets an intermodal feature. Since the antecedent is more plausible than its denial, typical cases support the claim that perception makes intermodal features available to subjects for use in action. Action thus supports the premise that typical subjects are perceptually aware of intermodal features. It thereby is evidence for irreducibly multisensory perceptual awareness.

Perception-guided actions therefore provide additional evidence that the exercise of perceptual capacities can fix which feature is available for thought and for action. Nevertheless, this argument also is not conclusive. So, it does not demonstrate that perceptual awareness attends sensitivity to intermodal features.

Moreover, even if perceptual sensitivity to intermodal features does guide action, there is a further reason to resist the conclusion I have drawn. A skeptic may reply that such actions could depend unconsciously on perception. Perception for action, after all, may be functionally distinct from perception for recognition and awareness. Thus, even if multisensory perception for action requires sensitivity to intermodal features, a subject still might wholly lack irreducibly multisensory perceptual awareness.

What matters for awareness is a special sort of accessibility. The subject of awareness can *make use* of a feature in thinking, reasoning, and *rationally* acting. Paradigms of rational action, like paradigms of thought and reasoning, are under a subject's control, and they are susceptible to reasons. They are normatively assessable as such.

However, the multisensorily guided actions I have described are not among the paradigms of rational action. Perception's enabling such actions therefore does not establish the kind of accessibility to a subject that suffices to demonstrate awareness. From the subject's point of view, these actions might as well stem from reflexes, learned associations, or snap judgments and implicit inferences. It is difficult not to act on multisensory perception, even when you possess contrary evidence.

Thus, it remains possible that the relevant awareness stems from extraperceptual cognition. Perception-guided action therefore is compatible with unisensory perceptual awareness.

4.3.3 Appearances

The concern just raised is that perception can guide action in a way compatible with unawareness. That is because prompting an action that is not a rational action does not show that perception makes any feature available to a subject in the way required for rational action. In light of this, it is possible that multisensory perception does not make intermodal features available for rational action guidance. If it does not, the perceptually-guided actions I have described do not guarantee multisensory perceptual awareness.

Appearances are evidence of the right sort of availability. How things appear can guide rational action and thought. Typically, subjects are able to make use of appearances in thinking and reasoning, and for acting in a considered way. How things appear to a subject thus is evidence of what perception can make available for use in thought, reasoning, and rational action. Therefore, appearances are evidence of perceptual awareness.

My claim is that appearances include features whose perception requires the joint use of multiple senses. Subjects can appreciate this. And they can make use of such features to rationalize actions. Appearances thus help show that perception makes novel intermodal features available to subjects in the right sort of way for use in reasoning and rationally guiding action. It follows that perceptual awareness is irreducibly multisensory.

Start with the distinction between how something is and how it appears. The two come apart, so they are distinct. Now, "appears" is a visual term, so it is useful to have something neutral among sensory modalities. Here, "seems" works fine. How something is can differ from how it seems. I'll treat how things seem in perceiving them as perceptual seemings. Appearances thus are visual perceptual seemings. That said, I'll mostly use the two terms interchangeably.

Appearances and seemings have two significant features. First, each can be misleading. Müller-Lyer lines can mislead subjects about their relative lengths, and Shepard tones can mislead subjects about their pitch trajectory over time. The sound-induced flash can mislead subjects about the number of visible events. Ventriloquism can mislead subjects about the source of a sound. Appearances or seemings in each case tend to lead naïve subjects to make errors.

Second, how things appear and seem is relatively independent from what a subject judges, infers, or otherwise comes to believe. If you know about a misleading appearance or perceptual seeming, you might inoculate yourself from cognitive errors. But that need not extinguish or alter how things appear or perceptually seem.

Multisensory perception sometimes is misleading. In a multisensory context, a perceiving subject earnestly can form false beliefs or act in ways that do not fit the facts. Thanks to ventriloquism, when a performer is lip syncing, you may believe she is singing. This contrasts with unsuccessful ventriloquism, in which it is evident that the performer's visible mouth movements are not responsible for what you hear.[2] Such beliefs and actions are not based on how things are—on the actual locations and sources of sounds. They are based on how things seem perceptually. The sound appears to come from the performer's lips—perceptually, the performer seems to make the sound. Thus, things perceptually seem to have intermodal features.

Failing to discern an intermodal feature also can mislead. For instance, visible and audible features belonging to one thing can seem perceptibly to belong to distinct things. In successful ventriloquism, the sounds appear to come from the dummy but in fact come from the ventriloquist you see. Or take the trick in which you cross your forearms, weave your fingers together, twist your hands inward and up, visually target a finger, and try to raise it. When the trick works, before you move anything, the seen but visually untargeted finger you surprisingly raise seems distinct from that finger as it is felt. More simply, before you wiggle it, the visible toe peeking out from under the sheet can fail to seem perceptually to be your own felt toe.

---

[2] It is noteworthy that Austin (1962) mentions ventriloquism as an example of illusion.

Then again there are the illusions produced by professional "illusionists", conjurors—for instance the Headless Woman on the stage, who is made to look headless, or the ventriloquist's dummy which is made to appear to be talking   (Austin 1962, 22–3).

Intermodal spatial, temporal, and causal relations also can remain undetected, leading to false perception-based judgments and intended actions founded on mistakes. Imagine hearing a moving sequence of beeps and seeing an interleaved series of visible flashes, while failing to discern the intermodal motion of a single drone passing overhead in the dark.

So, multisensory perception can be misleading. In a misleading multisensory scenario, perceptible things can seem to have intermodal features they lack or to lack intermodal features they have. The contrast between these two types of cases highlights how appearances of intermodal features can account for subjects' differing tendencies to judge, to believe, and to act in multisensory contexts.

In general, things appearing a particular way to a subject in perceiving is not a wholly cognitive condition. It does not require judging, believing, or acting as if things are as they seem. And knowing, thinking, or acting otherwise need not change how things seem perceptually. At a glance, Müller-Lyer lines tend to appear unequal to me after so many viewings.

Multisensory perceptual seemings are not an exception. The McGurk illusion remains striking even after learning the setup—specialist audiences typically still giggle. At the movies, you know that nothing in the theater utters the words you hear and is visible on screen. But that does not ruin the show. In the psychology lab, the clicks and flashes can seem simultaneous even to experimenters in the know. Multisensory seemings neither require nor inevitably cause corresponding endorsements, inferences, or actions.

Multisensory appearances thus are not just settled by clear forms of extraperceptual cognition. They can decouple from what a subject extraperceptually thinks, entertains, believes, and concludes. How things seem to a subject multisensorily can differ from that subject's preconceptions, judgments, and considered tendencies to act. However, in the key cases, perceptual seemings do align with the exercise of demonstrated multisensory perceptual capacities. This suggests that some perceptual appearances correspondingly are multisensory.

How things appear multisensorily thus is evidence of what perception makes available for use in thinking, reasoning, and acting rationally. If so, it is evidence for ineliminably multisensory perceptual awareness.

The next step is to show that subjects can make use of perceptually apparent intermodal features in their thinking, reasoning, and rational action. This secures their availability to subjects for use in thinking, reasoning, and acting rationally. What matters in establishing the availability of a feature is that a subject can make use of reasons involving that feature. So, I'll argue that the exercise of multisensory perceptual capacities makes intermodal features that figure in perceptual appearances available to subjects to serve as reasons in thinking and acting.

As a start, sensitivity to intermodal features does more than cause actions. It makes sense of them, in the following ways. Reorienting your head is a good idea if visible events cause the sounds you hear. How you edit the soundtrack and video is intelligible in light of apparent audiovisual synchrony. The rhythm of your foot tapping is an appropriate response to an audiotactual rhythm. Even a reflexive response can be apt in the face of a seeming intermodal feature.

Moreover, subjects can appreciate this. It is possible to recognize that one's response is called for in the face of an intermodal feature. You know that your tapping is fitting given the intermodal rhythm. You understand that looking first at a spot behind an airplane overhead is appropriate given where you hear its sound. You get that binding explains why ventriloquism is compelling.

So, your perceptual sensitivity to an intermodal feature can make sense of a response to it, and sometimes you are in a position to appreciate this. Doing so involves grasping the relation between a feature that appears to you and your response to it. This relation is not merely causal. It also has rational significance. The apparent feature can be a reason for the response.

A subject thus may employ it to rationalize an action. This may be overridden by other considerations, and the subject need not endorse it. But it can figure in reasoning. It follows that a subject can make use of a perceptible, perceptually evident intermodal feature in reasoning and as a reason for further actions.

The fashion in which intermodal features become available to subjects is noteworthy in two respects. First, intermodal features are manifest. They are present to perceivers, spatially and temporally, as in the environment. No apparent effort nor extraperceptual act of cognition needs to be implicated in their seeming to be there.

Second, apparent intermodal features are particular. Subjects become acquainted with instances or instantiations of features, not just their general kind or category. A specific instance of simultaneity, or events' being simultaneous, is before you, rather than just simultaneity in general or in the abstract. Unlike thought or pure imagination, perception makes particulars available to subjects for use in thought, reasoning, and action. Intermodal features thus are available to subjects in a way that typifies perception.

As further support for this claim, it is significant that how things appear is not alterable by a subject in the same way as thoughts, beliefs, and actions. Typically, appearances are responsive neither to direct, deliberate control nor to the consideration of reasons. Usually, we cannot change what we perceive on the spot just by trying. Ambiguous figures are exceptions, but even that switch can be difficult. Most often, illusions do not go away when you recognize them.

This is not just a descriptive claim. Even in an ideal case, perception need not be sensitive to reasons drawn from cognition. By this I mean that is not a strike against perceptual appearances to remain fixed when a subject endorses an incompatible claim. Of course, being under rational control is not the same as being available to guide reasoning and rational action. Perception can inform thinking and acting without being subject to deliberation. Indeed, that is part of its distinctive rational role. And that is part of what affords the reasons it provides their capacity to support judgments and beliefs.

This section offers reasons to think multisensory appearances involving intermodal features conform to this role. And this in turn supports the claim that perception makes such features available to subjects for use in thinking, reasoning, and acting rationally. It follows that perceptual awareness is constitutively and irreducibly multisensory.

In summary, intermodal features figure in perceptual appearances. And these are available to subjects for use in thinking, reasoning, and acting rationally. This all relies on the exercise of multisensory perceptual capacities. So, multisensory perception can make distinctive features available to subjects in the way required for use in thought, reasoning, and rational action. Therefore, the conditions for irreducibly multisensory perceptual awareness are met.

4.3.4 Dissociations

Skeptics may insist that appearances are not decisive. Despite misleading subjects and giving rise to reasons, appearances in multisensory contexts all could be sense specific. That is, each aspect of an appearance that is perceptual might at root be associated with just one sense. In that case, intermodal features are aspects of how things seem awareness of which is fixed by extraperceptual resources. The resulting condition of awareness, while multisensory, may be hybrid or only partly perceptual. Such a condition could mislead a subject, inform rational action, and stand as relatively independent from beliefs, deliberation, and other aspects of cognition. But, such a condition is not perceptual in the relevant respect because its object is not settled by perception. If so, the upshot is that each case in which a subject is aware of an intermodal feature may involve only parallel unisensory perceptual awareness.

The skeptic can be more specific. The best option is to say that perceptual awareness of unisensory spatial and temporal features grounds extraperceptual awareness of intermodal features. This is the type of approach I discuss in what follows. Some skeptics add that associations between senses play a role. I take that up in a subsequent section. In either case, the skeptic claims that no subject is perceptually aware of an intermodal feature.

First, let's be clear what is at stake. An arrangement of unisensory spatiotemporal features does not guarantee intermodal identity, causality, or motion. Thus, being sensitive to the former does not suffice for being sensitive to the latter. So, when a subject endorses appearances involving the former, that entails distinct accuracy conditions from endorsing appearances involving the latter. Perceptual awareness of an intermodal feature thereby secures differing commitments from perceptual awareness of unisensory spatial and temporal features. Therefore, whether and how appearances warrant judgments and beliefs about the environment's multisensory organization are at stake.

Why think perceptual appearances involve intermodal features? A good indication is that awareness of unisensory spatiotemporal features dissociates from awareness of intermodal features. In this case, single dissociation suffices. There is a contrast between a case in which perception makes only unisensory spatiotemporal features available to a subject and an otherwise equivalent case in which perception also makes available an intermodal relational feature.

To illustrate, start with a typical human subject. Imagine watching a movie with a compelling, immersive soundtrack. You hang on the actors' words and jump from your seat at the explosions. It sounds like planes flying up behind you and overhead. Now, imagine the soundtrack's timing is off. It could be just a little bit, so that it is noticeable but not disturbing. It could be even more, so that the experience is jarring. Or it could be a lot, so that the sights and sounds seem wholly disconnected. In each of these four cases, the auditory and visual stimulation independently remain qualitatively the same, but the appearances differ unmistakably.

The alignment matters. However, the contrast is not just a difference in the alignment of appearances. My claim is that part of the difference concerns apparent intermodal features. The dramatic difference between the perfect soundtrack and the poorly aligned soundtrack stems in part from perceptual sensitivity to intermodal features, such as identity, causality, and spatiotemporal relations. As a result, only when the sounds and images align in the right way, something appears jointly to have audible and visible features, something visible perceptibly causes something audible, or intermodal simultaneity or motion is evident.[3]

This claim is not obvious. Notice that in this respect all of my cases parallel that of perceiving causality. Stimulus features that cue perceptual awareness of causality also are responsible for the scene's apparent spatiotemporal features. The main features that indicate causation just are spatiotemporal. So, it is difficult to control for perceptually apparent spatiotemporal features.

There is a further reason to maintain that we are sensitive perceptually to more than unisensory spatiotemporal features that happen to be aligned in a way that enables quick recognition of intermodal relational features. Intermodal feature perception is categorical. A perceptual

---

[3] A similar argument applies to dubbed foreign language films. In that case, the fine-grained structures mismatch. Speech and language, however, present extra confounds.

phenomenon is categorical to the extent that gradually varying a parameter that is diagnostic for a given perceptible feature corresponds psychophysically to a discontinuous or abrupt perceptual difference. In the case of intermodal feature perception, the shift is categorical, rather than gradual and uniform. For instance, varying unisensory spatiotemporal features gradually in relation to each other across senses leads to discontinuous differences in multisensory awareness. Unlike distinct, unisensory spatiotemporal features, which vary continuously in relation to each other, intermodal features can make an abrupt appearance. This discontinuity in how appearances vary with crossmodal alignment can be explained by selective perceptual sensitivity to configurations corresponding to intermodal structural features and specific types of intermodal relations.

Someone may object that the cases I have used to argue for the contrast differ in spatiotemporal respects. So, once we control for spatiotemporal differences, any difference in appearances—thus, in which features are available—could dissolve.

My reply is that fixing unisensory spatiotemporal features need not fix multisensory awareness. It may be atypical, but a subject could be sensitive independently to unisensory cues without integrating or perceptually discerning how they are related.

In support of this claim, start with the idea that spatial and temporal coincidence does not suffice to settle whether intermodal perception occurs. Vatakis and Spence (2007) say:

> At the same time, the perceptual system also appears to exhibit a high degree of selectivity in terms of its ability to separate highly concordant events from events that meet the spatial and temporal coincidence criteria, but which do not necessarily "belong together."
>
> (Vatakis and Spence 2007, 754)

For typical subjects, awareness of intermodal features does not just depend on unisensory spatiotemporal features. It also has been reported to depend on other factors, such as the concordance between those cues, whether and how the subject is attending (Talsma et al. 2010), whether the subject expects one event or multiple events, and the plausibility of the combination or compellingness of the match (Bertelson and de

Gelder 2004). For instance, a female face more easily binds a female voice than does a male face (Vatakis and Spence 2007).

> The binding versus segregation of these unimodal stimuli—what Bedford (2001) calls the object identity decision; see also Radeau and Bertelson (1977)—depends on both low-level (i.e., stimulus-driven) factors, such as the spatial and temporal co-occurrence of the stimuli (Calvert, Spence, and Stein 2004; Welch 1999), as well as on higher level (i.e., cognitive) factors, such as whether or not the participant assumes that the stimuli should "go together." This is the so-called "unity assumption," the assumption that a perceiver makes about whether he or she is observing a single multisensory event rather than multiple separate unimodal events.   (Vatakis and Spence 2007, 744)

Now, it could be that fixing fine-grained unisensory spatial and temporal attributes (rather than just gross spatial and temporal coincidence) does suffice in typical subjects to determine apparent intermodal features, but the point stands that sensitivity to intermodal features requires more than parallel sensitivity to unisensory attributes. That is because the crossmodal correspondence between fine-grained unisensory structural attributes must be discerned. Thus, fixing unisensory spatiotemporal features need not suffice to fix whether a subject deploys the capacity to detect and differentiate an intermodal feature.

Therefore, it is possible to tease apart the appearance of an intermodal feature from that of unisensory spatial and temporal features. Fixing unisensory features need not fix whether an intermodal feature is perceptually apparent. Take a pair of cases that controls for unisensory spatiotemporal features and other aspects of perceptual awareness. A case in which you perceptually discern an intermodal feature may contrast with an otherwise similar one in which you do not.[4]

---

[4] This gives us a way to deal with an objection about the relation between empirical measures and binding awareness. Mitroff et al. (2005) demonstrate that empirical measures of visual feature binding, such as object-specific preview effects, under odd conditions diverge from subjective reports. Zmigrod and Hommel (2011) report a similar result in multisensory conditions.

If the system responsible for tracking objects (the "object-file" system) incorporates mechanisms that are responsive just to low-level spatiotemporal features, and if such mechanisms are selectively probed during creative experimental interventions, then the appearance of binding

This argument is not yet conclusive. The reason is that spatiotemporal cues in each sense need not fix corresponding unisensory spatiotemporal appearances (see Briscoe 2017). Crossmodal influences, for one, can affect unisensory appearances. So, showing that such spatiotemporal cues do not fix multisensory perceptual appearances does not demonstrate that perceptual appearances outstrip unisensory appearances. The latter requires that unisensory spatiotemporal appearances fail to fix multisensory appearances.

To establish this, it is enough to show a difference in multisensory appearances is compatible with common unisensory appearances. In other words, given the arguments of previous chapters, we need an argument that fixing each form of unisensory awareness does not also suffice to fix multisensory perceptual appearances. If so, then which determinate unisensory spatiotemporal features perception makes available does not by itself settle which features multisensory perception makes available to a subject.

Recent empirical evidence helps to make progress. This work supports the claim that the capacity to perceive an intermodal feature can be selectively disrupted. In such a case, while leaving extraperceptual capacities intact, it is possible to disrupt a subject's multisensory capacities and thereby to change what is available to that subject without affecting unisensory perceptual capacities or unisensory appearances.

In Chapter 2, I described research in which neuroscientists report "zapping" multisensory integration performance using brain stimulation. For example, Pasalar et al. (2010) show that transcranial magnetic stimulation (TMS) to posterior parietal cortex can selectively disrupt visuotactile sensory integration (see also Kamke et al. 2012; Zmigrod and Zmigrod 2015). This brain area is known to receive inputs from vision, audition, and somatosensation. Its outputs predominantly feed motor areas. It is believed to harbor a multisensory map of peri-hand space

may disagree with the verdicts of some low-level components of the overall system that is responsible for apparent intermodal binding.
  Suppose that extraperceptual factors sometimes play a role in determining whether or not intermodal feature binding awareness occurs. This implies neither that intermodal feature binding is extraperceptual nor that awareness of intermodal binding is wholly cognitive. Cognition may causally influence perception, and binding awareness need not require awareness of the relevant cognitive factors.

centered on the viewed hand. In a bimodal tactual and visual condition, subjects are faster and more accurate in discriminating congruent tactual and visual touches to the hand, as compared with a unisensory tactual stimulus or incongruent tactual and visual touches (the incongruent condition improves performance over the unisensory tactual condition). However, this multisensory advantage is eliminated with TMS to posterior parietal cortex. Nonetheless, stimulating this area does not impact subjects' capacity to perceive using each of their individual senses. And nothing suggests that it otherwise disturbs their extraperceptual capacities to recognize, infer, judge, think, or act. But, it does affect which intermodal features perception makes available to a subject. In particular, without figuring them out, visuotactual relational attributes, such as congruency and incongruency, become unavailable.

In neuropsychology, Hamilton et al. (2006) describe a patient who cannot integrate auditory and visual information about speech. "We propose that multisensory binding of audiovisual language cues can be selectively disrupted" (66). This subject's capacity to discern auditory and visual language cues independently is not affected, and the subject's language-related capacities otherwise are typical. A selective impairment "blinds" this subject to intermodal features of spoken language. In typical subjects, Beauchamp et al. (2010) report a similar effect using TMS to selectively disrupt the McGurk effect during audiovisual speech perception.

Further cases are suggestive. For instance, people with autism are reported to have difficulty integrating cues about emotion from vision and audition (see, for example, de Gelder et al. 1991; Mongillo et al. 2008). Attention Deficit Hyperactivity Disorder (ADHD) reportedly disrupts apparent intermodal simultaneity. Panagiotidi et al. (2017) observe a narrower temporal integration window with ADHD-like traits, which manifests as a narrower threshold for simultaneity judgments, even while temporal order judgments and just noticeable temporal differences remain typical. In such cases, sense-specific spatial and temporal capacities remain intact, but multisensory performance is disrupted. In the present argument, however, these cases are controversial because each condition also impacts other perceptual and extraperceptual capacities.

In a true case of selective disruption, specific types of information from distinct senses cannot be integrated. The relevant unisensory capacities remain intact, as do unisensory appearances. However, multisensory capacities are disrupted. This affects which intermodal features are available to the subject for use in thinking, reasoning, and acting rationally. Nonetheless, this change occurs without otherwise affecting the subject's capacity for extraperceptual cognition, nor the subject's general purpose capacity to recognize, attend, infer, judge, or act in the face of perception. Thus, in such a case, perception fails to make an intermodal feature available to the subject for use in thinking, reasoning, and acting rationally. Empirical evidence about actual disruptions and dissociations supports the claim that such a selective disruption is possible.

By contrast, in typical perceiving subjects, information sometimes is integrated across senses. In such a case, the same range of unisensory spatiotemporal features could appear. However, a typical subject also can exercise the capacity perceptually to detect and differentiate an intermodal feature, such as an intermodal relation that holds between something seen and something felt. When the subject is awake, alert, and attentive, selective sensitivity to an intermodal feature also can make such a feature available to the subject for use in thinking, reasoning, and acting rationally. In other words, perceptual sensitivity to an intermodal feature enables the subject to make use of that specific feature as a reason to think and to act. This is missing in selective disruption. If so, the subject is perceptually aware of intermodal identity, causality, rhythm, or motion.

I have argued that intermodal features figure in multisensory appearances or seemings. Thanks to the exercise of multisensory capacities, subjects are able to make use of such features in thinking, reasoning, and acting rationally. Selective perceptual capacities, rather than extraperceptual cognition or a general capacity to recognize, judge, attend, or infer in the face of perception, fix the objects of such awareness. However, unisensory spatial and temporal features do not exhaust the features that are available to a subject due to the exercise of perceptual capacities, and their appearances do not suffice to fix the appearance of intermodal features. Instead, multisensory perceptual capacities are responsible for the availability of intermodal features. I conclude that typical human subjects sometimes are perceptually aware of such features. Thus, perceptual awareness is irreducibly multisensory.

4.3.5 Associations

Which intermodal features are perceptually apparent decouples from what you think and from what you are inclined to judge on extraperceptual grounds. Their appearances are not due wholly to unisensory spatiotemporal features, nor to extraperceptual forms of recognition, cognition, or inference. The exercise of multisensory perceptual capacities makes intermodal features available to subjects in the manner this chapter requires for awareness.

A final skeptical maneuver remains unaddressed. Some have argued that multisensory perceptual consciousness involves only associations between sense-specific conscious perceptual episodes (Fulkerson 2011; Connolly 2014, 2019, chapter 5). Thus, perceptual consciousness leaves out awareness of intermodal features. If so, sense-specific awareness plus association, without irreducibly multisensory awareness, suffices to capture perceptual awareness and to account for its rational significance.

The arguments above provide the materials to reply. Part of the contrast between a conscious episode in which you deploy the capacity to discern an intermodal feature and one in which you do not concerns that of which you become perceptually aware. This is not simply a matter of relations between episodes of being aware. In particular, associations between such episodes by themselves are not capable of revealing objects or attributes. They do not impose conditions of accuracy or correctness. Endorsing associated appearances does not imply any commitments beyond those imposed by endorsing each associated appearance along with their "going together" in a generic respect. A mere conscious association between appearances is not itself an illusion or misperception.

Thus, while associations may come with a difference in perceptual awareness, they do not by themselves alter which features perception makes available to perceiving subjects for use in thinking, reasoning, and acting rationally. That is because, if perceiving unisensory features alone does not make available specific intermodal features, such as identity, causality, simultaneity, or motion, then perceiving unisensory features plus generic relations of association also does not suffice to make intermodal features available to perceiving subjects.

However, suppose that such associations could ground a difference in how things seem perceptually to be and thus may be illusory or misleading. If so, in order for this type of skepticism to have teeth, merely seeming to be associated or to tend to co-occur must differ from seeming to stand in a specific further relation to each other, such as being numerically identical, belonging to something common, being causally related, being parts of a rhythm, being simultaneous, or being co-located.

But, if seeming to be associated or to tend to co-occur does not guarantee seeming to share any specific further feature, then appearing merely as associated or as tending to co-occur also is too permissive to capture the distinctions among the differing cases I have described. For instance, a sound and an image may seem merely to be associated or to tend to co-occur without seeming perceptually to share a common source (this may be the case with a poorly dubbed soundtrack). A rough surface and a red surface can seem to be associated without their seeming perceptually to be one surface or to belong to one object (as with distinct tactual and visual surfaces repeatedly presented together). A sequence of sounds and taps can seem to be associated without appearing to have a rhythm or a metrical pattern (perhaps they start and stop at the same time while lacking the right coherence).

Seeming to stand in a generic or unspecified further relation fails to account for these discernible differences. Thus, mere associations do not suffice for an account of that to which one may be sensitive multisensorily. Therefore, they do not suffice for an account of multisensory perceptual awareness.

4.3.6 Attention

One last complication concerns the role of attention. I am attracted to the idea that intermodal attention is required for awareness of intermodal features. Identity and binding are especially compelling cases (see, for instance, Talsma et al. 2010).

Suppose there are differing ways of deploying attention. For instance, you might maintain distinct unisensory streams, or you might sustain a single intermodal focus. If so, differences in awareness associated with these differing ways of deploying attention might be thought to account for differences between contrasting cases that otherwise are alike. Thus, parallel unisensory awareness in contrast with constitutively, irreducibly multisensory awareness might be just a difference in ways of deploying attention.

Four replies serve here to defuse the objection. First, such attentional effects plausibly are regarded as contributing to perceptual awareness. According to prevailing empirical models, attention manifests differences in the distribution of perceptual resources. Thus, intramodal and intermodal forms of attention manifest differing ways of distributing resources in deploying perceptual capacities. Intramodal and intermodal attention therefore imply differences in intramodal and intermodal perception. So, appealing to attention does not make the difference wholly extraperceptual.

Second, given that perceptual attention targets individual entities or particular features, a single intermodal focus requires attention to a common item, feature, or relation. Therefore, to distinguish it from intramodal attention, intermodal singular attention requires intermodal items, features, or relations. Thus, the appeal to attention does not avoid recognizing awareness of novel intermodal features.

Third, attention alone does not suffice to make novel, imperceptible features available to subjects for use in thinking, reasoning, and acting. Some theoretical models treat attention as selection for cognition or action (Wu 2014); others treat attention as a novel phenomenal relation to a content (Speaks 2015); others treat it as just a way of perceiving or cognizing (Mole 2011). But in no such account does perceptual attention suffice to make a given object available to a subject in the absence of that object's being perceptible. Attention operates over perceptible objects.

Finally, in the case of intermodal features, multisensory perceptual capacities share objects with multisensory attention. Therefore, rather than attention alone, the exercise of multisensory perceptual capacities is part of what makes novel intermodal features available to subjects for use in thinking, reasoning, and acting rationally. For a subject to make use of such features may require attention. Even so, once attention is directed, multisensory perception itself fixes the objects of awareness. Perceptual sensitivity to intermodal features thus is part of what accounts for the contrast between parallel unisensory awareness and multisensory awareness. It follows that intermodal attention does not undermine this chapter's main conclusion. The conclusion is that perceptual awareness is constitutively, irreducibly multisensory.

4.3.7 Synopsis

Chapter 3 concluded that typical human subjects have the capacity to detect and differentiate things and features accessible only through the joint use of several senses. This chapter has argued that the exercise of multisensory perceptual capacities can make such novel intermodal features available to conscious subjects for use in thinking, reasoning, and acting rationally. Together, arguments from perceptual beliefs and judgments, perception-guided actions, perceptual appearances, and dissociations and selective disruptions converge to support this claim. Therefore, subjects meet this chapter's criterion for perceptual awareness of intermodal features. Typical human subjects sometimes are perceptually aware of things and features that are perceptible only thanks to the coordinated use of multiple senses.

It follows that some perceptual awareness is constitutively and irreducibly multisensory. By this, I mean, first, that perceptual awareness cannot fully be captured without recognizing aspects of awareness associated with distinct senses. Second, perceptual awareness is not exhausted by phenomena that are sense specific. Perceptual awareness is not just a matter of being aware with each of our various senses. Thus, if awareness is part of consciousness, not every aspect of perceptual consciousness belongs to one sense or another.

4.4 Conclusions

A limitation of the argument from Chapter 3 is that a perceptual capacity need not be reflected as such in consciousness. This chapter argues that exercising the capacity multisensorily to detect and differentiate a novel intermodal feature can ground corresponding perceptual awareness. That is because multisensory perceptual capacities sometimes play the right role in a conscious subject's psychology and mental life. In particular, the evidence described shows that multisensory perception can make a novel intermodal feature available to a subject for use in thought, reasoning, and action.

Multisensory phenomena thus are not limited either to subpersonal or to subconscious psychological states. Multisensory capacities not only can be attributed to persons, but also can impact what is occurrently accessible to a conscious subject. They are reflected in awareness from the first-person perspective.

According to a persistent picture, perceptual consciousness at its core is unisensory. If so, conciously registering or cognizing further features depends on inferring, associating, or conceptualizing what perception reveals. This chapter's arguments entail that, in the case of perceptual awareness, the picture is mistaken. Perception makes available to subjects features that are not accessible just by using one sense at a time or by using several senses simply in parallel. As a result, perceptual awareness is ineliminably multisensory.

One upshot concerns the study of conscious awareness. In light of this chapter's conclusions, human perceptual awareness has a multisensory nature—in particular, it has multisensory objects and structure. Thus, multisensory phenomena cannot be ignored in characterizing awareness. Indeed, multisensory effects overturn not just the picture of sensory functioning but also the model of subjective awareness that has dominated from the early modern era through the early twenty-first century. Multisensory perception therefore is not just a topic for empirical psychology and neuroscience. It earns a place as relevant to answering some of the most central questions in the philosophy of mind and perception.

A second upshot concerns the significance of multisensory perceptual awareness. In particular, consider its rational significance. Given what I have argued in this chapter, whether awareness is necessary or merely sufficient to make a rationally relevant difference, multisensory phenomena can affect the rational status of a perceptual episode. If awareness suffices for a rational difference, multisensory perception can make a rational difference. In particular, an episode in which a subject is multisensorily perceptually aware can differ in its capacity rationally to support beliefs and judgments, when compared with an otherwise equivalent episode in which a subject enjoys only parallel unisensory awareness, and when compared with an episode in which wholly unconscious perceptual processes that are multisensory fail to be reflected as such in perceptual awareness.

Similarly, if awareness is necessary for a rationally relevant difference, multisensory perception can make a rational difference. For instance, if awareness is required for a relation between thought and perception to be reasons sensitive, multisensory perception can enable subjects to appreciate new, otherwise inaccessible reasons. In general, perception can make a rational difference. Typically, it puts subjects in a position to appreciate new reasons. Multisensory phenomena thus occupy perception's typical rational role. Multisensory perception therefore matters in rational and philosophical psychology.

It follows from these arguments concerning perceptual awareness that multisensory phenomena have a place in philosophical debates about consciousness, perceptual epistemology, and rational psychology.

4.5 Limitation

Awareness is one aspect of consciousness. Phenomenality is another. Claims about availability do not entail corresponding claims about phenomenal consciousness and experience. One reason is that being accessible to a subject for use in thinking, reasoning, and acting rationally does not guarantee phenomenality. Another is that phenomenal features might vary independently from features of which subjects are aware.

Perceptual awareness as I have characterized it therefore does not guarantee multisensory perceptual experience. Suppose an experience is an episode with phenomenal properties. And suppose that perceptual awareness is constitutively, irreducibly multisensory. Multisensory perceptual awareness does not guarantee that the phenomenal character of any perceptual episode is constitutively or irreducibly multisensory.

The following chapter aims to establish that perceptual experience itself is constitutively, irreducibly multisensory. By this I mean that some conscious multisensory perceptual episodes have phenomenal features that are not associated with any specific sense and that do not accrue thanks to simple co-consciousness. Thus, not even all phenomenality is sense specific.

This requires saying what it is for a phenomenal feature to be associated with a specific sense modality and what it is for a phenomenal feature to belong to perception rather than extraperceptual cognition. The conclusion that follows is that perceptual consciousness is richly, deeply multisensory.

5

Experience

The previous chapter argued that some perceptual awareness is ineliminably multisensory. As I characterized it in Chapter 4, availability suffices for awareness, where being available is being occurrently accessible to a subject for use in thinking, reasoning, and acting rationally. Phenomenality is another aspect of consciousness. My arguments concerning awareness do not establish conclusions concerning phenomenality. They do not guarantee that perception itself involves ineliminably multisensory phenomenology. Therefore, nothing so far establishes that perceptual experience is multisensory.

This chapter argues that conscious perceptual experience is constitutively and irreducibly multisensory. The exercise of multisensory perceptual capacities can make a phenomenal difference to perceptual consciousness that cannot be captured in sense-specific terms. This requires specifying what it is for a phenomenal feature to be sense specific. According to my proposal, the phenomenal features associated with a given sense modality on an occasion include just those that could be instantiated by a corresponding unisensory episode.

My argument is that such features do not exhaust the character of each conscious perceptual episode. Its key claim is that fixing sense-specific phenomenal features need not fix the phenomenal features of a multisensory perceptual episode. This holds whether or not a phenomenal difference requires a difference that is discriminable by a subject from the first-person perspective. Thus, the phenomenal properties of a conscious perceptual episode are not all sense specific. By this, I mean that the phenomenal properties of some conscious perceptual episodes are not exhausted by those associated with each of the respective modalities along with what accrues thanks to mere co-consciousness. I answer two forms of skepticism.

A Multisensory Philosophy of Perception. Casey O'Callaghan, Oxford University Press (2019).
© Casey O'Callaghan. DOI: 10.1093/oso/9780198833703.001.0001

5.1 Experience

An experience is a phenomenally conscious episode. For each experience, there is something it is like for its subject to undergo it, rather than nothing at all. What a conscious episode is like for its subject is fixed by its phenomenal character, which is an attribute of a conscious episode or of its subject (Speaks 2015). Phenomenal character is the determinable of which a subject's phenomenal properties are determinates. Differences in what conscious episodes are like for their subjects require phenomenal differences. Phenomenal features are aspects of phenomenal character— determinants of what it is like.

Phenomenal properties are the focus of entrenched philosophical disputes. There is disagreement about their nature and their individuation. At the outset, and as far as possible, I want to remain neutral among such accounts. Whether you are an intentionalist, a relationalist, or a qualia theorist, I hope to convince you that perceptual phenomenal character is irreducibly multisensory. Accordingly, I'll operate with a minimal conception according to which discriminable differences in how things seem for subjects entail differences in phenomenal character. I will not assume that differences in phenomenal character require discriminable differences.

5.2 Multisensory Experience

A perceptual experience is a phenomenally conscious perceptual episode. A multisensory experience is a phenomenally conscious multisensory episode. An episode is multisensory just in case it is associated with or belongs to more than one sense. Perceptual experience typically is multisensory. People can use more than one sense at a time. Seeing a turtle while hearing a duck is associated with more than one sense modality. Thus, it is plausible that some conscious perceptual episodes are associated with more than one sense. So, some experiences are multisensory.

This is relatively innocuous, but some deny it. Spence and Bayne (2015) are skeptical whether perceptual experience is multisensory, even in this very minimal respect. They argue that perceptual consciousness switches quickly back and forth between senses but at any moment is unisensory.

The unisensory view is most plausible if conscious experience requires attention and if attention is restricted to one sense modality at each time. I set aside the controversy whether consciousness requires attention. If it does, whether consciousness is unisensory is a trivial consequence if attention is unisensory. But, attention need not be unisensory. It is plausible that attentional resources can be allocated to different modalities at one time. As evidence for this, a simultaneous sound can diminish visual attentional blink, repetition blindness, and backward masking (reviewed in Deroy et al. 2014). In these multisensory conditions, devoting attentional resources to audition affects how resources are devoted at once to vision. Moreover, it is plausible that there can be multisensory attentional objects, so object-directed attention can be multisensory (see Chapter 3; Kubovy and Schutz 2010; Talsma et al. 2010).

Even so, there is a more direct argument. What I'll call *the grain problem* is that the duration of a switch in consciousness between modalities can be less than that of the specious present. First, there need not be an apparent temporal gap between experiences associated with distinct senses—one sometimes seems seamlessly to follow another. Next, the temporal grain of the experienced present sometimes is coarser than that of such a rapid conscious shift between modalities. Thus, temporal segments of experiences associated with different senses sometimes seem to fall within the same experienced present. Since experiences that fall within the same experienced present seem to overlap or to occur at the same time, some temporal segments of experiences associated with different senses sometimes seem to overlap or to occur at the same time. Since seemingly simultaneous experiences typically are co-conscious, it follows that there are times at which one's experience is associated with more than one sense. So, not every perceptual experience at each moment is unisensory. Therefore, some experiences are multisensory.

As it stands, this is a weak claim. It does imply that, in a minimal respect, perceptual experience is constitutively multisensory: at some times, a subject's perceptual experience is associated with more than one sense. However, this is compatible with the spirit of the slogan that all perceptual experience is modality specific. A perceptual experience could have only parts or properties that belong to one sense each. So, a minimally multisensory experience is compatible with the claim that each phenomenal feature of a conscious perceptual episode is associated with exactly one sensory modality (for such a view, see Deroy et al. 2014). Thus, the phenomenal character of each perceptual episode may be exhausted by that which is associated with each of the respective senses.

The unity of consciousness presents a counterexample. Any phenomenal unity that accrues thanks to mere co-consciousness is not associated with any single sense (see, for example, Bayne and Chalmers 2003; Tye 2003; Bayne 2010). If phenomenal unity contributes to the character of a conscious perceptual episode, then not all perceptual experience is modality specific. But my concern is not the general unity of consciousness. Unity extends beyond exteroceptive sense perception. Bodily and affective experiences can be co-conscious with visual and auditory experiences, as can any distinctive phenomenology of thought. So, just revise the claim to accommodate the simple unity of consciousness. The slogan that all perceptual experience is modality specific then yields the claim that the phenomenal character of each perceptual episode is exhausted by that which is associated with each individual modality, along with whatever accrues thanks to mere co-consciousness.

There is another benefit to accommodating phenomenal unity in this way. It captures any phenomenal features that supervene on those are modality specific. For instance, it captures any complex audiovisual features that supervene on auditory and visual phenomenal features. Such complex features are not modality specific, but they accrue thanks to simple co-consciousness.

This chapter's question now can be restated. Is the phenomenal character of each conscious perceptual episode exhausted by features associated with each of the respective modalities along with those that accrue thanks to simple co-consciousness? My thesis is that it is not. Therefore, perceptual phenomenology is constitutively and irreducibly multisensory.

5.3 Being Sense Specific

My argument's first premise is that if the phenomenal character associated with each of the respective modalities along with whatever accrues thanks to mere co-consciousness does not exhaust the phenomenal character of a perceptual episode, then that episode's phenomenal character

is constitutively and irreducibly multisensory. That is, it has phenomenal features associated with several senses, but those features associated
with each of the respective senses (along with any further features that
stem from mere co-consciousness) do not exhaust its phenomenal
features. If so, there is more to perceptual phenomenality than what is
associated with the several senses.

This relies on a conception of *being associated with a sensory modality*.
Many philosophers say perceptual experiences of a given sense modality
have distinctive phenomenology. Grice (1962) famously appeals to "the
special introspectible character of the experiences of seeing and smelling"
to distinguish them (135). He talks about "a generic resemblance signal-
ized by the use of the world 'look', which differentiates visual from non-
visual sense-experience" (152). Peacocke (1983) says, "the sensational
properties of visual and tactual experiences are *toto caelo* distinct; in this
sense no ideas are common to touch and sight" (27–8). And Lopes
(2000) provides a clear statement of distinctiveness:

> [W]hat it is like to perceive in one sense modality is different from what
> it is like to perceive in others—each has a unique "phenomenal charac-
> ter"—and this is a fact of which any theory of perception must take
> account.... The senses differ because experiences in each sense have a
> phenomenal character unique to that sense.... It seems to me that tactile
> and visual experiences have distinctive phenomenal characters through
> and through. What it is like to see the shape of a cube is different from
> what it is like to touch the same shape.   (Lopes 2000, 439–45)

Now, distinctiveness does not require some specific qualitative feature
that is shared by all and only experiences of a given modality. Instead, a
perceptual experience of a given sensory modality has a distinctive
phenomenal character if and only if it could not be instantiated by any
experience that is not of that same modality. Accordingly, phenomenal
character may be associated with a sensory modality just in case it is
unique to that sense—that is, just in case it could not be instantiated by
an experience that is not of that same sense modality. The question is
whether phenomenal character is limited to what is distinctive in this
way to each of the respective senses.

This characterization faces an obstacle. Not every phenomenal feature must be distinctive to exactly one sensory modality. That is, it need not be the case that each phenomenal feature of a perceptual episode could be instantiated only by perceptual episodes of that same modality. This is so even if perceptual consciousness at each time is unisensory. If so, phenomenal character is not *locally distinctive*, or distinctive "through and through." Proper sensibles, such as hue, pitch, and warmth, present no difficulty. However, common sensibles make trouble. Common sensibles include spatial and temporal properties, causality, number, and numerosity. It is not obvious that a visual experience of, say, sphericity—when it is considered in abstraction from the experience of other visible features—must differ in respect of each phenomenal feature from a tactual experience of sphericity. If visual and tactual experiences may share phenomenal features, local distinctiveness fails.

There are good replies to this traditional argument from common sensibles. Phenomenal features could depend holistically on awareness of other sensible features within a modality. Differing modality-specific modes of presentation could generate a phenomenal difference. Or, the modality of experience, construed as a mode of representing, itself could partly determine phenomenal character. Nevertheless, this chapter's argument is independent from the traditional argument from common sensibles. I do not want my conclusion to turn on whether or not that argument works. Thus, I do not want my account of being associated with a given sensory modality to rely on being distinctive to that sense. We need other tools.

There is a way forward. First, set aside the idea that being sense specific requires a feature to be associated on every occasion exclusively with at most one sense. Focus instead on what it is to be associated with a given sense on an occasion. A feature may be associated with one sense on an occasion, even if on another occasion it could be instantiated by an experience that is not of that same sense. This chapter's question is whether features associated with one or another sense on each occasion exhaust the phenomenal features of a conscious perceptual episode.

Next, characterize what it is to be associated with a given sense on an occasion in terms of features of corresponding unisensory experiences. Start with the fact that experiences of different sensory modalities doubly dissociate. For a multisensory experience involving vision and audition, you could have a corresponding unisensory visual experience without audition, and you could have a corresponding unisensory auditory experience without vision. Say that the features associated with a given sense on an occasion include only those a corresponding unisensory experience could have.

What is a corresponding unisensory experience? The notion of a perceptual experience that belongs purely or wholly to one sense modality is coherent. In *Individuals* (1959), Strawson posits a purely auditory experience. A purely auditory experience is one that is auditory but not visual, tactual, olfactory, or gustatory. To avoid tainting by experiences of other senses, Strawson considers it to be presently and historically exclusively auditory. It is the sort of perceptual experience someone blind from birth would have if they also lacked taste, smell, and touch. According to Strawson, it involves hearing only sounds of varying pitch, timbre, and loudness. This subtractive conception is intelligible. Sensory deficits help us to fathom it. This is a diachronically unisensory perceptual experience.

However, typical subjects have a rich background of experience involving various senses. That can change the character of a unisensory experience on a later occasion. This is a genuine concern. Missing one sense or another measurably impacts both perceptual capacities and neural structures associated with differing senses (for example, Krubitzer 2009; Shams et al. 2011; Thaler and Goodale 2016). Thus, it is plausible that the auditory experience of a congenitally blind person can differ from that of a blindfolded sighted person. For instance, echolocation can improve directional acuity, but blindness distorts middle distance hearing and altogether disrupts the capacity to hear relative locations between objects (Gori et al. 2014; King 2014). For blind perceivers, spatial hearing is richer in some respects, but it is poorer in others.

Brain plasticity also causes physiological differences. For instance, typical visual areas subsume auditory functions in blindness. Krubitzer (2009) reports striking effects on the size and organization of sensory cortices in genetically altered mice and early enucleated (blinded) opossums (see, especially, figure 4, 51). Experiential differences are likely to accompany such physiological differences, given differing sensory capacities.

In light of this, it is plausible that, for a given pattern of sensory stimulation, the auditory experience of a subject whose perceptual experience over time is exclusively auditory can differ in character from the auditory experience of a subject who enjoys the usual range of visual, tactual, olfactory, and gustatory episodes. If you could only ever hear, but not see, touch, taste, or smell, then your auditory experience could differ from how it actually now is. If the other senses are blocked or anesthetized, an otherwise typical subject's perceptual experience at a time is wholly auditory. It follows that such a synchronically unisensory auditory experience may differ from the auditory experience of a subject with a diachronically (historically and presently) purely auditory experience.

Some perceptual experiences of a given sense modality thus may require prior perceptual experiences of another. Any such crossmodally dependent experience could have phenomenal character that a corresponding purely unisensory experience could not. Nevertheless, crossmodal dependence is compatible with a version of the claim that all perceptual experience is modality specific. That claim requires only that phenomenal character on each occasion is exhausted by what is associated with some specific sense or another.

So, consider a synchronically unisensory perceptual experience. Such an experience requires that a subject's overall perceptual experience remains solely, entirely of the relevant modality, but only while that experience takes place. For instance, a presently wholly auditory experience is auditory but not visual, tactual, olfactory, or gustatory. But it is compatible with a history of experiences employing other senses. To get a fix on it, consider the other sense organs as blocked or anesthetized. Or imagine subtracting one at a time. Once you lack vision, touch, taste, and smell, you are in a position to have a synchronically unisensory auditory perceptual experience.

A synchronically unisensory experience accommodates crossmodal dependence. A dependent phenomenal feature may be instantiated by a presently unisensory experience, given a history of multisensory experiences. A blindfolded sighted person may have auditory spatial experiences that depend on prior visual episodes.

Now, for any multisensory episode that involves a certain sensory modality, we can say that a corresponding synchronically unisensory perceptual experience of that same modality is a perceptual experience wholly or merely of that modality under equivalent stimulation. In light of crossmodal dependence, corresponding synchronically and diachronically unisensory experiences of a modality may differ phenomenally.

This enables us to operationalize what is required on an occasion for phenomenal character to be associated with a sensory modality. The phenomenal character associated with a given sense on an occasion includes just that which a corresponding synchronically unisensory experience of that modality could instantiate. Take a multisensory perceptual episode. The phenomenal character that is associated with audition on that occasion includes that which a corresponding synchronic unisensory auditory experience could have. The phenomenal character associated with vision on an occasion includes only that which a corresponding unisensory visual experience could have. And so on for each sense modality.

Now we can unpack the idea that each aspect of a conscious perceptual episode belongs to one sense or another: The phenomenal character of each conscious perceptual episode is exhausted by that which could be instantiated by a corresponding synchronically unisensory visual, auditory, tactual, gustatory, or olfactory experience, plus whatever accrues thanks to mere co-consciousness. This accommodates simple phenomenal unity, and it handles crossmodal dependence. By fixing overall stimulation, it accommodates crossmodal causal influences. It is a good way to capture the spirit of the claim that all perceptual experience is modality specific.

5.4 The Argument

Sometimes the phenomenal character of a multisensory perceptual episode is not exhausted by what is associated with each of the respective modalities along with what accrues due to mere co-consciousness. Whenever this is so, the phenomenal character of perceptual experience is constitutively, irreducibly multisensory.

Focus on the perception of intermodal relational features. Typical human perceivers are differentially sensitive to the presence of certain relational features that could only be perceived through the joint use of several senses (Chapter 3). For instance, it is possible multisensorily to detect and differentiate intermodal identity, spatial and temporal features, such as motion, synchrony, rhythm, or meter, causality, and complex attributes such as flavors. Moreover, subjects sometimes are aware of such novel intermodal features. The exercise of multisensory perceptual capacities makes them accessible to subjects for use in reasoning and rationally guiding action (Chapter 4).

Some intermodal feature perception is phenomenally conscious. Controlling for consciousness of other features, perceiving a novel intermodal feature can differ phenomenally from failing to do so. Perceiving a novel intermodal feature thus can impact the phenomenal character of a multisensory perceptual episode.

First, some feature instances are perceptible only through multisensory perceptual episodes. You just cannot get at them unisensorily. Thus, you cannot consciously perceive a novel intermodal feature through any corresponding unisensory experience. For instance, you cannot consciously perceive a novel intermodal instance of identity, causality, movement, synchrony, rhythm, or meter with one sense on its own. No wholly unisensory experience is a case of consciously perceiving a novel intermodal feature instance.

Next, adding mere co-consciousness to otherwise unisensory experiences does not suffice to consciously perceive a novel intermodal feature. Co-consciously seeing and hearing distinct events does not suffice for consciously perceiving audiovisual causality. Co-consciously hearing and feeling distinct rhythms is not consciously perceiving an intermodal rhythm.

Finally, consciously perceiving a novel intermodal feature can make a phenomenal difference. This difference concerns what it is like for a subject to undergo a conscious episode. In particular, an episode in which a subject consciously perceives intermodal identity, causality, motion, synchrony, rhythm, or meter can differ phenomenally from an episode in which a subject consciously perceives only distinct unisensory features, even when the perceptible unisensory features are held fixed between the two cases.

The difference does not stem solely from extraperceptual judgment, belief, or inference. Instead, it is a difference in phenomenal character between distinct perceptual experiences. What it is like for a subject co-consciously to perceive using more than one sense does not suffice to fix what it is like consciously to perceive a novel intermodal relational feature. As a consequence, consciously perceiving a novel intermodal feature may have phenomenal features that could not be instantiated by a corresponding unisensory perceptual experience of any specific sense modality and that do not accrue thanks to mere co-consciousness.

To illustrate, suppose you can consciously hear a given musical rhythm, f_1. And suppose that this is a unisensory auditory experience. You also can unisensorily tactually perceive a distinct rhythm, f_2. Finally, suppose you can consciously audiotactually perceive a distinct musical rhythm, f_3. Co-consciously hearing f_1 and feeling f_2 does not suffice for consciously audiotactually perceiving a more complex rhythm, f_3, whose constituents are those of f_1 and f_2. You could do the former without doing the latter. This difference could manifest phenomenologically. What it is like for a subject to hear f_1 while feeling f_2 can differ from what it is like to perceive f_3. So, co-consciously hearing f_1 while feeling f_2 may differ phenomenologically from audiotactually perceiving f_3.

Similar claims hold of intermodal spatial, temporal, and causal features. But the argument only requires one example. Consciously multisensorily perceiving that novel intermodal feature instance can differ phenomenologically from co-consciously perceiving distinct unisensory features. Thus, the phenomenal character of a multisensory perceptual experience need not be exhausted by that which is associated with each of the individual modalities along with that which accrues thanks to mere co-consciousness.

Thus, we have a counterexample to the claim that all perceptual experience is modality specific. That is because, for a multisensory perceptual experience that involves distinct modalities, m and n, of a perceptible intermodal instance of a relational feature, r, neither a corresponding unimodal experience belonging to m nor a corresponding unimodal experience belonging to n could have the phenomenal character of consciously perceiving r, and mere co-consciousness does not suffice.

Some multisensory experience thus has phenomenal character that no corresponding unisensory experience has and that does not accrue thanks to simple co-consciousness. So, not all phenomenal character on each occasion is associated with one sense or another. Therefore, perceptual phenomenology is richly, constitutively and irreducibly, multisensory.

5.5 Phenomenal Differences

This argument relies on a difference in phenomenal properties. Some conscious multisensory episodes differ phenomenally from any co-conscious collection of corresponding unisensory experiences. This requires a defense. My defense has two parts, corresponding to whether or not the relevant phenomenal differences are noticeable by a consciously perceiving subject. The first part argues that if comparable differences are noticeable within a sense, the intermodal cases present no special difficulty. Thus, the relevant multisensory episodes also differ noticeably. The second part argues that even if a subject could not differentiate two multisensory episodes, nevertheless, those episodes may differ phenomenally. Thus, whether or not a noticeable difference obtains, the relevant phenomenal features differ.

To start, grant that a difference in phenomenally conscious episodes that is discernible by a perceiving subject from the first-person perspective suffices for a phenomenal difference. You can tell seeing red from hearing a sound, and you can feel how sharp pain differs from throbbing. Each suffices for a phenomenal difference. But, you cannot differentiate otherwise equivalent phenomenally conscious episodes of seeing perfect twins or metamers just by undergoing them. Since we are not requiring that phenomenal differences must be discriminable by their subjects, the episodes may or may not differ phenomenally.

Some philosophers accept that perceptual phenomenology within a sense modality is moderately rich. Perceptual psychology provides good reasons to believe typical humans are sensitive to features beyond simple qualities like hues, pitches, and textures. These features include spatial and temporal relations, causality, identity, and numerosity. According to moderates, this sensitivity is reflected in perceptual phenomenology. (Exclude natural kind and semantic properties, which raise distinctive concerns.) Controlling for sensitivity to other features, exercising the capacity to detect and differentiate such a feature can impact the phenomenal character of a perceptual episode (see, for example, Bayne 2009; Siegel 2010; O'Callaghan 2011; Speaks 2015).

In such a case, what it is like for a subject to undergo a conscious perceptual episode could differ noticeably for its subject from a case in which no such feature is discerned. Plausibly, any such noticeable difference stems in part from sensitivity to differing features.

There are two main reasons to believe subjects in general can discern such differences. First, subjects sometimes notice a contrast. This holds for conscious episodes near enough in time not to raise doubts about memory or confabulation. And reports in some cases are consistent among subjects. Where the best explanation for a consistent reported difference rules out extraperceptual cognition, judgment, or inference, it is reasonable to accept that perceptual phenomenology differs noticeably.

Second, the difference detectably can break down. A subject may fail to attend as required to discern a relational feature. In addition, experience and perceptual learning cause differences in perceptual sensitivity that can affect perceptual phenomenology (see O'Callaghan 2011; Connolly 2019). Disorders cause changes in perceptual capacities that seem to impact the character of a subject's consciousness (Bayne 2009). And typical subjects can attest that direct interventions like transcranial magnetic stimulation (TMS) alter what it is like to undergo an experience in which the relevant perceptual capacities measurably are disrupted.

In comparison with the intramodal case, the intermodal case presents no special difficulty. I have argued that typical humans are differentially sensitive to intermodal relational features, such as identity, motion, simultaneity, meter, and causality. Moreover, human subjects sometimes are perceptually aware of such features. By parity with the intramodal case, what it is like consciously to perceive an intermodal relational feature in a multisensory scene may differ noticeably from what it is like consciously to perceive an otherwise common set of sense-specific features.

As with relational features perceived using one sense, subjects may notice that otherwise indiscernible conscious multisensory episodes differ from the first-person perspective when one but not the other involves sensitivity to an intermodal feature. This is true especially during a short time interval. In some noteworthy cases, such as intermodal rhythm and causality, reports indicate such a noticeable difference, and they are consistent across subjects.

Moreover, the difference can break down. Attention and cognitive influences can affect whether or not a subject is sensitive to an intermodal feature (Chapters 3 and 4). In addition, experience and perceptual learning affect such sensitivity over time. Thus, they can impact the target perceptual phenomenology (O'Callaghan 2017; Connolly 2019, chapter 5). It also is plausible that disorders and experimental disruptions to multisensory perceptual capacities using TMS can change what it is like for a subject to perceive multisensorily.

Each of the cases I have discussed involves a relational feature that holds between things consciously perceived using different senses. The empirical results can establish that it is possible to detect and respond differentially to such a feature. Philosophical and rational psychology can support access consciousness and awareness. The claim being considered is that experiences contrasting in respect of sensitivity to such a feature sometimes are discriminable by their subjects.

The best reasons to deny that subjects consciously perceive any such intermodal feature in a way that detectably affects perceptual phenomenology *also* support skeptically denying that subjects consciously perceive any such relational features, even through a single modality, in ways that detectably affect perceptual phenomenology. However, saying that binding, spatial, temporal, and causal relations never are consciously perceived, even unimodally, leaves us with an implausibly sparse picture of perceptual experience and its character. In both intramodal and intermodal cases, we have evidence to support the claim that the difference sometimes is noticeable from the first-person perspective.

Thus, according to a moderately liberal general account of perceptual phenomenal consciousness, there is no compelling reason to deny that perceiving some such relation noticeably affects the phenomenal character of a conscious multisensory episode. There is nothing especially problematic about the intermodal cases.

Since an experiential difference that is discernible by a conscious perceiving subject from the first-person perspective suffices for a phenomenal difference, we have reasons to extend a moderately liberal account of perceptual experience to multisensory perceptual consciousness. If so, a conscious multisensory episode can differ phenomenally from each co-conscious collection of corresponding unisensory experiences.

5.6 Skepticism

Skepticism about multisensory experience nevertheless remains intelligible. Throughout this book, I have spoken of multisensory processes and capacities. This notoriously does not establish claims about consciousness, especially phenomenal consciousness, if it is distinct from access consciousness. Multisensory perception does not avoid the explanatory gap (Levine 1983). Descriptions of multisensory processes leave open questions about experiences and phenomenal properties.

Some skeptics about multisensory experience exploit the gap. They grant that processes associated with different senses interact extensively and satisfy criteria for being multisensory (such as superadditivity) (Deroy et al. 2014; Spence and Bayne 2015). However, skeptics say that perceptual consciousness remains unimodal. Any distinctive multisensory phenomenology or awareness depends on inference, association, or extraperceptual cognition (see Fulkerson 2011; Connolly 2014).

One obstacle in responding is that beyond a few focal examples—cases like seeing red and feeling pain—it is hard to identify specific characteristics of consciousness. This holds in particular of phenomenal consciousness, in contrast with access consciousness. It is even harder to establish that an aspect of consciousness is perceptual rather than extraperceptual. Any cognitive phenomenology accentuates this difficulty.

Here is a glib response. During a phenomenally conscious multisensory episode, sometimes you are perceptually sensitive to a novel intermodal feature instance, such as identity, motion, synchrony, or causality. You are perceptually aware of an intermodal feature: the same event's being seen and heard, flashing and banging, an intermodal rhythm, synchrony, or a flavor that goes beyond a smell and a taste. You can report that this episode differs subjectively from an otherwise comparable one in which you are not sensitive to an intermodal feature. A perceptual process, one that manifests a perceptual capacity, is responsible for the differing aspect of your experience. So, it is a case of perceptual phenomenality. And it is irreducibly multisensory.

This response faces a further obstacle. It is hard to tell which state or process is responsible for an aspect of consciousness. Set aside technical limitations, such as limited resolution in mapping brain function. Testing for features of experience typically means relying on introspection, verbal reports, or performance of an action in a task. Each invokes cognition and general conscious awareness. Perceptual sensitivity thus could drive either cognition that is not marked phenomenally or conscious awareness that is extraperceptual. Tests might probe one of the latter instead of perceptual phenomenality.

If, as skeptics challenge, multisensory processes are not reflected as such in perceptual experience, then the role they play in the psychological lives of subjects differs from paradigm examples of phenomenal consciousness. For instance, in that case, multisensory perceptual phenomena lack any distinctive epistemic force stemming from phenomenality. Their relevance to aesthetics is sharply limited (cf. Nanay 2012). And they fail to figure in the debate concerning what it is like to be a subject, from that subject's perspective. If so, they simply do not register for a big part of the philosophy of mind.

This dispute hinges on a third variety of psychological explanation. What Robbins and Jack (2006) dub *the phenomenal stance* involves ascribing phenomenal states to subjects. This enterprise aims to capture what it is like for a conscious subject. It has to account for how things are from the subject's point of view. It does so by describing features that constitute the phenomenal character of a conscious episode and how they hang together. We might call this the descriptive metaphysics of consciousness.[1]

Assuming this enterprise needs the distinction, what marks perceptual phenomenality in contrast with that of extraperceptual cognition? First, we cannot just say that all phenomenology is perceptual. Consciousness is full of other stuff. There is emotion, imagery, and mere sensation, which Strawson (2010) calls *sensory-affective*. Others admit phenomenology associated with thought, agency, and mental effort (further, see Kriegel 2015). Second, it just begs the question to say that all perceptual phenomenality is modality specific. Third, what about distinctive marks of the perceptual? Hume appealed to vividness. Some describe apparent independence from experience (Strawson 1959; Siegel 2006a). Others rely on phenomenal intentionality (Loar 2003). Many appeal to presentational phenomenology—being right

---

[1] This phase is Benj Hellie's (personal communication).

there before you, temporally and spatially present, available for attention and demonstration (Valberg 1992).

Do multisensory episodes bear those marks? The McGurk effect,
ventriloquism, Sekuler's streaming–bouncing illusion, and intermodal
binding, rhythm, synchrony, and causality all are good candidates for
cases in which subjects undergo vivid, subject-independent, presentational
multisensory phenomenology. The multisensory demonstrations really do
work. And my best effort at a sincere experience report is that I am just
consciously presented with that audiovisual event; or, that intermodal
rhythmic sequence, apparent intermodal motion, causality, or temporal
ordering of occurrences. None of these experiences is secured just by sense-
specific phenomenal features and co-consciousness.

Still, these are tough cases. There are differences among them, and
there is room for doubt. Skepticism remains a threat. In this respect,
intermodal cases are like other examples of relational feature awareness.
We can doubt whether the relevant bit of consciousness is perceptual,
and we can argue about the details of its character. Given the explanatory
gap, nothing we say about processes and capacities wholly extinguishes
the doubt.

Here is the first step in responding. Forget about satisfying skeptical
standards about phenomenology. That requires certainty—no room for
doubt—about phenomenal character. If we had privileged, incorrigible
access to phenomenology, we might hope to meet that standard. As it
stands, claims about phenomenology and appearances are theoretical
claims. We make them to account for a range of evidence. Sometimes we
get phenomenology altogether wrong, or only partly right. It is a difficult
enterprise (see Siewert 1998). In these types of disputes, we cannot hope
to satisfy ourselves that we have reached certainty.

Consider the methodology. Naïve introspection is deeply flawed (see
Schwitzgebel 2008). It is poorly suited to the task, and it is prone to
errors. That is because experience reports require judgment, interpretation, and conceptualization that may not mirror the features instantiated,
their structure, or their psychological roles, such as being perceptual or
not. Reports of phenomenal contrasts, especially synchronic, intrapersonal
ones, are better than naïve introspection. But, they can only reveal differences, not the respects in which experiences differ or whether the difference is perceptual or extraperceptual. Contrast arguments, like the one

I have described, are an improvement. However, they are abductive (see Siegel 2006b). They require ruling out other factors as better explanations for the evidence. They appeal to empirical considerations, such as the possibility of dissociations. They rely on assumptions about the functional roles of things that might be responsible for reported contrasts, such as inference, judgment, or familiarity. And they treat subjects as rational agents, trying to make the best sense of what they think, say, and do. So, claims about phenomenology are fallible, theoretical claims.

Now consider a skeptical position about multisensory phenomenal character. Here are Spence and Bayne (2015) on intermodal binding awareness:

> However, we think it is debatable whether the "unity of the event" really is internal to one's experience in these cases, or whether it involves a certain amount of post-perceptual processing (or inference). In other words, it seems to us to be an open question whether, in these situations, one's experience is of an MPO [multisensory perceptual object] or whether it is instead structured in terms of multiple instances of unimodal perceptual objects. (Spence and Bayne 2015, 119)

First, the skeptic we are considering says that empirical psychology reveals integrative mechanisms that are differentially responsive to features across sense modalities. These ground relatively early perceptual processes. They yield measurable effects, such as object-specific preview effects (see Chapter 3). Second, these processes crossmodally guide attention and actions like reaching and orienting. They also reflexively lead to appropriate beliefs and make possible demonstrative thoughts—*that is a single event, it is loud and bright*, or *that rhythm comprises taps and sounds*. Third, subjects are aware of the relevant features. It is not as if people are confused about where they get multisensory beliefs or why they act as they do. They do not comport themselves like blindsighters. Still, acquiring these beliefs is not cognitively demanding. These phenomena behave like perception in enabling thought and action.

Nevertheless, skeptics deny that perceptual experience is richly multisensory. They contend that phenomenality itself is unimodal.

That is odd. A conscious condition of the subject counts as perceptual for the purposes of empirical and rational explanation, but not for the purposes of phenomenology. Skepticism is not incoherent. It just demands we meet a certain evidential standard. The claim that we lack richly multisensory phenomenal consciousness is compatible with the evidence. This is unsurprising. Naïve introspection is unreliable as an empirical method, and we have not yet closed the explanatory gap. Thus, our argument does not meet the highest skeptical standard. But consider the skeptic's commitments. There is a domain of experiences, characterized phenomenologically, some of which are distinguished as perceptual, and some of which are not. This domain is the target of a variety of psychological explanation that is relatively independent from empirical and rational explanation. The skeptic grants multisensory processes and capacities that play the typical functional and rational roles of perceptual awareness, but denies multisensory perceptual experiences and phenomenal features.

What independent purchase do we have on such a domain to support these skeptical claims? I am saying that there is no distinctive, self-contained phenomenological enterprise that stands on its own, evidentially, apart from empirical and rational psychology. I am tempted to subsume phenomenology to the other two varieties of explanation. So, more radically, as a mode of psychological explanation, it just collapses into the empirical and the rational. This does not deny the reality of phenomenal consciousness. It says that the details of what it is like to be you are targets of theoretical claims in those enterprises. Given this, we should set aside this form of skepticism about constitutively, irreducibly multisensory perceptual consciousness as a genuine explanatory concern.

Here, then, is a sufficient condition for ascribing richly multisensory perceptual phenomenal consciousness. (i) An irreducibly multisensory capacity involves differential sensitivity to the presence of novel features of the environment. (ii) Processes and states involved in the exercise of such sensitivity play the right causal-functional role with respect to stimulation, cognition, and action. (iii) Its exercise is apt to rationally ground thoughts, beliefs, and actions in the manner characteristic of perception. (iv) Episodes involving such processes and states bear the causal-functional and rational marks of phenomenal consciousness. (v) Moreover, they are implicated as part of the best explanation for features of phenomenal consciousness in the following way: where the conditions on phenomenal consciousness are met, the relevant feature of a subject's conscious life depends in a suitably counterfactual-supporting way on such a process or state.

5.7 Indiscriminability

This chapter's argument depends on the claim that the phenomenal character of a conscious multisensory perceptual episode need not be exhausted by that which is associated with each of the respective modalities plus what accrues thanks to simple co-consciousness. This relies on a difference in phenomenal properties.

A noticeable difference of the right sort suffices for a phenomenal difference. The previous section considered the case that a conscious perceiving subject sometimes can notice such a difference. It relied on a moderately liberal view about perceptual phenomenality. Nevertheless, a distinct form of skepticism remains. Someone may maintain that no difference of the sort my argument requires is discernible by any conscious perceiving subject.

Here is why. To take an example, you need not be able to tell apart an episode in which you multisensorily perceive an intermodal rhythm from an otherwise equivalent episode in which you perceive distinct audible and tactual rhythms. Or, controlling for other differences, you may not be able to differentiate multisensorily perceiving a common audiovisual object from perceiving distinct but co-located audible and visual objects. And so on, for each intermodal feature. If no such difference is discernible from the first-person perspective, why say the experiences differ phenomenally?

In answering, it helps to understand motives. Phenomenal features of perceptual episodes are aspects of what it is like to be a perceiving subject. It is natural to think that recognizing, categorizing, and attributing features to objects are part of what it is like to undergo a conscious perceptual episode. Thus, they help fix the character of a perceptual experience. These psychological capacities—recognizing, categorizing, ascribing features to individuals—are more cognition-like than capacities that paradigmatically belong to perception, such as detecting objects or features, differentiating between distinct objects or features, and being differentially sensitive to the instantiation of attributes by objects. Nonetheless, their exercise can depend on the presence of a stimulus. And, it can be relatively insulated from judgment, belief, action, inference, and deliberative control. Thus, it is plausible that such factors can affect the phenomenal character of a perceptual episode. Even Fodor and Pylyshyn, who champion perception's immunity from cognitive influence, say its phenomenology includes contributions from cognition.[2] According to this conception, perceptual phenomenology is relatively replete. If so, the previous section's arguments have a lot of force. A case in which you quickly, effortlessly appreciate, recognize, or ascribe an intermodal feature (even if you do not judge or believe it is present) plausibly differs noticeably for you from the first-person perspective from an otherwise equivalent case in which you do not.

But the typical cues and indications need not be conclusive. They may not enable you to differentiate a scene in which an intermodal feature is instantiated from an otherwise equivalent scene with only parallel unisensory features. So, for instance, you might not be able to tell apart a perfectly coordinated multisensory virtual reality rig from the real world of nonvirtual things and happenings. Nothing about just the appearances of things before your senses, unsupplemented by statistical information or other assumptions about the environment, would warrant your differentiating them.

Once we have factored out any contributions from recognition, categorization, or predication, two options present themselves. One option is to maintain that perceptual phenomenal differences require differences that a subject occurrently is in a position to appreciate. For reasons that will emerge, this is not my favored option. Nevertheless, this conception does make room for multisensory phenomenology. But defending this claim requires further resources. I take that up in the next section. The other option, which I pursue now, is to maintain that

---

[2] Their reasons, however, differ. Pylyshyn (1999, 362) says belief shapes phenomenology. Fodor (1983), on the other hand, argues that basic categorizations, such as *dog*, are "phenomenologically given" (96).

the phenomenal features of two conscious perceptual episodes may differ even if they do not differ in a way that is noticeable as such by a subject from the first-person perspective. This is the route I prefer, and I defend it in the remainder of this section.

There is a conception of perceptual experience according to which nothing an experience itself noticeably provides suffices to enable you to discriminate such scenes. The difference between them is not something evident as such to you as a consciously perceiving subject. Treating a scene as perceptibly containing an intermodal feature may make a noticeable difference, but that stems from how you take it, not just the appearance it presents to you. To be warranted in treating it as instantiating an intermodal feature, rather than just unimodal features, may require more support.

Some philosophers say perceptual experiences therefore lack content (Travis 2004). That is because they hold that no experience determines, in a way that is evident to its subject, how it ought to be taken. It has no face value that settles the scenes with which it is compatible. Thus, it does not fix conditions under which it is assessable as correct or incorrect, and thus as accurate or inaccurate. One might say that experience, unlike thought or judgment, does not ascribe or predicate features of individuals in the environment (since that would entail correctness conditions) but instead involves sensitivity to the instantiation of features by individuals.

Relying on what a subject can differentiate under controlled conditions is an advance over murky talk of what it is like for a subject. In the right controlled conditions, a subject could not tell two coinciding unisensory features from a unified multisensory feature. This is a respect in which two conscious perceptual episodes do not differ in a way a subject could notice just in virtue of undergoing them.

Here is my response. First, perceptually experiencing an individual or an attribute requires consciously being sensitive perceptually to that individual or attribute. That involves consciously standing in a sensory relation to a perceptible item or feature. What you perceive by means of your senses depends in part on the objects and features before you, to which you stand in that relation. Thus, two otherwise equivalent conscious perceptual episodes might differ if only their subjects stand in sensing relations to distinct objects and features. Consciously being sensitive to an intermodal relational feature instance therefore may differ from consciously being sensitive only to distinct unimodal feature instances.

What, then, are the conditions under which a subject is sensitive to one type of feature rather than another? This question is pressing, especially for co-occurring features. One concern is that if a subject responds no differently, this is a distinction without a relevant difference.

In the intermodal case, consciously perceiving an intermodal feature requires sensitivity to a type of configuration, and perceiving parallel intramodal features does not. Whether or not you are sensitive to that configuration, rather than just to each of its constituents, depends not just on your current reaction but also on how you would respond in a variety of other conditions. For example, being sensitive to a configuration characteristic of intermodal identity requires the capacity to differentiate between identical and distinct objects across senses in at least some conditions—such as when spatial and temporal constraints are met in contrast with when they are unmet. Being sensitive just to the constituents of a configuration, rather than to the configuration itself, requires only that a subject is differentially sensitive to each of those features independently and that such sensitivity can be exercised in parallel at the same time. Earlier chapters have argued that subjects sometimes are differentially sensitive to intermodal configurations and other features.

Still, from your perspective, on a given occasion, you may not be able to differentiate coinciding but distinct objects from a case of intermodal identity just in virtue of undergoing episodes in which you are sensitive to each. Past experience, scene statistics, regularities, insider knowledge, or a gut leaning may lead you to take things one way or another. But, the appearance each scene presents on that occasion need not enable you to notice a difference. And phenomenology need not make evident which perceptual capacities you exercise.

Some experiential differences thus are not discriminable. That is, just on the basis of undergoing them, a conscious subject may be unable to differentiate two conscious perceptual episodes whose characteristics differ. Nevertheless, each of the differing features may be indispensable in accounting for what it is like for a subject to undergo a conscious perceptual episode. For instance, each may be needed to capture the apparent particularity or the demonstrative character of a perceptual episode. Moreover, each may be needed to capture what it is like for a subject in other conditions, or to give a more systematic account of what a subject consciously can detect and differentiate. If so, then the respects in which experiences that are not discriminable may differ can qualify as phenomenal features.

So, consider the case of multisensory perception. Even if a subject cannot tell the difference in a carefully controlled pair of conditions, the features to which the subject is consciously related during distinct multisensory episodes can differ. Consciously being perceptually sensitive to an intermodal feature instance differs from consciously being sensitive only to distinct unisensory features. For instance, consciously being sensitive multisensorily to something visible's causing something audible differs from co-consciously being sensitive only to something visible and something audible. Likewise, consciously being perceptually sensitive to a single audiovisual object differs from consciously being perceptually sensitive to distinct but coinciding audible and visible objects.

In each of these examples, the former but not the latter requires being differentially sensitive to an intermodal feature. At the very least, this requires sensitivity to a special type of configuration. Whether or not you are sensitive to that configuration, rather than just its constituents, depends on how you would respond in a variety of other conditions. So, being sensitive (on an occasion) to an intermodal feature depends on how a subject would respond in a range of circumstances and not just on details that can be read off from the present episode.

Now, each of these differing characteristics—being sensitive to an intermodal feature, in contrast with being sensitive just to independent unimodal features—also is relevant to capturing what it is like for a subject to undergo a whole range of conscious multisensory episodes in various conditions. And each is needed to capture a pattern of conscious discriminations. So, they are not coextensive, and they are not explanatorily equivalent. Thus, there is a corresponding difference in phenomenal features. This is the relevant phenomenal difference.

According to this conception, two conscious multisensory episodes can differ phenomenally even if a subject could not tell which is which—that is, even without a noticeable difference. So, it is possible for there to be a phenomenal difference between perceptual episodes that could not be evident to a subject just in virtue of undergoing those episodes.

Some may object that phenomenal differences require discernibility by a conscious subject. First, we ought to distinguish individuating distinct phenomenal features from attributing distinct phenomenal features to pairs of experiences. What is required for phenomenal features to be distinct may differ from what is required for perceptual episodes to instantiate distinct phenomenal features. Discriminability under some conditions may be required for the former, even while discriminability of distinct episodes is not required for the latter. Put another way, possessing distinct phenomenal features may require possessing a feature that suffices for a discriminable difference in some but not every otherwise equivalent pair of cases in which it is instantiated. Thus, two otherwise equivalent episodes might possess distinct phenomenal features without being discriminable from each other.

Second, more generally, we ought to accept that episodes can differ phenomenally without being discriminable. Consider, for instance, a phenomenal sorites. Suppose you cannot differentiate between any two adjacent color chips in a stack. If a phenomenal difference requires discriminability, no two experiences of adjacent chips differ phenomenally. Thus, if property identity is transitive, no two experiences of distinct chips differ phenomenally. However, you can tell the difference between pairs of distant chips. Thus, if a noticeable difference suffices for a phenomenal difference, experiences of some chips differ phenomenally. Rejecting that being discriminable is necessary for distinct episodes to instantiate distinct phenomenal properties avoids the contradiction. Thus, a subject need not be capable of discriminating two conscious episodes that differ phenomenally (Williamson 1990; Speaks 2015).

So, suppose that a subject could not, just in virtue of undergoing two episodes, discriminate or tell the difference between consciously perceiving an intermodal feature instance and co-consciously perceiving otherwise identical unisensory features. Nevertheless, that subject may in each case consciously be sensitive to distinct features, each of which is relevant to capturing what it is like for that subject across a range of differing conditions. If so, two indiscriminable conscious perceptual episodes may differ phenomenally.

5.8 Qualities

A loose end needs tying. Suppose perceptual phenomenology is sparse. In particular, suppose that sensitivity to a relational feature never makes a phenomenal difference to a conscious perceptual episode. This denies the moderate liberal view of perceptual phenomenality, even within a sense. And it opposes the arguments of the previous section, blocking its conclusion. In support of this view, one might maintain that phenomenal differences must be discriminable by a perceiving subject, while relational features make no discriminable difference. According to such a sparse view, must all perceptual phenomenality be sense specific? My answer is no.

According to a most austere sparse view, perceptual consciousness reveals only a small collection of basic qualitative features. Other qualitative features stem from their co-conscious combinations. For instance, sensible qualities may include hues, pitches, warmth, scents, and the like. Each such basic feature, like a Lockean simple quality, consistently has a single, uniform appearance. It is a discernible respect of similarity and difference, and it grounds a sensory ordering. Sensitivity to such qualities exhausts perceptual phenomenology.[3]

Proponents of a sparse view may not find my arguments compelling. The intermodal relational features I have discussed lack clear qualitative characteristics that are simple or uniform and shared across instances. Each involves a complex array of sensible qualities. And distinct experiences of an intermodal feature can vary phenomenally. Consciously perceiving such a feature thus need not be marked by any simple, consistent qualitative phenomenology. Thus, a sparse theorist may reject that perceiving any novel intermodal relational feature impacts phenomenal character in a way that is not captured by sensitivity to basic qualitative features and co-consciousness.

Such a view is compatible with the claim that all phenomenal character is modality specific. Suppose that every basic sensible quality is perceptible unisensorily. Accordingly, suppose that every basic phenomenal feature instantiated by a conscious multisensory episode also is instantiated by a corresponding unisensory experience. If so, the phenomenal character of each perceptual episode is exhausted by that which is associated with each of the respective senses, along with

---

[3] Corresponding to each such sensible quality, some think there is an inherently qualitative phenomenal feature, or phenomenal quality (cf. Peacocke 1983). Qualia, according to some accounts, are examples of such features. See, for instance, Goodman (1951).

whatever accrues thanks to simple co-consciousness. If each phenomenal feature in fact is associated with exactly one sense on each occasion, or else stems from mere co-consciousness, the sparse view entails that all phenomenal character is modality specific.

My first reply is general. This conception of phenomenal character is too sparse, and it ought to be enriched. First, sensitivity to simple qualities need not exhaust phenomenal character. Structural and relational characteristics—spatial, temporal, binding—also matter to what it is like for a consciously perceiving subject. The arrangement into configurations of co-conscious qualities matters. Second, its inventory of features is too austere. For instance, it rejects that sensitivity to shapes, as distinct from pluralities of quality instances, ever impacts what it is like to perceive. The same holds for motion, simultaneity, causality, individuals, numerosity, and other categorical features. Otherwise, the march to enrich is on. Moreover, hard questions about how to individuate phenomenal features remain. Even a paradigmatic sensible quality, such as a hue, does not consistently present a single, uniform appearance. And the phenomenal sorites blocks using indiscriminability as a criterion for instantiating identical phenomenal features.

But, set aside these concerns, and focus on sensible qualities. Must each be sense specific? There is a good reply on the sparse theorist's own terms.

Consider again the case of flavor. Flavors are paradigm examples of perceptible qualitative features (Lewis 1983, 1988). Examples include the flavor of mint ice cream, red wine, hatch chilis, blood oranges, dark chocolate, and Vegemite.

Flavors are complex. They include components drawn from taste, smell, and somatosensation. Thus, flavors are fully perceptible only through the joint use of multiple senses. Flavors are significant because they provide an example of a wholly novel type of feature whose instances are perceptible in the first instance only multisensorily (Chapter 3).

Nevertheless, flavor might involve only sensible qualities associated with each of the respective senses. Menthol is olfactory, tingling is trigeminal, sweetness is gustatory. Thus, according to a sparse account of perceptual phenomenality, the phenomenal features of a multisensory flavor experience might be exhausted by those that could be instantiated by corresponding unisensory episodes plus those that accrue due to mere co-consciousness. If so, flavor experience is just minimally multisensory.

However, Chapter 3 described an intriguing prospect. Using multiple senses in coordination could enable a subject to be sensitive to a new qualitative component of flavor that could not be perceived using any sense entirely on its own. Such features could have a simple, uniform character that grounds a sensory ordering distinct from that of sense-specific qualities. The perception of flavor therefore could involve sensitivity to a novel qualitative component or dimension beyond various sense-specific characteristics. For instance, a distinctive, recognizable quality inherent to *mintiness* could be evident only thanks to the coordinated use of several sensory systems. If so, conscious flavor perception correspondingly could involve a novel phenomenal feature associated with sensitivity to such a quality. Thus, consciously perceiving flavor could involve phenomenal features that no unisensory episode of any sense could have.[4]

Therefore, a sparse account of perceptual phenomenality does not require that all phenomenal character is sense specific. By this I mean that even the phenomenal features of a perceptual episode need not be exhausted by those associated with each of the respective senses along with what accrues thanks to mere co-consciousness. It is not the case that every characteristic needed to capture what it is like to undergo a multisensory episode must be associated with one sense or another. Some qualities can emerge only thanks to the joint use of multiple senses.

If this is counterintuitive, compare it to unisensory perception of a sensible quality. Sensitivity to a phenomenologically simple or basic quality, such as a hue or a pitch, in fact depends on a complex process. That process integrates information from multiple sources. For instance, apparent hue relies on comparing differing cone responses, and apparent pitch involves harmonic analysis across audible frequency bands. By analogy, an aspect of flavor whose appearance is simple and uniform could rely on integrating chemical information from taste, smell, and

---

[4] Sweetness enhancement provides evidence. This occurs when a degree of sweetness not otherwise perceptible is evident only thanks to an olfactory contribution from vanilla scent. However, this is a novel determinate quality, akin to supersaturated red; it is not a novel determinable quality. Alternatively, if there are feature types to which retronasal olfaction is sensitive only when a tastant is present, and which contribute constitutively to flavor, this provides evidence for such a novel type of quality. True integration between olfaction and gustation strengthens the evidence to the extent that it obscures its sources.

somatosensation. So, discerning apparently simple qualities multisensorily does not differ in kind from doing so unisensorily.

Multisensory perception therefore could reveal new sensible qualities. It thus presents novel candidates for phenomenal features that are not instantiated by any conscious unisensory perceptual episode. Not even all qualia must be sense specific.

5.9 Conclusions

This chapter argues that perceptual experience is richly multisensory. Phenomenal consciousness, in particular, is constitutively and irreducibly multisensory. By this, I mean that the phenomenal character of a conscious perceptual episode sometimes may include more than what is associated with each of the respective senses on an occasion plus whatever stems from simple co-consciousness. Exercising multisensory capacities thus can make a phenomenal difference to perceptual experience. This difference can obtain whether or not it would enable a subject to discriminate between two otherwise equivalent experiences.

First, intermodal features present no special difficulty for a moderately liberal account of perceptual phenomenality. Being sensitive to an intermodal feature can make a difference that is noticeable from the first-person perspective. According to the best explanation, this difference stems from the exercise of multisensory perceptual capacities.

However, a subject may be unable to differentiate a scene containing intermodal features from an otherwise matching scene with only unimodal features. Nonetheless, in each condition a subject may be sensitive to distinct features. This sensitivity to distinct features depends on how the subject would respond in a variety of other conditions. Moreover, sensitivity to distinct features may be indispensable in a systematic account of what it is like for such a consciously perceiving subject. Being sensitive to distinct features can mean having distinct phenomenal properties. We ought to reject that phenomenal differences between episodes require their discriminability.

Finally, even a sparse account can admit novel sensible qualities. Multisensory flavor perception could disclose novel qualities not accessible using any one sense on its own. Accordingly, even if sensitivity to basic qualities exhausts phenomenal character, that does not require that all phenomenal character is sense specific. Even qualia freaks should accept that multisensory perception could reveal novel qualia.

It follows that the character of a perceptual episode is not exhausted by that which is associated with each of the respective senses, along with whatever accrues due to mere co-consciousness. Therefore, not all perceptual experience is modality specific. Perceptual consciousness in this respect is richly multisensory. Coordination among the senses thus makes possible new forms of perceptual consciousness. Subjects could not enjoy these experiences if their senses only worked independently and in parallel. In these respects, multisensory perception extends the varieties of experience.

5.10 Limitations

Two limitations remain. The first concerns whether or not any basic or fundamental sensible quality is revealed only multisensorily. The second concerns how to individuate sensory modalities in the face of richly multisensory perception and consciousness.

5.10.1 Uniqueness

Some perceptible intermodal features belong to types with instances that are perceptible using one sense at a time. You can see, hear, or feel binding, simultaneity, motion, rhythm, and causality unisensorily. Experiencing such a feature multisensorily is not unique. Thus, consciously perceiving an intermodal instance of such a feature might involve only phenomenal features of determinate types that also have unisensory instances. That is, each determinate phenomenal feature of such a multisensory episode might also be instantiated by some actual or possible unisensory visual, auditory, tactual, olfactory, or gustatory episode, or else stem from simple co-consciousness. If that is the case, each such phenomenal feature could be instantiated by some unisensory episode. If so, none is wholly novel. None is unique to multisensory perception.

However, some perceptible intermodal features do belong to novel types. Flavors are wholly novel features whose instances are fully perceptible in the first instance only multisensorily. Flavors are not perceptible unisensorily. Accordingly, if flavor perception involves a distinctive sort of experience, then it may have some phenomenal feature no wholly unisensory episode could instantiate.

One such feature is structural. It involves a relation among sense-specific components drawn from taste, smell, and somatosensation. Perhaps it is an organic unity. So, on one hand, what is distinctive about flavor could be the nature of the relation that holds among sense-specific components. Perhaps, unlike spatial, temporal, and causal relations, this relation does not hold among any collection of attributes accessible at the same time using only one sense. If so, corresponding to this unique structural feature, flavor perception involves a phenomenal feature that is distinctively multisensory.

On the other hand, what is distinctive about flavor could stem from how sense-specific components are arranged. Rather than the nature of the relation, the constituents of flavor plus their organization jointly are novel. If so, neither the constituents nor the structure must be unique to multisensory perceptual experience. Therefore, it is possible that the character of a multisensory flavor experience is exhausted by phenomenal features that could be instantiated by some unisensory gustatory, olfactory, or somatosensory episode plus those due to mere co-consciousness. And, again, this is a respect in which multisensory flavor perception is not a wholly unique sort of experience.

Nevertheless, as I have described it, flavor perception also could involve sensitivity to a wholly novel quality. If so, a novel type of phenomenal feature characterizes flavor experience. It is not instantiated in any unisensory episode, and it does not accrue thanks to simple co-consciousness. This does yield a uniquely multisensory experience.

This book offers no conclusive case that any such novel quality is perceptible by humans only multisensorily. Thus, it may be that no novel, basic or fundamental sensible quality is revealed to us only multisensorily. Accordingly, it could be that any basic phenomenal quality is of a type that could be instantiated by some unisensory episode.

I am agnostic about the nature of the relation that unifies a flavor's sense-specific characteristics in order to constitute a single, complex attribute of stuff in the mouth. Therefore, it remains possible that each determinate phenomenal feature instantiated by a multisensory perceptual episode either could be instantiated by some unisensory episode or else stems from mere co-consciousness. My arguments in this book do not address this limitation. It may be a real limit. This may mark just the extent to which perception and perceptual consciousness are multisensory.

I want to emphasize that this does not establish that all phenomenal character is modality specific. And it does not undermine the conclusion that perceptual consciousness is richly multisensory. Here is why. If, for instance, flavor experience is *sui generis*, then that is fuel for my fire—it supports this chapter's central claim. And it topples the limitation.

If not, the main conclusion nevertheless stands. Suppose multisensory perception reveals no entirely novel quality among flavor's constituents. That leaves alive the claim that no perceptual experience reveals a sensible quality (in contrast with complex qualitative attributes) that is not revealed by some possible unisensory visual, auditory, tactual, olfactory, or gustatory experience.

But that is a far weaker claim than this chapter's target. First, it does not imply that all phenomenal features originate within a sense or that being instantiated multisensorily depends on being instantiated unisensorily. It means only that each basic sensible quality could be perceived during some unisensory experience, and that each basic phenomenal feature—each building block of experience—possibly is instantiated during some conscious unisensory episode. Alternatively, each belongs to a determinate type with unisensory instances. But this deflates the claim that every phenomenal feature of each conscious perceptual episode is associated with one of the sense modalities.

Moreover, it just cannot establish that all perceptual consciousness is modality specific. It does not imply that the phenomenal character of each multisensory perceptual episode is exhausted by that which could be instantiated by a corresponding unisensory visual, auditory, tactual, olfactory, or gustatory experience under equivalent stimulation, along with what stems from mere co-consciousness. Such features do not exhaust multisensory phenomenal character on each occasion.

5.10.2 The Senses

This all has presupposed that perceivers possess distinct senses. The arguments throughout this book have relied on it. This chapter's account of what it is for a feature to be associated with a given sense on an occasion appeals to the intelligibility of a corresponding unisensory episode—one that belongs to a single sense. And the characterization of a richly multisensory phenomenon depends on features beyond those each sense could contribute on its own. To be genuinely multisensory requires more than one sense.

All the while, I have offered no account of what makes something a sense nor of what differentiates senses from each other. Moreover, my arguments challenge the distinctness of our senses. Senses are not causally independent from each other. Even from the earliest stages, sensory systems cooperate extensively and perform joint functions. Perceptual consciousness is not segmented into discrete, experientially encapsulated components whose boundaries align with the senses. Experiences cannot be carved without remainder into their sense-specific parts.

Should we abandon talk of distinct senses? Perceptual capacities divorced from particular senses could take the spotlight. And, perhaps, as Speaks (2015) maintains, there is just one fundamental conscious mode of sensing, rather than distinct modalities of sensory consciousness. The next chapter tackles these concerns and addresses this remaining limitation.

6

Senses

Genuine multisensory perception presupposes multiple senses. The phenomena I have discussed challenge the independence of our senses. This chapter defends their distinctness. It presents an account of the nature of the senses and of what differentiates them that accommodates richly multisensory perception and consciousness.

According to common sense, human beings and other creatures have several senses. Theorizing about perception and the mind has taken this for granted. Two approaches to understanding the senses can be discerned. Scientists focus on the machinery, investigating sensory systems, processes, and capacities. Philosophers focus on experiences.

Multisensory perception challenges the distinctness of our senses. First, sensory systems interact extensively. Their coordination enhances the reliability and extends the reach of human perceptual capacities. Multisensory mechanisms and functions suggest that the senses are not separate information-processing systems. Shimojo and Shams (2001), for instance, maintain that crossmodal interactions, integration, and plasticity show that senses are not distinct modalities.

Second, perceptual consciousness is constitutively, irreducibly multisensory. The boundaries between senses are not evident in perceptual experience. This undermines conceiving of the senses as distinct experiential modalities. Speaks (2015), for instance, argues that there are not distinct attitudes or relations of sensing corresponding to each of the senses. He rejects "the view that each sense involves its own phenomenal relation" (178). Thus, the senses are not distinct modes of consciously entertaining contents. Speaks instead admits only a single conscious way of perceiving—a single relation of *sensing*. Tye (2003) says that discernible sense-specific experiences are "figments of philosophers' and psychologists' imaginations" (28).

Moreover, we lack a good account of what individuates senses. What makes something a sense? What differentiates senses from each other?

A Multisensory Philosophy of Perception. Casey O'Callaghan, Oxford University Press (2019).
© Casey O'Callaghan. DOI: 10.1093/oso/9780198833703.001.0001

In virtue of what do experiences belong to sensory modalities? A number of candidates have been proposed. Grice's influential essay, "Some Remarks about the Senses" (1962), articulates and assesses four distinct criteria: features perceived, special introspectible character, physical stimuli, and internal mechanisms. Each faces destructive objections (Nudds 2003). No agreement since has been reached concerning how best to differentiate the senses. No criterion yet offered is satisfying. This compounds skeptical worries raised by multisensory phenomena.[1]

One response is despair. Some reject hope for an account according to which the senses are real psychological kinds, deserving a place in our best theorizing about the mind. Nudds (2003), for instance, attributes how we carve up the senses to convention. Sensory taxonomy thus answers ultimately to the practical.

Another response is pluralism. Macpherson (2011), for instance, is pluralist about the types of senses that could exist. Each criterion yields a dimension, and each of many actual and possible senses corresponds to a location in a complex multidimensional space. Fulkerson (2014) is pluralist about criteria for classifying senses. Differing explanatory purposes, such as those of neuroscientists and of philosophers, warrant differing ways of dividing sense modalities. Matthen (2015b) is pluralist about conceptions of the senses. Appealing to transducers and appealing to perceptual systems as criteria for differentiating senses rely on different sorts of concepts but generate no real disagreement about the nature of the senses.

I am optimistic about the prospects for a principled, informative account of the senses, according to which perception and perceptual consciousness are genuinely multisensory, and which appreciates insights of conventionalism and pluralism. This relies on an account of

---

[1] A number of more specific criteria have been proposed. (i) Aristotle famously distinguishes senses by proper or special sensibles—colors, sounds, tastes, smells, warmth, and pressure (Aristotle 1984, II.vi–x). (ii) Grice (1962) appeals to the full range of features revealed by each of the respective senses. (iii) Heil (1983, chapter 1) relies on kinds of physical stimulation to sensory receptors and types of energy transduced—light, sound, heat, chemical, and mechanical. (iv) Keeley (2002) invokes evolutionarily dedicated sense organs. (v) Psychologists and neuroscientists delineate senses according to functionally or physiologically distinct systems responsible for sensory processing. (vi) Representationalists appeal to differing contents associated with various senses. (vii) Clark (1993) and Rosenthal (2015) rely on quality spaces determined by patterns of discrimination distinctive to each sense. (viii) Peacocke (1983), Lopes (2000), and, ultimately, Grice (1962) himself, cite distinctive experiential character associated with each of the senses. As Nudds (2003) makes evident, each more specific criterion faces difficulties familiar from those Grice's original four criteria confront.

what differentiates senses and in virtue of what experiences belong to distinct senses.

This chapter presents an account of the nature of the senses and what differentiates them. According to the account I propose, senses are ways of perceiving. Each is a faculty that comprises a collection of perceptual capacities. What each sense shares and what differentiates one sense from another is the manner in which its capacities are exercised. Each way of perceiving involves a distinct type of information-gathering activity.

Differentiating senses and attributing experiences to sensory modalities are distinct tasks. Perceptual experiences are episodes in which perceptual capacities are exercised. Conscious perceptual episodes thus may be ascribed distinct sensory modalities, according to the manners in which perceptual capacities are deployed on an occasion. In this account, subjects may have only limited first-person knowledge of the senses they employ.

This framework illuminates psychological taxonomy for multisensory perception and consciousness. In multisensory perception, distinct sorts of information-gathering activity are engaged in a coordinated manner in order jointly to deploy perceptual capacities. Nothing in this account rules out attributing an episode to multiple senses, nor associating its features with more than one sense at a time. Furthermore, multisensory phenomena demonstrate that no exclusive, exhaustive taxonomy types experiences by sensory modality, even according to phenomenology. Belonging to one sense does not preclude belonging to another. And experiences cannot be carved without remainder into sense-specific parts.

According to this account, typical human perceivers have multiple senses. Thus, it resists skepticism about the senses. And it accommodates the richly multisensory nature and character of perception. So, it preserves the distinctness of our senses, but it scraps their independence.

6.1 Senses as Capacities

My proposal takes its lead from two insights. One is due to Matthew Nudds (2003), who says, "Senses are ways of perceiving" (47, see also 44–9). The other is due to Mohan Matthen (2015b), who says, "The senses constitute a group of information-gathering faculties" (567). Together, these insights suggest that the senses are distinct ways of gathering information.

If perception is or involves a type of psychological faculty, the senses are its modes or modalities. A faculty is a collection of capacities. Thus, senses may be understood in terms of perceptual capacities. My proposal is that senses are families of perceptual capacities. This is the core of a capacities account of the senses.

Chapter 3 explicated the notion of a capacity. Here are the highlights. A capacity is an ability or capability. Capacities are distinct from their exercises or manifestations. Capacities are standing characteristics rather than episodes or events. A capacity is a matter of potential or disposition. You have the capacity to hold your breath and to understand the last word of this chapter, even if you currently are breathing and reading this sentence, and even if you never hold your breath nor read beyond this page.

Perceptual capacities are psychological, and they belong to subjects. A perceptual capacity, in the first instance, is a capacity to perceive a thing or feature, such as a sound, a texture, a hue, or causality. Perceiving requires being differentially sensitive to a thing or feature in one's environment. Differential sensitivity to a thing or feature requires the capacity to detect it and to differentiate it from other things and features. This requires responding appropriately to it in a variety of actual and possible conditions. To be perceptual, this responsiveness also must play the right role in one's psychology, enabling other capacities, such as memory, imagination, and judgment.

Given this, we may individuate perceptual capacities in part according to their objects. Perceptual capacities differ when they target distinct objects or features. Accordingly, a difference in what subjects can detect and differentiate diagnoses a difference in their perceptual capacities.

My proposal is that each sense is a distinct collection of perceptual capacities.

6.2 Individuating Senses

Aristotle said a capacity is a principle of change that explains activities. Characterizing a capacity so that it can be used to predict and explain requires specifying what is done. What can be accomplished? What is the outcome of the capacity's successful exercise?[2] For instance, you have the capacity to understand the last word of this chapter, which involves being able to grasp its meaning. Ascribing this capacity enables me to predict how things will be if you reach that word: you will comprehend it.

That outcome, however, is not inevitable. Specifying a capacity more completely typically requires saying in what conditions it can be exercised, or in what conditions the relevant disposition is manifested. You can only grasp the meaning of this chapter's last word while awake and attending to it. Ascribing a capacity, so described, helps to make more accurate claims about future and hypothetical performance.

In characterizing a capacity, it also is valuable to specify how it works— the manner in which its bearer carries out the achievement. How are things done? Specifying the manner in which a capacity is exercised matters because it helps explain the achievement. Unless capacities are grounded in inherently powerful dispositional properties (Heil 2012), citing a capacity and its conditions adds little in accounting for an accomplishment. Specifying what is done and in what circumstances does not explain why it takes place or further illuminate the result. It would be best not to tie an account of the senses to a contentious metaphysics of properties and capacities.

Capturing the manner in which a capacity is exercised does help to explain an accomplishment. For instance, you can understand this chapter's last word by means of reading the English inscription, touching the Braille letters, seeing the ASL sign for it, reading it in translation, or listening to the sound of the spoken utterance. Describing the manner in which you exercise the capacity for understanding helps to account for why you grasp the meaning when you do. One way it can do so is by describing the subcapacities that explain your performance (Cummins 1983).

According to the capacities account, each sense is a collection of perceptual capacities exercised in a common manner.

---

[2] For generality, assume a capacity can be exercised unsuccessfully. This seems appropriate in the case of perception given the possibility of illusion and hallucination (see Schellenberg 2016, especially section 2, and 2018, chapter 2). See also Miracchi (2017); cf. O'Callaghan (2020).

6.3 Ways of Perceiving

My proposal is that each sense is a family of perceptual capacities. Each is unified and distinguished by the way or manner in which those capacities are exercised or implemented. Senses comprise perceptual capacities deployed in a common manner. This calls for an account of sensory manners.

Sensory manners must individuate senses at the right grain. It is possible to deploy the same capacity in distinct manners. For instance, one can perceive shapes by vision or by touch. And it is possible to deploy distinct capacities in the same manner. One can perceive shapes and colors in vision, and one can perceive texture and warmth in touch.

Matthen (2015b) appeals to the actions or exploratory activities involved in perceiving to individuate senses (for a related view, see O'Regan and Noë 2001). This approach appeals to activity types to differentiate the senses. Differing exploratory activities bring to light differing manners in which perceptual capacities are exercised. However, the class of information-gathering activities is vast and diverse. It lacks neat structure, and its joints are not clearly marked. Exploratory activities alone are too amorphous to deliver an account of the senses.

Perceiving is enabled by extracting information contained in a stimulus. Humans extract information from various physical sources in part by means of receptors that respond selectively to each. These tuned receptors are distributed unevenly over our bodies, collected in our sense organs. We exercise perceptual capacities by doing things that enable us to detect and differentiate objects and features through the use of our sense organs. When we exercise perceptual capacities, we do so by behaving so as to facilitate information gathering. We explore, and we glean details about our surroundings.

Exercising a perceptual capacity thus involves deploying a sense organ in order to detect and differentiate things and features in the environment by exploiting or taking advantage of its propensity to transduce and thereby to help extract information contained in a medium or stimulus. This is a kind of information-gathering activity. Call it sensory information gathering.

Perceptual capacities are exercised in the same sensory manner just in case they are deployed using the same type of sensory information-gathering activity. So, the relevant way or manner in which perceptual capacities belonging to a given sense may be exercised is a specific sort of sensory information-gathering activity. And each sense involves a distinct sort of sensory information gathering.

A number of features characterize sensory information-gathering activities. These include the sense organ deployed, the medium or form of energy mined, the information extracted, and the objects and attributes discerned. Sensory information-gathering activities thus belong to a range of distinct types corresponding to such features individually or in combination. Our question is which such types individuate senses.

Suppose we understand a sense organ as a collection of receptor types. Thus, a sense organ is a device that transduces energy of specific sorts. Unlike a biological organ, this does not require a cellular makeup or evolutionary history. This allows for prosthetic sense organs. Nevertheless, employing a common sense organ understood in this way carves actual sensory information-gathering activities at a relatively natural joint. The sense organ employed marks a type of activity in which energy of a specific kind is transduced, information of a given sort is thereby extracted, and even bodily movements of a similar form are performed.

These features do not go together accidentally. They point to a joint function. The function of the activity they characterize is to extract from a medium of transmission information of a specific sort. That is the role the activity plays. That is its purpose. We may call this its information-extraction function. My claim is that this function individuates the relevant types of sensory information-gathering activity. Thus, it individuates sensory manners.

Sensory manners thus are aspects of exercises of perceptual capacities. Each sense is a family of perceptual capacities exercised in a common sensory manner. That is, each capacity belonging to a sense can be exercised by means of the same sort of information-gathering activity. What marks the relevant sort of information-gathering activity is the variety of information it functions to extract and the medium from which it does so.

Therefore, a sense is a bundle of perceptual capacities whose exercise involves a common sort of information-gathering activity, individuated by the type of information it functions to extract from a given medium. Questions about numbers of senses turn on questions about perceptual capacities and the differing manners in which they are exercised. Specifying capacities and manners is a task for empirical and rational psychology.

This approach illuminates disputes about difficult cases, such as sensory substitution, haptic touch, and alien senses. Hard cases turn on predictable disagreements about what individuates activity types. For instance, tactile–visual substitution systems (TVSS) rely on a subject's actively using a device that transduces and thereby enables extracting information encoded in light in order to discern and distinguish three-dimensional objects, illumination, and spatial features at a distance. The information-extraction function of this activity thus corresponds to that of typical vision. But, the tactile array stimulates mechanoreceptors in the skin, which is typical of touch. To which type does this information-gathering activity belong? According to the account I have described, this activity functions to extract information about distal objects and spatial features from the light, but it relies on mechanical transduction to do so. However, it is not the type of information-gathering activity typical of touch, because it does not function to extract from the contact that takes place information about shapes, textures, temperatures, and configurations of objects in one's peripersonal space. Thus, in its skillful use, TVSS is a form of vision that implicates the organ of touch, rather than haptic touch.

One virtue of this schema is that it allows for some flexibility in individuating and counting senses. Differing explanatory projects have differing purposes. Rough-and-ready, day-to-day psychologizing relies on what is at hand. Thus, it gets by using observable sense organs and introspection to discriminate distinct sorts of information-gathering activity, yielding five familiar exteroceptive senses. Some projects benefit from differentiating sensory manners more finely. Empirical psychology, whose aim is a species of causal-functional explanation, focuses on the details of transduction, the process of information extraction, and patterns of dissociation. Each can yield a finer-grained taxonomy of activity types, with potential explanatory gains. Thus, scientists may wish to distinguish mechanical from thermal haptic touch. Rational psychology, a species of normative explanation, focuses instead on how perceivers use their senses and sense organs, their intentions and aims, and the information thereby gathered and thus made available. Such features have explanatory pull in rational psychology, which aims to make sense of subjects and what they do. Thus, we may wish to distinguish active echolocation from typical hearing. Despite their differences, each such project nonetheless includes means for targeting information-gathering activity types of the sort I have described.

This approach permits pluralism about criteria used to identify sensory information-gathering activity types. But it is a principled pluralism. It stems from general features of activity individuation. Functions, objects, intentions, means, and mechanisms are relevant criteria for identifying and differentiating distinct types of activities. And it is a constrained pluralism, since it applies to sensory information-gathering activities, individuated in the first instance by information-extraction functions. Furthermore, it is amenable to empirical and theoretical revision and refinement. The point is that there are legitimate ways to distinguish distinct senses.

In summary, a sense is a bundle of perceptual capacities. Each distinct bundle shares a common sensory manner. A sensory manner is a sort of information-gathering activity. Each such activity type is marked by its function to extract information from a medium.

6.4 The Significance of the Senses

Nudds (2003) says an account of the senses must address their significance. Why does it matter that we possess distinct senses rather than just a long list of perceptual capacities? What explanatory gain stems from distinguishing various senses?

The account I have described captures six reasons why distinct senses matter. First, there are vastly different ways to exercise the same perceptual capacity, and there are noteworthy similarities in how subjects exercise distinct capacities. Sensory manners thus capture salient features of sense perception's landscape and its grain.

Second, differing sensory manners reveal distinct collections of features that help achieve distinctive ends. Each sensory manner enables the exercise of a given collection of perceptual capacities: those targeting features about which the sense organ deployed can transduce information. Thus, each is suited to reveal a certain range of features, and those features serve differing sets of needs. For instance, deploying your eyes exploratorily enables the exercise of a set of perceptual capacities. This serves to reveal colors, shapes, and patterns by extracting information about them from the light. This enables you to distinguish material bodies from their surroundings and to identify objects. It is valuable if you want to find a ring on the carpet or to recognize a person you have met before. By contrast, attentively using your ears, taking advantage of their capacity to extract information from sound waves, is a different sort of information-gathering activity. If you want to pursue a lost bunny moving across dried leaves in the dark, or to know who is on the other end of a phone call, this sort of sensory information-gathering works better.

Third, this has epistemic import. Multiple ways of exercising perceptual capacities can improve your epistemic position. Having different sources of information gives you another angle. It can help to make you a more reliable perceiver, and it can improve on perceptual capacities you already possess. In particular, it can improve your range, acuity, accuracy, and recognitional capacities. This accrues to your epistemic standing.

Fourth, it has practical import. Redundancy improves resilience. Distinct sorts of sensory information gathering can target the same things and features. This can make a perceiver more flexible. A subject can continue to function after losing one or more ways of exercising perceptual capacities.

Fifth, differing senses provide valuable third-person information. Knowing what sort of sensory information-gathering activity someone employs reveals the way in which they exercise perceptual capacities. This enables a person to infer what sorts of things and features a subject likely perceives (Nudds 2003). Knowing that Frances saw the cardinal, beyond just knowing she perceived it, you can reasonably infer she perceived its coloration, size, and shape, rather than its song. In turn, grasping which sensory manner was involved enables you more informatively to attribute specific experiences, beliefs, and knowledge.

Sixth, it illuminates multisensory phenomena. Distinct sensory manners can be employed jointly, in contrast with independently and in parallel, to enhance and extend our perceptual capacities. Employing distinct information-gathering activities in coordination is a novel, complex form of activity. It enables the joint exercise of perceptual capacities that otherwise could be deployed only separately. For instance, it allows subjects perceptually to discern novel intermodal instances of causality. More generally, this book has argued that the coordinated use of multiple senses makes perception more reliable and coherent, reveals novel features, and grounds new forms of experience. Distinct manners of perceiving thus are a more informative guide to our surroundings jointly than independently.

6.5 Taxonomic Payoff

Understanding senses as capacities organized by manners has taxonomic payoff in characterizing multisensory perception. Start with the *senses*. In this scheme, a *sense* is a collection of perceptual capacities. A *token sense*, such as a particular human's sense of vision, is a bundle of perceptual capacities instantiated by a perceiver. A *determinate sense*, such as human vision (or human vision just like mine), is a determinate collection of perceptual capacities, which may characterize a range of perceivers. A *determinable type of sense*, such as vision (of humans or honeybees), is a range of determinate senses that involve a common type of way of perceiving.

Belonging to the same sense, token or determinate, amounts to employing a common sensory manner. For discerning various things and features, you may have distinct capacities, each of which can be exercised in the same manner. Such capacities belong to one bundle. They are exercised by means of information-gathering activities that share an information-extraction function. This function organizes senses for each class of perceivers. A perceiver's distinct senses are collections of perceptual capacities employing distinct sensory manners. You may exercise distinct capacities in differing sensory manners, in which case they belong to distinct senses. Or you may exercise a single capacity, such as the capacity to perceive a given feature, in differing sensory manners. If so, the same capacity belongs to distinct collections. Belonging to distinct collections requires that distinct information-extraction functions individuate the activities involved in its exercise on varying occasions. Determinable senses require types of ways of perceiving, since distinct species rely on differing information-gathering activities. For instance, human and honeybee vision are distinct determinate senses. Each involves a distinct sensory manner, since each extracts differing information from the light. Accordingly, their information-extraction functions differ, while each nonetheless belongs to a broader shared type. The distinct information-extraction functions that fix such types most naturally are delimited by the range of information encoded in a specific medium, to which perceivers may be differently sensitive.

Now consider *sensible features*. A *proper sensible* is a feature accessible with only one sense. It is a feature targeted by a perceptual capacity that can be deployed in only one sensory manner. For typical humans, pitch is a feature perceptible only by using the ears, exploiting their capacity to transduce and thereby to extract information about relative frequency from pressure waves by means of the cochlea. Pitch is perceptible by means of a single sensory information-gathering activity— that is, one that functions to extract information about events and features such as pitch, timbre, loudness, and location from sound waves. A *common sensible* is accessible with multiple senses. It is a feature targeted by a perceptual capacity that can be deployed in more than one sensory manner. For instance, shape, location, and motion are perceptible not only through an activity type that involves the use of the eyes but also through a type of activity that implicates the skin and mechanoreception. Each has a distinct information-gathering function. *Multiple proper sensibles* of one sense are distinct proper sensibles accessible in a common sensory manner. They are distinct features perceptible with the same sense, none of which is accessible with a distinct sense. Such features are targeted by distinct perceptual capacities exercised in the same sensory manner, each of which can be deployed in only one such manner.

Turn to *multisensory perception*. Specifying a perceptual capacity for the purposes of prediction and psychological explanation involves specifying what is accomplished, in what conditions, and in which manner. The senses are bundles of perceptual capacities individuated in terms of a common way or manner of perceiving. Making some choices in terminology, this enables us to characterize what makes a *perceptual capacity* unisensory, unimodal, or multisensory.

Say that a *unisensory*, or *sense-specific*, *perceptual capacity* is one that can be exercised in only one such manner. For instance, there is only one sensory manner each in which one can be differentially sensitive to a proper sensible, such as a color, a sound, a pitch, or saltiness. That is, the information-extraction function corresponding to each differs. Unisensory capacities need not be limited to those targeting proper sensibles. Multiple object tracking, for example, is a sense-specific capacity if it is only deployed visually. Joint attention may be another. A *unimodal capacity*, as I understand it, is one for which each exercise occurs in a single manner. Like a unisensory capacity, one such way exists per token exercise. However, in contrast with a unisensory (sense-specific) capacity, a unimodal capacity can be deployed in distinct ways. Thus, a unimodal capacity may belong to multiple senses. For example, texture perception is a candidate unimodal capacity that can be deployed separately in vision and in touch.

A *multisensory capacity*, in this choice of terminology, is one that can be deployed multisensorily, or in a way that relies on more than one sensory manner. A capacity that can be exercised unimodally nevertheless may have exercises that jointly employ more than one sensory manner. This is the case when a subject multisensorily perceives an intermodal spatial, temporal, or causal relation, as discussed in Chapter 3. You can perceive space, time, and causality with just one sense, but you also can exercise each of these capacities by jointly using several senses. However, a multisensory capacity may be a perceptual capacity that cannot be deployed originally using only one sensory manner. Flavor perception and balance are examples. Call these *novel* multisensory capacities. Each is distinctively, irreducibly multisensory.

Lastly, we may wish to characterize capacities that can be deployed perceptually, in one or more sensory manners, but that also can be deployed in ways that are not sensory or perceptual, such as in thought, judgment, or inference. For instance, if it is possible to perceive numerosity or semantic properties of spoken utterances, then this could involve capacities that could be deployed in manners that are not sensory or perceptual. If perception were to involve conceptual contents, this might implicate such perceptual capacities. We might call these *amodal* perceptual capacities. If so, being amodal in this way is not simply failing to be sense specific (unisensory) or even unimodal, since a capacity could be multisensory but not unisensory, unimodal, or amodal. Moreover, involving an amodal capacity is not a simple test for cognition in contrast with perception.

6.6 Episodes

What about experiences? If senses are bundles of perceptual capacities, perceptual capacities belong to sense modalities. Experiences, however, also are said to come in modalities. They can be visual, auditory, gustatory, olfactory, or tactual. But experiences are not capacities. In virtue of what do experiences belong to senses? Here, multisensory phenomena pose special trouble. How do we pry apart experiences constitutively involving several senses?

Experiences are conscious perceptual episodes. The first step is to specify the modality of a perceptual episode. Perceptual episodes are events or occurrences that involve the exercise of one or more perceptual capacities. Therefore, perceptual episodes belong to types corresponding to the manners in which subjects manifest perceptual capacities. For instance, an episode is auditory just in case it involves the exercise of perceptual capacities in the manner characteristic of audition—that is, by means of an information-gathering activity with the function to extract information about features such as sounds, pitch, timbre, loudness, duration, and location from pressure waves. Accordingly, one perceives auditorily, visually, tactually, olfactorily, or gustatorily. Manner, and thus modality, is an attribute or aspect of a perceptual episode.

This proposal ascribes modality to an episode. Most perceptual episodes involve the exercise of multiple perceptual capacities in several sensory manners. Therefore, each such episode must belong to several sensory modalities.

This raises two potential concerns. Someone might object that no experience can be both visual and tactual. Intuitively, being visual rules out being tactual. Furthermore, someone might think that this proposal deflates the project of differentiating senses and analyzing perception in terms of sense modalities. What good is an account that attributes most perceptual episodes to all of the senses?

These are features rather than bugs. We ought to forget about carving up perceptual episodes and analyzing them in terms of sense-specific parts. First, it is contentious whether perceptual episodes decompose into events which themselves are perceptual episodes belonging to a single modality. Second, it may be indeterminate to which sense some proper part of a perceptual episode belongs, especially in cases of multisensory perception. Third, if some perception is richly, or constitutively and irreducibly, multisensory, no such segmentation is exhaustive. My account thus abandons sensory atomism.

This classificatory scheme distinguishes distinct senses, and it sorts perceptual episodes by modality. To do so, it distinguishes the project of differentiating senses from that of ascribing modalities to perceptual episodes. Multisensory perception presents an obstacle to distinguishing sense-specific components of a complex multisensory episode. But it does not undermine the project of differentiating the senses. And it does not undermine ascribing modalities to perceptual experiences.

A multisensory episode may be ascribed various modalities because it may at once manifest perceptual capacities in several sensory manners. A single perceptual episode can involve both vision and touch. Rejecting the intuitive decomposition of perceptual episodes into sense-specific parts thus means rejecting the intuition that vision rules out touch.

This account therefore rejects exclusivity. Belonging to one sensory modality does not preclude belonging to another. Just as a capacity can belong to more than one sense, a perceptual episode can have multiple sensory modalities. Being visual does not preclude being tactual. This taxonomy yields overlapping rather than exclusive classes associated with each of the senses.

This has further taxonomic payoff in characterizing multisensory *perceptual episodes*. A *unisensory episode* involves the exercise of perceptual capacities in just one sensory manner. Touching a rough surface in darkness and silence is one example. A *multisensory episode* is one in which perceptual capacities are deployed in more than one sensory manner. A *minimally multisensory episode* is one that involves the exercise of perceptual capacities in more than one sensory manner but in which each of the capacities exercised is unimodal, relying on no more than one sensory manner. A *richly multisensory episode* involves deploying a multisensory capacity, relying for this exercise on more than one sensory manner. This book has argued that that some perceptual episodes are richly multisensory.

6.7 Experiences

The next step is to address experiences. A perceptual experience is a phenomenally conscious perceptual episode. For each such episode, there is something it is like for its subject to undergo it. Perceptual experiences thus involve phenomenal character, whose determinates are phenomenal properties.

Experiences bear a range of attributes beyond their phenomenal features. Thus, experiences belong to a variety of types. Depending on the project, we may want to focus on experiences that share objects, contents, etiology, character, or modality. For instance, we may wish to determine the impact of modality on phenomenal character when controlling for content. This project requires attributing experiences to sense modalities. Since experiences are conscious perceptual episodes, we can classify them according to the sensory manners in which perceptual capacities are exercised, as in the previous section.

Some philosophers, however, maintain that phenomenology suffices to determine the modality of an experience. For instance, Grice (1962) holds that experiences of each sense possess a distinctive and recognizable phenomenal character that distinguishes perceiving with that sense from perceiving with each other sense (see also Peacocke 1983; Lopes 2000). According to such a view, to each sense corresponds an identifiable phenomenal type. The senses thus are experiential modalities. If so, then sensory manners are dispensable, or even undermined, in attributing experiences to sense modalities.

In replying, two distinct claims ought to be distinguished. The weaker claim is that phenomenal features suffice to fix the modality of an experience. The stronger claim is that each experience belonging to a given sense shares a distinctive, sense-specific phenomenal character that, in principle, can be discerned and recognized by its subject. We should reject the stronger claim, even if the weaker claim stands. However, the weaker claim does not undermine using sensory manners to ascribe modalities to experiences. I'll argue that sensory manners maintain an explanatory advantage when compared with an adequate phenomenological criterion.

Start with the weaker claim. Just in virtue of their phenomenology, do experiences belong to types that correspond to sensory modalities? The argument from intermodal identity and binding demonstrates that not every phenomenal feature is distinctive to some sense modality (Chapter 5; see also O'Callaghan 2015). Thus, not every experience is exhausted by features distinctive to one sense or another. Common sensibles present a similar but less acute challenge.

Thus, to type experiences by modality according to their phenomenal character, it is natural to invoke the proper sensibles. If an episode involves consciously perceiving a proper sensible, then it has some phenomenal feature that is unique to one sense. If you consciously perceive an olfactory proper sensible, such as a scent, that experience has a distinctive, olfaction-specific character. It is phenomenally olfactory. If you consciously perceive pitch, that episode is phenomenally auditory. And so on for each proper sensible. Since we already have characterized proper sensibles in other terms, phenomenal features provide a way to type experiences by modality that is not viciously circular. If each conscious episode of a given sense involves experiencing one of its proper sensibles, this maps experiences to sensory modalities.[3]

Multiple proper sensibles of one sense still present a problem. Pitch, timbre, and loudness are proper sensibles of hearing; temperature, hardness, and pressure are proper sensibles of touch; hue, brightness, and saturation are proper sensibles of vision. If our typing scheme hews to distinctive phenomenal features, then a distinct experiential modality ought to correspond to each proper sensible. Otherwise, something further must account for distinct proper sensibles' belonging to one experiential modality. Call this *the problem of multiple proper sensibles*.

The best hope for a reply is to appeal to dependent awareness. For typical humans, it is always possible to experience a proper sensible of one sense without experiencing any proper sensible of another sense. If you do not have synesthesia, you can see colors without hearing sounds

---

[3] However, it imperfectly maps experiences to sensory manners. The two criteria need not completely agree. A synesthetic color experience may be phenomenally visual even though it does not involve exercising the capacity to perceive color by deploying the eyes to discern features of the environment. Thus, the extensions of typing schemes may not perfectly match.

and feel temperature without smelling odor. However, in typical conditions, it is not always possible consciously to perceive a proper sensible of one sense without consciously perceiving any other proper sensible of the same sense. For instance, experiencing pitch and experiencing timbre each depend on experiencing loudness. Experiencing hue depends on experiencing lightness and saturation but not pitch. Experiencing hardness may depend on experiencing temperature but not color.

Nevertheless, this relation of dependence need not be symmetric or transitive. For instance, some sounds lack pitch, so experiencing loudness does not depend on experiencing pitch. The claim is only that if a sense has multiple proper sensibles, experiencing each of its proper sensibles requires experiencing some other proper sensible of that same modality but does not require experiencing proper sensibles of any other modality.

This is similar to what Grice describes as "detection-links" among features perceptible with a given sense (139). So, say that experiences of distinct proper sensibles are *dependence linked* just in case a dependence relation holds between them or if there is a further proper sensible experience to which each is dependence linked. This handles symmetry and transitivity. It yields equivalence classes, such that experiences of distinct proper sensibles are dependence linked to all and only experiences of other proper sensibles of the same sense. Proper sensibles of distinct senses are not dependence linked. Therefore, an experience belongs to a given sense just in case it belongs to such an equivalence class. Such equivalence classes correspond to experiential modalities.

This proposal requires that dependence links corresponding to sense modalities obtain. Assume for the argument that they do. Nonetheless, what depends on what need not be evident at a moment. For instance, it is not obvious from listening to a tone at a time that loudness could be heard without pitch. Nor must it just be evident to a naïve subject of multisensory experience that perceiving sound does not rely on perceiving color. Thus, the proposal being considered also requires that such dependence relations are fixed by the phenomenal character of conscious perceptual episodes over time. If so, then it is possible to type perceptual experiences by modality according to momentary phenomenal features plus facts about diachronic phenomenology. Otherwise, the criterion relies on more than phenomenology.

In my view, this is the most promising way to sort experiences by modality according to phenomenology. Nevertheless, even if it succeeds, it does not subvert using sensory manners to attribute experiences to sense modalities.

First, the phenomenological approach does not block using sensory manners to ascribe experiences sense modalities. In an ecumenical approach, the two can coexist. On one hand, phenomenology and sensory manners need not disagree. If they agree, we can ask what are the further benefits of one or the other. Explanatory purposes and overall theoretical success can inform this assessment. On the other hand, if they conflict, we may wish to adjudicate.

My position is that shared ways of exercising perceptual capacities have an explanatory advantage. They can account for dependence relations that hold among experiences of distinct proper sensibles of one sense. Dependence links correspond to perceptual capacities from a bundle exercised in a given manner. Thus, they involve a common type of information-gathering activity, individuated by its information-extraction function. So, each relies on extracting information about a shared range of features that is encoded in a medium. Experiential dependence relations obtain because information about one feature is encoded or extracted in a way that depends on encoding or extracting information about another feature. Sensory manners thus illuminate why experiences with one character seem to depend on those with another character. There is a common factor that accounts for their being experienced together, rather than a direct, brute, or phenomenological dependence relation between them. Sensory manners thus are more fundamental than the phenomenological criterion.

According to this proposal, the modality of an experience may not be evident synchronically to its subject. A naïve subject may be unable to recognize on phenomenological grounds alone that distinct phenomenal features are distinctive to a single sense rather than distinct senses. It may take time and experience to learn the proper sensibles and their sense-specific dependencies.

Thus, the stronger claim fails. Experiences of a given sense need not share distinctive phenomenal character in virtue of which they belong to a single sense and that distinguishes them from experiences of each other sense. Dependence relations also play a role.

Given this, it also follows that, controlling for other features, such as which objects and properties consciously are perceived, a difference in modality alone need not suffice for a phenomenal difference. If so, modality as such is not among the fundamental determinants of phenomenal character. Modality is not fundamental, phenomenologically.

Finally, I have maintained that perceptual episodes belong to multiple senses. Typing experiences by phenomenology does not preclude ascribing a single conscious episode more than one sense. In virtue of its phenomenal character, an experience of a given sense also can belong to another sense. An episode that is phenomenally visual also can be phenomenally auditory. Phenomenology in this respect is not exclusive.

6.8 Features

What about parts of experiences? It is common to assume that perceptual experiences comprise component experiences of the various sensory modalities (for instance, Siegel 2010, 20–1). From this perspective, your current perceptual consciousness includes as proper parts distinct visual, auditory, tactual, olfactory, and gustatory experiences. When you see a red cube while hearing a high-pitched sound, this includes distinct but co-conscious visual and auditory experiences.

I have maintained that experiences are conscious perceptual episodes. Thus, I resist the claim that they apportion into component experiences of specific sense modalities (see also Tye 2003; Bayne 2009). Someone nevertheless might maintain that phenomenology supports the claim that experiences include modality-specific components. After all, consciously seeing a cardinal does seem like one part of my current conscious life. Thus, it might be thought to count against my proposal that it does not associate parts of perceptual experiences with specific sense modalities.

Appealing to phenomenology to associate components of experiences with sense modalities faces difficulties as long as it treats a visual experience as a conscious episode that is an individual proper part of one's overall perceptual consciousness. So, I avoid that approach. Nonetheless, some aspects of my current experience are visual, some are auditory, and some are tactual. Aspects of perceptual episodes may be associated—in some cases, exclusively—with specific senses. In particular, features of perceptual episodes, including their phenomenal properties, can be associated with one sense or another.

Here is how phenomenal features may be associated with specific senses. Chapter 5 proposed that a unisensory visual episode is one that is visual but not auditory, tactual, gustatory, or olfactory. It involves the exercise of perceptual capacities only in the visual sensory manner. For a given multisensory episode, the features that are associated with vision on that occasion include just those that a corresponding uni-sensory visual episode could have under equivalent stimulation. Thus, the phenomenal character associated with vision on an occasion includes just those phenomenal features that a corresponding unisensory visual experience could have under equivalent stimulation. In this account, some features of a perceptual episode, including some of its phenomenal features, may be associated with one sense or another on an occasion. This captures the obvious fact that some phenomenal aspects of particular perceptual experiences may be visual, auditory, tactual, gustatory, or olfactory.

This, too, has a taxonomic payoff. An innocuous, *minimally multi-sensory experience* is one whose phenomenal features are exhausted by those associated on an occasion with each of the respective sense modalities, along with whatever accrues thanks to simple co-consciousness. On the other hand, a *richly multisensory experience* is one whose phenomenal features are not exhausted by those associated with each of the respective senses. The former, but not the latter, entails having only phenomenal features that are compatible (given actual psychophysics) with the exercise of perceptual capacities in at most one sensory manner or that accrue thanks to their independent exercise in distinct sensory manners.

I have argued that not every phenomenal feature of a conscious perceptual episode is associated with one sense or another or else accrues thanks to mere co-consciousness (Chapter 5). Examples include con-sciously perceiving intermodal binding, causality, rhythm, and flavor. Thus, I have rejected exhaustiveness as a claim about the phenomenal features of conscious perceptual episodes. That is, even if every conscious perceptual episode belongs to at least one sense, not every aspect of each perceptual episode is associated with some specific sense or another. Perceptual experience therefore is richly multisensory.

6.9 Knowledge of Modality

How do we know the modality of a perceptual episode? The manner of perceiving—the way in which a subject exercises perceptual capacities—needs to be determined. That is the route to knowing which bundles are in play and which senses are used.

According to the account I have described, third-person knowledge of modality is not a problem, in principle. Empirical observation, casual or experimental, can support such claims. Behavioral evidence from action patterns and reports may reveal the capacities exercised and the manner in which a subject perceives. For instance, it may be observed that specific things and features in the surroundings are detected and differentiated by means of using a particular sense organ, thereby exploiting that organ's capacity to transduce and thus to enable extraction of information from its stimulating medium.

Since, in this account, phenomenology is not essential in determining the modality of a perceptual episode, observers may meet even a very high threshold for justification. Nonetheless, familiar barriers to knowing others' activities and intentions remain in place.

In the first-person case, similarly, you can know the modality of a perceptual episode by discerning which features you perceive and the manners in which you perceive them (cf. Byrne 2012). In some situations, knowing the perceptual capacity you deploy suffices to know the modality. If an object or a feature is perceptible only by means of a given sense, then its perception involves a unisensory capacity. If so, then knowing that fact and knowing which object or feature you perceive suffices to know which sense you have used.

However, not every perceptible feature is a proper sensible. Beyond that, the specific perceptual capacities you exercise and the sensory manners in which you deploy them need not be obvious to you. But, the manner in which you exercise a perceptual capacity is a kind of activity. Frequently, it is subject to your intentional control. You can scan a scene for the maroon binding of a favorite book, angle your head to focus your listening on the upright bass from stage left during a performance, sniff out the rosemary in a fragrant kitchen, or sweep your hands across grass to find a tennis ball while blindfolded. In such cases, you are in a position to know which sense you are using because you can know what you are doing. You knowably direct your eyes around the scene, get your ears in a position to spatialize the sound, move your nose and sniff around the kitchen, or promote contact with an obstacle by skimming the grass with your hands (cf. Matthen 2015b).

Asking about the conditions in which you can know the manner in which you perceive raises delicate questions about the conditions for knowledge of intentional action (Anscombe 1957). But, I am only trying to establish that sometimes you are in a position to know the manner in which you perceive because you know what you are doing. Thus, you can know a perceptual episode's modality.

Nevertheless, simply by introspecting the character of a perceptual episode, you may not be in a position to know the modality by which you perceive some particular object or feature. Moreover, you may not be in a position to know on an occasion the sense with which a given feature of your experience is associated. For instance, in cases of inter-modal binding awareness, consciously perceiving intermodal causality, or perceiving complex flavors, it is difficult to discern through intro-spection which phenomenal features are associated with which sense modalities. Is the vanilla flavor attributed to ice cream in your mouth just obviously associated with olfaction, with taste, or with neither? Is the causal impression when perceiving a talking face an aspect of your visual experience, your auditory experience, or neither? The answers are not clear based on unsupplemented, synchronic perceptual phenomenology.

In particular, the boundaries between the senses need not be intro-spectible. In having a multisensory experience, it is not clear where one sense ends and another begins. To resolve these questions requires evidence about perceptual capacities and the manners in which they are exercised. My account therefore rejects that the sense modality by which you consciously perceive some object or feature is self-evident.

I do endorse a more limited claim about first-person knowledge of modality. Typically, if you undergo a conscious episode of a given sense, you can know that you have an experience of that sense, even on the basis of its synchronic phenomenal character. Thus, if you undergo a phe-nomenally conscious visual episode, typically you will be in a position to know that you have a visual experience. This need not be just because you introspect the manner in which you exercise perceptual capacities. Instead, conscious episodes involving a given sense generally involve consciousness of its proper sensibles. Thus, they involve phenomenal character distinctive to that sensory modality. So, once you know the assignment of proper sensibles to modalities, discerning a visual proper sensible, such as color, suffices to know your experience has phenomenal features associated with vision and, so, is visual. However, it should by now be clear that this does not rule out that the experience also involves another sense. Being visual does not rule out being tactual.

6.10 Synopsis

According to the account this chapter describes, a sense is a collection of perceptual capacities exercised by means of an information-gathering activity whose function is to extract information of a specific type from a medium of transmission.

Senses are bundles of perceptual capacities. These include the capacity to detect and differentiate a thing or feature in one's environment in a way that enables recognition, thought, and action. Senses are unified and differentiated by distinctive ways of exercising perceptual capacities. A perceptual capacity can be exercised in differing manners, and differing capacities can be exercised in the same manner.

To exercise a perceptual capacity is to engage in a kind of information gathering. Sensory information gathering involves deploying a sense organ exploratorily in order to detect and differentiate things and features, thereby exploiting that organ's capacity to transduce and thus enable extracting information about the environment from a stimulus.

A way or manner of exercising perceptual capacities is a type of sensory information gathering. The relevant sort of way—a sensory manner—is a kind of activity. In particular, it is a kind of activity individuated by the information it functions to extract and the medium from which it does so. Differing explanatory purposes can shape how we identify and differentiate more specific sensory manners. This is a principled pluralism of activity types.

In this scheme, determinable senses, such as vision, share a common type of sensory manner. Their determinates, such as human vision, may collect differing capacities. Token senses, such as an individual perceiver's sense of vision, are instantiated collections of such capacities.

Multisensory phenomena stem from the coordinated use of multiple senses. This amounts to coordination among distinct ways of gathering information. Interactions among senses, such as those described in Chapter 2, are a kind of information sharing.

Multisensory capacities are those whose exercise sometimes relies on the joint use of multiple senses. Accordingly, a multisensory perceptual capacity is one whose deployment can jointly involve more than one sensory manner. For instance, typical humans can perceive an intermodal rhythm by jointly using hearing and touch. Some perceptual capacities, including some that target flavor, cannot be deployed unimodally. These are novel, distinctively multisensory capacities.

A perceptual episode is an event or occasion in which perceptual capacities are exercised. Sensorily perceiving is exercising perceptual capacities in some such manner. Perceptual episodes may be typed by modality according to the manners in which they manifest perceptual capacities. A perceptual episode belongs to a given sense if it involves exercising a perceptual capacity in its distinctive sensory manner. Multisensory episodes are occurrences implicating more than one such way of perceiving.

A perceptual experience is a phenomenally conscious perceptual episode. Experiences, too, belong to types that correspond to the manners in which perceptual capacities are exercised. If we wish to classify perceptual experiences by modality according to their phenomenal character, the best approach is to appeal to awareness of proper sensibles and to dependence links in experiencing distinct proper sensibles of one modality.

Features of perceptual episodes, including phenomenal character, also may be associated with specific senses on an occasion. This requires considering the features of corresponding unisensory episodes.

Multisensory consciousness requires a conscious perceptual episode whose features are associated with more than one sense. A richly multisensory episode is one whose features are not exhausted by those associated with each of the respective senses.

This account of the senses has three important features. First, the senses are not exclusive. A perceptual capacity can belong to more than one sense if it can be deployed in differing sensory manners. Moreover, a perceptual episode may be attributed to each of several senses. Being ascribed one sense does not preclude being ascribed another.

Second, individual senses are not exhaustive. Some perceptual capacities cannot be exercised in just one sensory manner at a time. Thus, unimodal capacities do not exhaust human perceptual capacities. In addition, sense-specific attributes do not exhaust the features of each perceptual episode. Not every feature of a perceptual episode, including its phenomenal features, must be associated with some sense or another.

Third, sensory modalities need not be evident. Both the capacities that comprise a given sense and the details concerning sensory manners are open to empirical investigation and theoretical refinement. Accordingly, which sense is deployed on an occasion need not be evident to a perceiving subject. In particular, the sense with which a feature is associated need not be obvious from the first-person perspective based solely on synchronic phenomenology. A corollary is that modality is not a fundamental determinant of phenomenal character. Modality is not an experientially basic category. Nonetheless, sensory manners are activities in which a subject can knowably engage.

6.11 Conclusion

Let me return to the challenge posed at the start. Multisensory perception undermines the independence of our senses. However, it does not threaten their distinctness. According to the account of the senses and of perceptual episodes that I have described, accommodating richly multisensory perception and consciousness requires abandoning neither the idea that we possess distinct senses nor the idea that experiences belong to various sensory modalities. However, we should give up the idealization according to which we can carve up perceptual consciousness into its sense-specific components and theorize one sense at a time. The key to this approach is distinguishing the project of individuating senses from that of ascribing modalities to perceptual episodes.

7

Conclusion

Unisensory approaches until recently have dominated the science and the philosophy of perception. Such an approach investigates perception one sense at a time. This isolates each sense in a unisensory context, or it abstracts from perception in a multisensory context. Unisensory approaches have presumed that each sense is explanatorily independent from the others and that assembling accounts of each individual sense yields a complete understanding of perception and perceptual consciousness.

This book argues that the sense-by-sense approach is incomplete and that it distorts our understanding of perception. This applies even when considering perception in a specific sense modality, such as vision or audition, and even in a unisensory context. A unisensory approach fails to consider the ways in which features associated with a given sense modality may depend on another sense, at a time and over time, as a result of their joint use. And it is not able to capture forms of perception that would not be possible using distinct senses working wholly independently from each other.

The preceding chapters argue for the thesis that the coordinated use of multiple senses enhances perception. In particular, the joint use of our senses makes perception more coherent and reliable, it extends perceptual capacities, and it makes possible novel forms of perceptual consciousness. Given how perceptual processes, capacities, awareness, and consciousness impact debates that turn on how we understand perception's structure and role, this makes the case for a multisensory approach to perception and perceptual consciousness.

This chapter recounts the arguments and the conclusions reached so far. And it describes the consequences, negative and positive. It concludes with implications and future directions for a multisensory philosophy of perception.

A Multisensory Philosophy of Perception. Casey O'Callaghan, Oxford University Press (2019).
© Casey O'Callaghan. DOI: 10.1093/oso/9780198833703.001.0001

7.1 Processes

The thesis that coordination among senses enhances and extends human sense perception in the first instance relies on claims about perceptual functions and capacities.

7.1.1 Function

The first claim is that some perceptual processes are multisensory. Establishing this is the aim of Chapter 2. Crossmodal illusions and related effects provide behavioral, neural, and introspective evidence that causal interactions take place between processes associated with distinct senses. This impacts resulting experiences. However, mere causal interactions hold little interest in psychological explanation. A causal interaction might be an accident of implementation, rather than an aspect of perceptual functioning. Or it could just be noise. Mere accidents or implementation details matter in perceptual psychology only insofar as they illuminate the functions a system realizes.

Chapter 2 argued that crossmodal interactions are not accidents or mere causes. They stem from processes of a sort that in most typical conditions do not cause illusions. Such processes generally compensate for imprecision, ambiguity, and mismatched timing in differing modes of sensory responsiveness. They help deal with noisy, fallible stimulation stemming from multiple sensory sources.

Crossmodal interactions satisfy a variety of criteria that have been proposed for differentiating functions from accidents and mere causes. They are principled. In particular, in resolving conflicts between senses, they conform to the principle of deferring to the more reliable modality. Such interactions also play a role in accounting for other perceptual capacities, such as capacities to perceive space, time, and number. Moreover, they have a believable purpose. Eliminating conflicts and weighting in deference to the modality that is more reliable with respect to a given feature improves coherence and increases the overall reliability of perception, even if it sometimes results in illusion. And it is plausible that such effects occur because they serve that purpose. Indeed, they are intelligible as adaptive.

Sensory interactions therefore bear the marks of functions. In particular, they are processes that serve to coordinate and to enhance responses across senses. They improve the coherence and reliability of human sense perception. Moreover, I argue, sensory interactions implement processes that count as perceptual according to criteria employed in empirical explanation. Therefore, there are multisensory perceptual processes of the sort that is relevant in empirical psychological explanation.

This conclusion has an important limitation. It does not follow from the claim that perceptual systems implement multisensory functions that subjects possess novel multisensory perceptual capacities. First, multisensory functioning is compatible with the claim that none of the perceptual capacities involved is distinctively multisensory. For instance, it could be that multisensory functioning simply improves or alters capacities already in place, such as the capacity to perceive space by means of vision or touch, or the capacity to perceive spoken language by hearing or by sight. Sensory interactions thus might tweak existing parallel unisensory capacities without conferring any novel capacity to perceive multisensorily.

Second, sensory interactions typically go undetected by subjects. They are subpersonal. Establishing that a subject's perceptual systems operate in accordance with intermodal organizing principles or implement multisensory functions does not establish that an individual subject possesses multisensory perceptual capacities. For instance, this conclusion is compatible with the claim that what is available centrally for the direction of action, or that what is manifest in awareness, remains wholly sense specific. If so, multisensory capacities need not be attributed to the subject.

7.1.2 Capacities

The second claim is that some perceptual capacities are multisensory. In particular, multisensory perceptual processes contribute to implementing perceptual capacities that can be deployed in ways that rely on the joint use of multiple senses.

Perceptual capacities of subjects matter in psychology and in philosophy. If multisensory effects occurred only among subpersonal perceptual processes, their interest for questions concerning the nature of perception and its theoretical role would be severely limited. For instance, they would have little bearing on questions concerning justification, responsibility, and consciousness.

Chapter 3 argued, first, that empirical evidence supports the claim that perceptual systems are differentially sensitive to the presence of things and features that could not be discerned using any single sense nor through several senses working merely in parallel. The evidence comes from cases in which subjects detect and differentiate novel intermodal feature instances, such as identity, motion, rhythm, or causality between items that are perceptible using distinct senses. For example, subjects can detect a novel intermodal rhythm comprising sounds and touches and differentiate it from distinct audible and tactual rhythms. Due to the coordinated use of multiple senses, we are sensitive to more of the world than otherwise would be possible.

Furthermore, the capacity to detect and differentiate a novel inter-modal feature instance sometimes plays the right role in a subject's psychology to count as a perceptual capacity rather than as a matter of extraperceptual cognition. For instance, it supports beliefs, anchors demonstrative thoughts, and guides action in the manner typical of perception. This holds when considering perception's role for the purposes of empirical psychology or for the purposes of rational psychology. Therefore, Chapter 3 argues, the capacity to detect and differentiate such a novel intermodal feature is a perceptual capacity.

Moreover, because it plays this role, the capacity to detect and differentiate intermodal features satisfies criteria for belonging to the individual rather than just to the individual's subpersonal perceptual systems. For instance, information about such features impacts an individual's capacity to form beliefs about them and to act on their presence in accordance with the goals of a task. Therefore, the relevant capacity is one that some subjects possess.

Perceiving a novel intermodal feature relies on the joint use of multiple senses. For instance, perceiving a collision's making a sound means perceiving causality by means that require both vision and audition. This is not just putting unisensory perceptual capacities to use in parallel. Instead, the capacity to perceive such a feature is exercised in a way that relies on the joint use of multiple senses. It is deployed multisensorily.

In the taxonomy I propose, if a perceptual capacity can be deployed multisensorily, then it is a multisensory perceptual capacity. Therefore, typical human perceivers possess multisensory perceptual capacities.

Unlike spatial, temporal, and causal features, which can be perceived using one sense at a time, some features are perceptible only through the coordinated use of multiple senses. Flavors, for instance, are complex qualitative properties with gustatory, olfactory, and tactual constituents. To fully perceive flavor requires taste, smell, and somatosensation working in concert. Flavor perception thus implicates perceptual capacities that could only be deployed multisensorily. Such a capacity could not be exercised using just one sense. Thus, some perceptual capacities are originally and invariably multisensory.

It follows that the coordinated use of multiple senses can extend the perceptual capacities of a human subject, when compared with a subject who possesses only parallel unisensory capacities. In particular, it enables the perception of otherwise imperceptible feature instances and features types. It reveals more of the world.

This argument has an important limitation. Claims about perceptual processes and capacities do not suffice to establish claims about perceptual consciousness. In particular, showing that a subject is differentially sensitive to the presence of a feature that impacts thoughts and actions does not by itself demonstrate awareness of that feature's presence. And it does not demonstrate that such sensitivity impacts perceptual phenomenal character. Thus, multisensory perceptual capacities need not be reflected as such in perceptual consciousness.

This has two consequences. First, perceptual awareness might remain wholly sense specific, even in the face of multisensory perceptual capacities. Given how awareness affects evidence, warrant, and rationality, this limits the impact of the claim that multisensory capacities enhance and extend human sense perception. It also threatens to undermine the claim that such capacities belong to individual subjects, if belonging to a subject requires consciousness (Phillips 2018).

Second, perceptual experience might remain modality specific. In particular, the phenomenal character of each conscious perceptual episode might be exhausted by that which is associated with each of the respective senses, along with whatever stems from simple co-consciousness. If so, there is an important respect in which all perception is sense specific.

In that case, multisensory perception has little impact on philosophical questions about experience, phenomenal consciousness, and what it is like. Its relevance to the philosophy of mind and perception thus is severely restricted.

7.2 Consciousness

The thesis that coordination among senses enhances and extends human sense perception also applies to perceptual consciousness. Chapters 4 and 5 address ways in which sensory interactions are reflected in the conscious lives of perceiving subjects. One facet of consciousness is awareness, and another is experience.

7.2.1 Awareness

Awareness is a variety of consciousness. It is a condition in which a subject or a person consciously has access to an object or feature. For instance, it enables a subject to make use of an object or feature in thinking, reasoning, and acting rationally. Perceptual capacities, even those that impact belief and action, need not guarantee corresponding perceptual awareness. Awareness has a distinctive rational and epistemic role.

Chapter 4 argued that the joint use of several senses makes possible novel forms of multisensory perceptual awareness. In particular, some perceptual awareness is constitutively and irreducibly multisensory. That is, multisensory perceptual awareness implicates several senses, but it is not always just a coordinated collection or simple fusion of what could occur using individual senses on their own. This meets the bar for ascribing to subjects richly multisensory awareness.

In order to bracket whether or not awareness requires phenomenal consciousness, it is useful to focus on what Block (1995) dubs access consciousness. Access consciousness encompasses what is occurrently available for use in reasoning and directly controlling speech and rational action. Since the role of awareness includes making things and features available for use in thinking, reasoning, and acting rationally, it satisfies criteria for access consciousness. Putting aside any role for phenomenality, Chapter 4 treats occurrent availability as sufficient for awareness. Alternatively, it relies on the more conservative claim that availability is evidence for awareness. In a slogan, awareness minus phenomenality is availability.

It is not enough to show that some awareness is multisensory. That is because awareness may occur in thought, emotion, or action. Thus, the relevant awareness could stem from extraperceptual cognition rather than perception itself.

Perceptual awareness occurs thanks to or in virtue of sense perception. It is a condition of awareness that is constituted or causally sustained by perceiving. While it requires perception, it need not belong wholly or fully to sense perception. According to this understanding, perceptual awareness admits hybrids. A condition of perceptual awareness may involve attention, demonstration, recognition, or even snap judgment.

Therefore, it is important to focus on perception's contribution to a condition of multisensory awareness. The question is not just whether awareness implicates perception or cognition. Instead, the critical question is whether or not perception fixes the object or feature that becomes available to a subject for use in thought, reasoning, and rational action. In particular, does perception itself settle that a novel intermodal feature is available to a subject, rather than just sense-specific features, or does that fact always rely on further contributions from extraperceptual cognition? So, the relevant issue is not whether awareness requires extraperceptual contributions; it is whether whether perception determines the object of multisensory awareness.

Perceptual beliefs, perception-guided actions, appearances, illusions, and dissociations converge to support the claim that perceiving subjects sometimes are aware of things and features that could not be perceived through individual senses nor through several senses working independently in parallel. In particular, the best explanation for the evidence is that the exercise of multisensory perceptual capacities can make such novel intermodal features available for use in thinking, reasoning, and guiding speech and rational action. Because sense perception is what makes these features so available, Chapter 4 concludes that some perceptual awareness is constitutively and irreducibly multisensory.

Multisensory perception therefore is not limited to subpersonal perceptual processes or to perceptual capacities that are not manifested in awareness. Thus, multisensory phenomena are poised to impact debates in which awareness matters. For instance, in the epistemology of perception, perceptual justification and perception's role in rationally supporting beliefs each may turn on multisensory awareness.

However, this conclusion, too, has an important limitation. It does not guarantee that phenomenal consciousness is multisensory. All phenomenal character might remain sense specific. In the first place, claims about awareness and access consciousness do not by themselves establish claims about experience and phenomenal consciousness. Multisensory perception provides an instance of the dreaded explanatory gap. So, multisensory perceptual awareness as I have characterized it does not guarantee multisensory perceptual experience. Even if awareness did secure phenomenality, perceptual awareness of an intermodal feature does not guarantee corresponding ineliminably multisensory phenomenal features. Therefore, each conscious perceptual episode that is implicated in multisensory awareness itself might have only sense-specific phenomenal features belonging to perception. If so, that is a respect in which all perceptual experience is modality specific.

If the phenomenology of perceptual consciousness is wholly sense specific, then multisensory phenomena do not touch the core of the metaphysics of mind and perception. For instance, in that case, multisensory perception is irrelevant to cracking the mind–body problem.

7.2.2 Experience

An experience is a phenomenally conscious episode. Phenomenality is a facet or a variety of consciousness. The phenomenal character of an episode determines what it is like from the first-person perspective for a conscious subject to undergo it. It is typical to point to examples. There is something distinctive it is like consciously to see crimson in good light, to hear an oboe play B-flat, or to feel the searing pressure of an advanced toothache. Each involves the instantiation of phenomenal character, whose determinates are phenomenal properties. Phenomenal features are aspects of what it is like.

Phenomenal consciousness matters. Beyond its role in constituting the mental life of a subject, phenomenality presents the most difficult instance of the mind–body problem. Chalmers (1996) calls it *the hard problem*. Phenomenal properties perennially resist attempts to be reduced, identified, or understood in terms of the kinds of properties that figure in the simplest complete inventories of reality described by theories in the physical and biological sciences.

Phenomenality is not easy to dismiss. It is not plausible to deny that typical human subjects are phenomenally conscious. For most human subjects, experience inevitably accompanies waking life. Some philosophers maintain that it provides a distinctive form of epistemic warrant. Certainly it matters a great deal in aesthetics and in appreciating our encounters with art. How it feels is a key part of what makes pain bad and pleasure good. Whole realms of value depend on the character of consciousness.

Awareness, as I have characterized it, relies on availability to a subject for use in thinking, reasoning, speaking, and acting rationally. Playing this role in a subject's psychology need not require corresponding phenomenal consciousness, even if phenomenality typically accompanies awareness (Block 1995). Thus, claims about awareness do not readily secure claims about phenomenality. This is especially acute when considering phenomenal features that belong specifically to perceptual consciousness rather than to cognition.

Chapter 5 argued that perceptual experience is constitutively and ineliminably multisensory. In particular, it argued not all perceptual experience is modality specific. By this, I mean that it is not the case that the phenomenal character of each multisensory perceptual episode is exhausted by that which is associated with each of the respective modalities, along with whatever accrues thanks to the simple unity of consciousness.

This argument relies on a conception of what it is for phenomenal features to be associated with a given sensory modality. If every phenomenal feature were distinctive to just one sense, this would be straightforward. However, that claim faces compelling challenges. Instead, what is needed is an account of what it is to be associated with a given sense modality on a particular occasion. Chapter 5 develops an account that relies on the features of a corresponding unisensory experience.

Not just any unisensory experience will do. Even holding fixed sensory stimulation, this leaves too much variety. Ample evidence shows that the character of experience belonging to one sense can change over time thanks to other senses. For instance, as I argue, a history of sight can affect auditory spatial experience. So, in a specific unisensory context, the experience of a congenitally blind person can differ from that of a sighted person.

The relevant comparison therefore is not an historically and presently purely unisensory experience (Strawson 1959). Instead, it is an experience that belongs wholly or fully to one sense and not to any other, but in a subject with a history of perceiving using other senses. The features of a multisensory episode that are associated with a given sense modality on an occasion include just those of such a corresponding unisensory experience of that modality under equivalent stimulation.

Chapter 5 argued that when a subject multisensorily perceives an intermodal feature, perceptual consciousness can be sensitive to the presence of a feature that could not be discerned using individual senses working independently. This is reflected in the phenomenal character of a multisensory perceptual episode. In particular, its phenomenal features are not exhausted by those associated with each of the respective sense modalities along with those that stem from mere co-consciousness. Thus, not all perceptual phenomenal character on each occasion is sense specific.

This argument relies on a contrast. A conscious multisensory episode may differ phenomenally from a co-conscious collection or mere fusion of unisensory experiences. And this claim requires a defense. According to some accounts, a phenomenal difference must, in principle, be noticeable by a subject from the first-person perspective. I argue that, if comparable differences are noticeable within a sense, as moderately liberal accounts of conscious perception contend, intermodal cases present no special difficulty.

In response to skepticism about this claim, I concede that it cannot be established beyond the possibility of doubt. However, we ought to abandon the skeptical standard for phenomenology. Phenomenological claims are fallible, theoretical claims that must answer to a range of evidence. Phenomenology is not a wholly distinctive explanatory project that stands apart from empirical and rational psychology.

A distinct form of skepticism holds that no difference of the sort I describe is noticeable to a subject from the first-person perspective. Consider an example. Just by consciously perceiving them, a subject may be unable to differentiate a sound that follows a flash from a flash that causes a sound. The two perceptual episodes may be indiscriminable for that subject. If so, no noticeable difference of the sort that suffices for a perceptual phenomenal difference obtains.

In my view, we ought to reject that this type of discriminability is necessary for a phenomenal difference. Phenomenal sorites arguments, for example, show that some phenomenal differences need not be discriminable. Accordingly, there are good reasons to maintain that being sensitive to an intermodal feature can differ in respect of what it is like for a subject from being sensitive only to sense-specific features, even if a subject cannot discriminate two such episodes just by relying on perceptual appearances and the first-person perspective.

A final form of skepticism stems from a very sparse view of perceptual phenomenality. An account may require discriminability and admit only a small collection of features. According to some accounts, for example, sensitivity to simple qualities and their arrangement exhausts phenomenal character. In others, phenomenality ends with qualia. For all I have said, experience might in the following respect be sense specific: each qualitative characteristic evident in perceptual consciousness might belong to exactly one sense.

Chapter 5 argued that some novel qualitative components of perceptible features could be revealed only thanks to the joint operation of several senses. Just as consciousness of some qualities, such as color and timbre, relies on integrating information within one sense, consciousness of other qualities, such as flavor, may rely on integrating information from multiple senses. For instance, experiencing qualities that constitute the mintiness of mint or the smoky heat of a green hatch chili may require drawing on information from taste, olfaction, and somatosensation. The apparent simplicity of the quality belies the complexity of the multisensory process responsible for revealing it.

Thus, the joint use of multiple senses adds to the qualities that are evident during perception. It thereby augments the qualitative character of phenomenal consciousness. Not even all qualia must be distinctive to a specific sense.

Multisensory perception therefore extends perceptual phenomenality. It makes possible novel forms of experience, when compared with independent senses working in parallel. Phenomenal consciousness is richer thanks to coordination among the senses.

Multisensory perception thus enhances and extends human sense perception. Perceptual processes, capacities, awareness, and phenomenality are altered and enriched, at a time and over time, thanks to the joint use of the senses.

7.3 Taxonomy

Multisensory perception raises two central questions of psychological taxonomy. The first concerns the senses. Multisensory perception and consciousness challenge the distinctness of our senses. What, if anything, differentiates one sense from another?

The second concerns the distinction between perception and cognition. What makes a process or an experience a matter of perception rather than extraperceptual cognition? We must mark the boundary without relying on what is sense specific.

7.3.1 Senses

This book's central thesis is that coordination among the senses enhances perception. My arguments presuppose that perceivers possess distinct senses. What it is for a feature to be associated with a given sense on an occasion assumes several senses. And genuinely multisensory perception requires multiple sensory modalities.

However, multisensory phenomena threaten to undermine the distinctness of the senses. In the science of perception, sensory integration and plasticity have been used to argue that the senses are not distinct information processing systems (Shimojo and Shams 2001). In philosophy of perception, the experience of unity and binding has been used to argue that the senses are not distinct experiential modalities—senses are not fundamentally distinct conscious ways of perceiving (Tye 2003; Speaks 2015). Skepticism that perceivers possess distinct senses is compounded by a consensus that we lack a satisfactory criterion that individuates senses. This drives some to conventionalism or to pluralism about the senses.

Chapter 6 described an account of the senses that is compatible with richly multisensory perception and consciousness. My approach treats separately two distinct tasks. The first is characterizing the nature of the senses and what differentiates them. The second is attributing experiences to sensory modalities.

A sense is a way of perceiving. According to the account I propose, each sense is a family of perceptual capacities. What unifies and distinguishes each collection is a distinctive manner in which those capacities are exercised. Across the senses, the same perceptual capacity, such as the capacity to perceive shape, can be exercised in distinct ways. And distinct capacities, such as the capacity to perceive color and the capacity to perceive shape, can be exercised in the same way.

Exercising perceptual capacities typically involves deploying a sense organ exploratorily in order to detect and differentiate things and features in the environment by extracting information from a medium. For instance, in human vision, perceivers deploy the eyes as a means to discern objects, colors, shapes, and motion, thereby exploiting the capacity to extract information about such things from the light. In audition, we use our ears to discern sounds, pitch, timbre, and loudness, thereby taking advantage of a capacity to extract information from pressure waves.

Accordingly, ways or manners of exercising perceptual capacities are activity types. In particular, they are types of information-gathering activity. Each functions to extract information from a medium. Sensory information-gathering activities belong to distinct types corresponding to the sorts of information those activities function to extract and the medium from which they do so. Their information-extraction functions individuate sensory information-gathering activity types. Touch, for instance, involves a kind of activity that functions to extract information about objects, shape, texture, and temperature from contact and pressure. So, to each sense corresponds a distinct information-gathering activity type. A sense, therefore, is a bundle of perceptual capacities whose exercise involves a distinctive sort of information-gathering activity.

Experiences, however, are not capacities. Experiences are conscious episodes. In virtue of what do experiences belong to differing senses?

Each perceptual episode involves the exercise of perceptual capacities. Perceptual episodes can be ascribed modalities according to the manners in which such capacities are exercised. This approach rejects exclusiveness. Belonging to one sense does not preclude an experience from belonging to another sense. An experience can be both visual and tactual. We ought to give up on carving experiences into their sense-specific parts.

Some philosophers say that experiences of each sense have a distinctive and recognizable phenomenological character. Chapter 6 argues that, since some senses have more than one proper sensible (the problem of multiple proper sensibles), phenomenal features at a time do not suffice to determine the modality of a conscious perceptual episode. They do so only given dependence relations among phenomenal features of a given sense. These dependence relations rely on further facts, such as facts about phenomenology over time. Sensory manners thus have an advantage over accounts that rely on phenomenology alone. They can explain such dependence relations in terms of shared ways of deploying perceptual capacities, rather than brute phenomenology. In this account, modality is not a fundamental determinant of phenomenal character. Modality is not experientially basic.

This account rejects self-evidence of modality. In particular, the sense modality with which a given feature is associated on an occasion need not be evident to a subject just in virtue of having an experience. Nonetheless, this does not rule out self-knowledge of modality. Most of the time, if you are having an experience of a given sense, you are in a position to know you are having an experience of that sense. First, experiences of proper sensibles typically have character distinctive to one sense. Second, perceiving with a given sense involves a distinctive type of information-gathering activity in which a subject can intentionally and thus knowably engage.

The capacities account of the senses is designed as safe for multisensory perception and consciousness. A capacity that can be deployed in only one sensory manner is a unisensory capacity. One that can be deployed in ways that rely on the joint use of several senses is a multisensory capacity. This book claims that coordination among our senses can alter and enhance unisensory capacities. Furthermore, some perceptual capacities are multisensory. Indeed, some are distinctively multisensory.

An episode is multisensory just in case it deploys capacities in more than one sensory manner. A multisensory experience is one with phenomenal features associated with more than one sensory modality. That is, each of at least two senses has at least one phenomenal feature associated with it. A richly—constitutively and irreducibly—multisensory experience is one with features associated with more than one sense but whose features are not exhausted by those associated with each of the respective senses along with whatever accrues due to mere co-consciousness.

This book argues that perceptual consciousness is richly multisensory. Thus, we ought to reject exhaustiveness. This holds even as a claim about phenomenal character. Not every phenomenal feature of a conscious perceptual episode must belong to one sense or another.

Multisensory perception and consciousness therefore are compatible with the distinctness of our senses. However, not every phenomenon associated with a given sense is wholly independent from each of the other senses. And collecting accounts of each of the senses on their own does not suffice for a complete account of sense perception and consciousness. Therefore, we ought to reject both the independence and the completeness of the senses.

With the right approach to individuating senses, multisensory phenomena do not pose trouble for the project of differentiating senses. A proper understanding of the senses illuminates the nature and the purpose of multisensory phenomena.

7.3.2 Perception

Multisensory processes, capacities, and experiences belong to perception. By this, I mean that the phenomena used to establish this book's main thesis are perceptual. They are not wholly a matter of extraperceptual cognition—not just inference, snap judgment, knowledge, association, confabulation, memory, or imagination. Instead, perception.

This relies on a distinction between perception and cognition. Thus, it turns on a challenging foundational dispute. This is especially pressing, and it must be addressed. Some multisensory effects do occur very early in perceptual processing and rapidly in response to a multisensory stimulus. However, some to which I appeal occur later and farther along the subsequent cascade. Each relies on something sense specific, but some are borderlands phenomena. Their impact on consciousness is not always obvious. They are not perfectly in line with paradigms of sense perception, like seeing redness or hearing a high-pitched sound, but they do not fit with the clear paradigms of inference, judgment, conceptualization, or learning.

Characterizing multisensory phenomena as perceptual thus relies on an understanding of the distinction between perception and cognition. One way to address this would be to adopt my favorite criterion and to argue that these phenomena satisfy it. That would not convince many philosophers or scientists, since each specific criterion that has been offered is contentious.

This book takes a different approach. Rather than pick my favorite criterion, I focus instead on the explanatory purposes for a distinction between perception and cognition. Differing purposes, which have divergent aims and success criteria, impose distinct contraints. Throughout the book, I argue that multisensory processes, capacities, and consciousness satisfy relevant constraints.

The preceding chapters distinguish three sorts of role for the distinction between perception and cognition. These correspond to three differing explanatory enterprises. In particular, empirical psychology, rational psychology, and phenomenology each have differing aims in theorizing about the mind. Empirical psychology aims to explain and predict behavior in the face of stimulation in terms of internal states and causal-functional relations. Rational psychology aims to make sense of subjects and what they do in the light of theoretical and practical norms. Phenomenology aims descriptively to capture what it is like for a subject, from that subject's own perspective.

Each of these explanatory projects deploys the distinction between perception and cognition. Given their aims, each places differing constraints on that distinction. My approach is to focus on the explanatory purposes for the distinction between perception and cognition in each of these enterprises and to identify the constraints each places on candidate phenomena.

Chapters 2 through 5 argued that multisensory phenomena, including processes, capacities, awareness, and experiences, meet criteria for being perceptual that are appropriate for the relevant type of explanation. By these lights, whether the context concerns empirical, rational, or phenomenological considerations, multisensory effects count among those that belong to perception.

This way of adjudicating questions about perception and extraperceptual cognition fits with a more general approach to the mind. According to this picture, the mind comprises faculties that are collections of psychological capacities. Perception is a collection of capacities unified and distinguished by the way in which those capacities are exercised. In particular, it is plausible that each differing sensory manner shares the characteristic of being a stimulus-dependent way of exercising psychological capacities. This, in turn, helps to account for perception's distinctive functional and rational roles, when compared with extraperceptual cognition.

7.4 Consequences

The arguments and the conclusions reached in this book have both critical and constructive consequences for the philosophy of perception and consciousness.

7.4.1 Negative

Multisensory perception means unisensory approaches face a methodological obstacle. If perceptual processes and perceptual consciousness typically are multisensory, theorizing one sense at a time risks impoverishing or distorting our understanding of perception.

In the first place, one sense can influence or depend on another sense, at a time or over time. In particular, this book argues that a feature of a perceptual process or of perceptual consciousness involving one sense modality may depend causally or constitutively on a feature associated with another sense modality. This applies to aspects of perceptual functioning, capacities, awareness, and experience. The dependence may hold during a brief interval, as in crossmodal illusions or in perceiving novel intermodal features. Or it can occur over a longer period of time, as with perceptual learning and flux.

This implies that unisensory approaches are incomplete. There is more to be said about sense perception after we have examined each sense on its own and grappled with the unity of consciousness. At the very least, we would like to know the respects in which a form of perception associated with a given sense depends on another sense, and in which respects perception outstrips individual senses working on their own. Extant accounts are incomplete to the extent they do not accommodate these multisensory phenomena.

In my view, things are worse. Perceiving with a given sense typically occurs while perceiving with others. For instance, seeing typically happens in a multisensory context. Thus, to understand vision on its own, a unisensory approach has two options.

The first is to consider seeing in a purely unisensory context. This eliminates influences from other senses. However, typical vision is shaped by influences from other senses, at a time and over time. Stripped of changes that take place thanks to senses beyond vision, visual processes and visual consciousness differ from what they otherwise would have been. These changes are not just peripheral. To take one example, vestibular and bodily influences are crucial to core aspects of visual space, such as up, down, left, and right. So, as compared with typical vision in a multisensory context, vision in the unisensory context is impoverished. The same holds for each of the senses.

The second option is to abstract away from other senses, ignoring their contributions in a multisensory context. In the case of vision, we bracket the respects in which other senses are relevant to explaining the features of a visual process or experience. This, however, affects how we understand visual capacities and visual consciousness. If, in abstracting, we imagine that the features of a visual episode in a multisensory context rely on vision alone, we may take for granted that each has a sense-specific and wholly visual characterization. This overestimates vision's resources, and it underestimates the contributions of other senses. What is a purely visual take on up, down, left, or right? Moreover, it is possible to mistake a feature of richly multisensory perception for a feature of vision itself. Each of these mistakes distorts what counts as a visual phenomenon. Similar concerns apply to each of the senses.

Unisensory approaches that risk impoverishing or distorting perceptual phenomena associated with a given sense therefore face a skeptical, undercutting concern. In a multisensory context, a feature that is taken to belong to one sense modality may rely on another sense. Crossmodal dependence therefore is a confound. It must be ruled out by any uni-sensory account of what it is to perceive with a given sense in typical conditions. Doing so, however, requires a multisensory approach.

7.4.2 Positive

This approach has constructive consequences. The coordinated use of multiple senses enhances and extends human perceptual capacities. Start with enhancement. Sharing information across senses can improve coherence and the acuity and reliability of perceptual capacities we already possess, such as the capacity to perceive spatial and temporal features by means of vision, audition, or touch. We are better perceivers in these respects thanks to multisensory perception.

Jointly using several senses also can extend the reach of our perceptual capacities. It can enable us to perceive intermodal identity and novel intermodal instances of relational features, such as simultaneity, motion, rhythm, speech, and causality. It also can reveal wholly new types of features, such as flavors and balance. We perceive more features of the world thanks to multisensory perception.

Coordination among senses also makes possible new varieties of perceptual consciousness. Some types of experience that are associated with a given sense are possible only due to the influence of other senses. For instance, vision enables typical hearers auditorily to discern the relative spatial locations of distinct sources. A history of hearing speech enables surprisingly fluent visual phoneme perception and speechread-ing. More exotic cases, like visually experiencing the solidity of an object thanks to a history of haptic touch, provide intriguing examples, though collecting direct evidence is challenging. The secure lesson, however, is that perceptual consciousness associated with one sense can change over time thanks to the influence of another sense.

Moreover, the joint use of several senses makes possible varieties of perceptual consciousness that outstrip what belongs to each of the respective senses. Consciously perceiving novel feature instances and novel feature types, for instance, can amount to more than just parallel awareness in several senses at once. Such episodes can have phenomenal features that no corresponding unisensory experience could have and that do not just stem from mere co-consciousness. Thus, they do not supervene on and are not fully grounded in what is sense specific. Perceptual consciousness is richer thanks to multisensory perception.

Multisensory bootstrapping thus enhances perception and perceptual consciousness. Our senses work better when they work together. Beyond its epistemic upshots, this has aesthetic and practical significance. Lots of what we enjoy when we enjoy sensory pleasures relies on multisensory perception. Music, dance, and art, but also food and wine, sports and exercise, conversations and arguments all are more vivid perceptually given their joint engagement of multiple senses and the coordination that takes place among senses.

A multisensory approach may even help to crack some of the most challenging theoretical and philosophical questions about perception. Handel (2006) says perceiving is about solving correspondence problems. A correspondence problem is one of identifying an individual or feature, at a time or over time, given varying and fluctuating sensory informa-tion.[1] Perceiving, in this view, involves using contrasts and changes in noisy and variable sensory stimulation to discern things with relatively stable characteristics. Burge (2010) argues that perceptual capacities differ from mere sensation in registering such constancies. This is the source of perception's objective purport.

One important lesson of multisensory phenomena is that a corres-pondence problem holds between senses. Perceiving involves determin-ing that what you hear is what you see, that the shape you see is the one you touch, or that what you feel on your tongue is what tastes sweet. It can mean discerning that sounds and touches have a rhythm or a pattern of motion, or that something visible causes a sound. An empirical account of perception should explain how this is accomplished. Philo-sophers should ask what makes it significant.

Here is a start. Just as perceiving colors and visual objects involves detecting constancies in hue and shape despite variation due to lighting and viewpoint, perceiving ordinary objects, events, and features using

---

[1] The original correspondence problem is how to reconcile two retinal images to yield information about depth.

several senses involves detecting constancies despite differences due to the modality with which one perceives. The appearance of an object or event, and of its spatial and temporal features, can differ from sense to sense. Without crossmodal constancies, shifting sense modalities would seem perceptually to result in altogether different features and objects of consciousness. As perceived through distinct senses, the world's cohesiveness depends on our perceptually keeping track of common items and features.

There is a complementary philosophical application. Perceptual consciousness is marked by the impression that we are acquainted with a world of things and happenings independent from ourselves and our experiences. This is central to the philosophical puzzle of perception. Multisensory perception plays a role in accounting for this aspect of experience. Each sense is a distinct way of perceiving. Each provides an angle on the world. Thus, our senses offer differing perspectives on individuals and features that we nevertheless perceive to be common. Deploying differing perspectives as perspectives on a common subject matter is treating them as perspectives on something independent from each individual perspective. Doing so regards its objects as having features beyond those revealed from any one perspective.

This is a key part of the impression that what is perceived is distinct from oneself and one's own consciousness. It is not a surprise that sense-specific phenomena—colors, tastes, rainbows, sounds, and odors—serve as footholds for subjectivism. Accessibility to multiple senses can make something seem more real, less subject dependent. Multisensory perception thus contributes an important ingredient to the sense of perceptual objectivity.

7.5 Coda

This establishes the book's central claims. The coordinated use of multiple senses enhances and extends human perceptual capacities, when compared with several senses operating independently and in parallel. And the exercise of multisensory capacities makes possible new forms of experience. Therefore, perception and perceptual consciousness cannot be captured fully in sense-specific terms.

What hangs on this? According to this approach, typical human exteroceptive sense perception is constitutively and irreducibly multisensory. In the first instance, this is a claim about perceptual processes. Perceptual mechanisms perform functions that span senses. They resolve conflicts and defer to the more reliable modality. Moreover, some perceptual capacities are exercised in ways that rely on the joint use of several senses. It is possible perceptually to detect and differentiate otherwise imperceptible intermodal feature instances—identity, simultaneity, motion, rhythm, causality, and flavors—only through the coordinated use of several senses.

But this also is a claim about perceptual consciousness. In particular, perceptual consciousness outstrips the individual senses taken separately. Some forms of perceptual awareness require the joint use of several senses, and perceptual phenomenology is not exhausted by what is associated with each of the respective sensory modalities. These claims are not just grounded in introspective phenomenology. Instead, they are theoretical claims. They are part of the best systematic explanation for the evidence from what people do.

These results are not trivial. Senses might have been fully independent systems, functionally modular and informationally encapsulated. Conscious sense perception might have been exhausted by distinct, parallel modes or relations of sensing. Its character might have been wholly distinctive and proprietary to each individual sense. The boundaries between senses might have been introspectible. Each of these ideas has shaped conceptions of perception, experience, and phenomenology from the early modern era to the present. Multisensory phenomena demonstrate that this traditional picture is not adequate. It falls short as an account of perceptual processes, capacities, awareness, and phenomenology. It is incomplete, and it is distorting. It ought to be abandoned.

In its place, the science and the philosophy of perception suggest an alternative way to understand the senses and sense perception. Our senses are deeply cooperative, collaborative faculties whose workings cannot fully be disentangled. We need not give up the idea that we possess distinct senses, but we should scrap the idealization according to which perception and perceptual consciousness can be apportioned neatly and exhaustively into sense-specific aspects and parts.

In diverse domains, sense perception and consciousness matter. Some, like epistemology, phenomenology, cognitive architecture, and the mind–body problem, are theoretical. Some, like art, virtual reality, artificial intelligence, and crafting sensory prosthetics, are more practical. Wherever perception and perceptual consciousness matter, multisensory perception matters. The science and the philosophy of perception thus stand to gain by appreciating the ways in which our senses flexibly shape each other and work jointly to meet shared aims. To come to grips with the nature, character, and function of sense perception calls for a multisensory approach.

References

Alais, D. and Burr, D. (2004). The ventriloquist effect results from near-optimal bimodal integration. *Current Biology*, 14: 257–62.

Allen, P. G. and Kolers, P. A. (1981). Sensory specificity of apparent motion. *Journal of Experimental Psychology: Human Perception and Performance*, 7: 1318–26.

Anscombe, G. E. M. (1957). *Intention*. Cambridge, MA: Harvard University Press.

Anscombe, G. E. M. (1965). The intentionality of sensation: A grammatical feature. In R. J. Butler (ed.), *Analytical Philosophy, Second Series*, pp. 158–80. Oxford: Blackwell.

Aristotle (1984). De Anima. In J. Barnes (ed.), *The Complete Works of Aristotle: The Revised Oxford Translation*, volume 1. Princeton: Princeton University Press.

Austin, J. L. (1962). *Sense and Sensibilia*. Oxford: Clarendon Press.

Baron-Cohen, S., Burt, L., Smith-Laittan, F., Harrison, J., and Bolton, P. (1996). Synaesthesia: Prevalence and familiality. *Perception*, 25: 1073–9.

Batty, C. (2011). Smelling lessons. *Philosophical Studies*, 153: 161–74.

Baumgartner, F., Hanke, M., Geringswald, F., Zinke, W., Speck, O., and Pollmann, S. (2013). Evidence for feature binding in the superior parietal lobule. *NeuroImage*, 68: 173–80.

Bayne, T. (2009). Perception and the reach of phenomenal content. *The Philosophical Quarterly*, 59: 385–404.

Bayne, T. (2010). *The Unity of Consciousness*. Oxford: Oxford University Press.

Bayne, T. J. and Chalmers, D. J. (2003). What is the unity of consciousness? In Cleeremans (2003), pp. 23–58.

Beauchamp, M. S., Nath, A., and Pasalar, S. (2010). fMRI-guided TMS reveals that the STS is a cortical locus of the McGurk effect. *Neuroscience*, 30: 2414–17.

Beauchamp, M. S. and Ro, T. (2008). Neural substrates of sound–touch synesthesia after a thalamic lesion. *The Journal of Neuroscience*, 28: 13696–702.

Beck, J. (2018). Marking the perception–cognition boundary: The criterion of stimulus-dependence. *Australasian Journal of Philosophy*, 96: 319–34.

Bennett, D. J. and Hill, C. S. (eds.) (2014). *Sensory Integration and the Unity of Consciousness*. Cambridge, MA: MIT Press.

Bennett, D. J., Trommershäuser, J., and van Dam, L. C. J. (2014). Bayesian modeling of perceiving: A guide to basic principles. In Bennett and Hill (2014), pp. 1–13.

Bertelson, P. (1999). Ventriloquism: A case of cross-modal perceptual grouping. In G. Aschersleben, T. Bachmann, and J. Müsseler (eds.), *Cognitive Contributions to the Perception of Spatial and Temporal Events*, pp. 347–62. Amsterdam: Elsevier.

Bertelson, P. and de Gelder, B. (2004). The psychology of multimodal perception. In Spence and Driver (2004), pp. 141–77.

Blauert, J. (1997). *Spatial Hearing: The Psychophysics of Human Sound Localization*. Cambridge, MA: MIT Press.

Block, N. (1995). On a confusion about a function of consciousness. *Behavioral and Brain Sciences*, 18: 227–47.

Block, N. (2014). Seeing-as in the light of vision science. *Philosophy and Phenomenological Research*, 89: 560–72.

Bolognini, N. and Maravita, A. (2011). Uncovering multisensory processing through non-invasive brain stimulation. *Frontiers in Psychology*, 2: 1–10.

Botvinick, M. and Cohen, J. (1998). Rubber hands "feel" touch that eyes see. *Nature*, 391: 756.

Bregman, A. S. (1990). *Auditory Scene Analysis: The Perceptual Organization of Sound*. Cambridge, MA: MIT Press.

Brewer, B. (2011). *Perception and Its Objects*. Oxford: Oxford University Press.

Briscoe, R. E. (2017). Multisensory processing and perceptual consciousness: Part II. *Philosophy Compass*, 12: e12423.

Burge, T. (2010). *Origins of Objectivity*. Oxford: Oxford University Press.

Busse, L., Roberts, K. C., Crist, R. E., Weissman, D. H., and Woldorff, M. G. (2005). The spread of attention across modalities and space in a multisensory object. *Proceedings of the National Academy of Science*, 102: 18751–6.

Byrne, A. (2001). Intentionalism defended. *The Philosophical Review*, 110: 199–240.

Byrne, A. (2012). Knowing what I see. In D. Smithies and D. Stoljar (eds.), *Introspection and Consciousness*, pp. 183–210. New York: Oxford University Press.

Calvert, G., Spence, C., and Stein, B. E. (2004). *The Handbook of Multisensory Processes*. Cambridge, MA: MIT Press.

Campbell, J. (2002). *Reference and Consciousness*. Oxford: Clarendon Press.

Carnap, R. (1928/2003). *The Logical Structure of the World and Pseudoproblems in Philosophy*. Chicago: Open Court.

Chalmers, D. J. (1996). *The Conscious Mind*. New York: Oxford University Press.

Chen, L. and Zhou, X. (2011). Capture of intermodal visual/tactile apparent motion by moving and static sounds. *Seeing and Perceiving*, 24: 369–89.

Choi, H. and Scholl, B. J. (2006). Measuring causal perception: Connections to representational momentum? *Acta Psychologica*, 123: 91–111.

Cinel, C., Humphreys, G. W., and Poli, R. (2002). Cross-modal illusory conjunctions between vision and touch. *Journal of Experimental Psychology: Human Perception and Performance*, 28: 1243–66.

Clark, A. (1993). *Sensory Qualities*. Oxford: Clarendon Press.

Clark, A. (2011). Cross-modal cuing and selective attention. In F. Macpherson (ed.), *The Senses: Classical and Contemporary Philosophical Perspectives*, pp. 375–96. Oxford: Oxford University Press.

Clark, A. (2016). *Surfing Uncertainty: Prediction, Action, and the Embodied Mind*. New York: Oxford University Press.

Cleeremans, A. (ed.) (2003). *The Unity of Consciousness: Binding, Integration, and Dissociation*. Oxford: Oxford University Press.

Cohen, J. (2004). Objects, places, and perception. *Philosophical Psychology*, 17: 471–95.

Conee, E. and Feldman, R. (1998). The generality problem for reliabilism. *Philosophical Studies*, 89: 1–29.

Connolly, K. (2014). Making sense of multiple senses. In R. Brown (ed.), *Consciousness Inside and Out: Phenomenology, Neuroscience, and the Nature of Experience*,
pp. 351–64. Dordrecht: Springer.

Connolly, K. (2019). *Perceptual Learning: The Flexibility of the Senses*. New York:
Oxford University Press.

Crane, T. (ed.) (1992). *The Contents of Experience*. Cambridge: Cambridge University Press.

Craver, C. F. (2007). *Explaining the Brain*. Oxford: Oxford University Press.

Cummins, R. (1983). *The Nature of Psychological Explanation*. Cambridge, MA: MIT
Press.

de Gelder, B., Vroomen, J., and van der Heide, L. (1991). Face recognition and
lip-reading in autism. *European Journal of Cognitive Psychology*, 3: 69–86.

de Vignemont, F. (2014). A multimodal conception of bodily awareness. *Mind*, 123:
989–1020.

Deroy, O. (ed.) (2017). *Sensory Blending: On Synaesthesia and Related Phenomena*.
Oxford: Oxford University Press.

Deroy, O., Chen, Y., and Spence, C. (2014). Multisensory constraints on awareness.
Philosophical Transactions of the Royal Society B, 369: 20130207. DOI = 10.1098/
rstb.2013.0207

Dickie, I. (2015). *Fixing Reference*. Oxford: Oxford University Press.

Djordjevic, J., Zatorre, R. J., and Jones-Gotman, M. (2004). Effects of perceived and
imagined odors on taste detection. *Chemical Senses*, 29: 199–208.

Dretske, F. I. (1969). *Seeing and Knowing*. Chicago: University of Chicago Press.

Ernst, M. O. and Banks, M. S. (2002). Humans integrate visual and haptic information in a statistically optimal fashion. *Nature*, 415: 429–33.

Firestone, C. and Scholl, B. J. (2016). Cognition does not affect perception: Evaluating
the evidence for "top-down" effects. *Behavioral and Brain Sciences*, 39: 1–77.

Fodor, J. A. (1983). *The Modularity of Mind*. Cambridge, MA: MIT Press.

Fodor, J. A. and Pylyshyn, Z. W. (1981). How direct is visual perception?: Some
reflections on Gibson's "ecological approach." *Cognition*, 9: 139–96.

Fowler, C. A. (1986). An event approach to the study of speech perception from a
direct-realist perspective. *Journal of Phonetics*, 14: 3–28.

Fujisaki, W., Shimojo, S., Kashino, M., and Nishida, S. (2004). Recalibration of
audiovisual simultaneity. *Nature Neuroscience*, 7: 773–8.

Fulkerson, M. (2011). The unity of haptic touch. *Philosophical Psychology*, 24:
493–516.

Fulkerson, M. (2014). *The First Sense: A Philosophical Study of Human Touch*.
Cambridge, MA: MIT Press.

Gendler, T. S. and Hawthorne, J. (eds.) (2006), *Perceptual Experience*. Oxford:
Clarendon Press.

Gibson, J. J. (1966). *The Senses Considered as Perceptual Systems*. Boston: Houghton
Mifflin.

Gibson, J. J. (1979). *The Ecological Approach to Visual Perception*. Hillsdale, NJ:
Erlbaum.

Gick, B. and Derrick, D. (2009). Aero-tactile integration in speech perception.
Nature, 462: 502–4.

Goldman, A. I. (1979). What is justified belief? In G. S. Pappas (ed.), *Justification and Knowledge*, pp. 1–25. Dordrecht: Reidel.

Goldman, A. I. (1986). *Epistemology and Cognition*. Cambridge, MA: Harvard University Press.

Goodman, N. (1951). *The Structure of Appearance*. Cambridge, MA: Harvard University Press.

Gori, M., Sandini, G., Martinoli, C., and Burr, D. C. (2014). Impairment of auditory spatial localization in congenitally blind human subjects. *Brain*, 137: 288–93.

Grice, H. P. (1962). Some remarks about the senses. In R. J. Butler (ed.), *Analytical Philosophy, First Series*, pp. 133–53. Oxford: Blackwell.

Guest, S., Catmur, C., Lloyd, D., and Spence, C. (2002). Audiotactile interactions in roughness perception. *Experimental Brain Research*, 146: 161–71.

Guski, R. and Troje, N. F. (2003). Audiovisual phenomenal causality. *Perception and Psychophysics*, 65: 789–800.

Hamilton, R. H., Shenton, J. T., and Coslett, H. B. (2006). An acquired deficit of audiovisual speech processing. *Brain and Language*, 98: 66–73.

Handel, S. (1993). *Listening: An Introduction to the Perception of Auditory Events*. Cambridge, MA: MIT Press.

Handel, S. (2006). *Perceptual Coherence*. New York: Oxford University Press.

Harman, G. (1990). The intrinsic quality of experience. In J. Tomberlin (ed.), *Philosophical Perspectives*, volume 4, pp. 31–52. Atascadero, CA: Ridgeview.

Harrar, V., Winter, R., and Harris, L. R. (2008). Visuotactile apparent motion. *Perception and Psychophysics*, 70: 807–17.

Hay, J. C., Pick, H. L., and Ikeda, K. (1965). Visual capture produced by prism spectacles. *Psychonomic Science*, 2: 215–16.

Heil, J. (1983). *Perception and Cognition*. Berkeley, CA: University of California Press.

Heil, J. (2012). *The Universe as We Find It*. Oxford: Oxford University Press.

Hill, C. S. (2009). *Consciousness*. Cambridge: Cambridge University Press.

Hohwy, J. (2013). *The Predictive Mind*. Oxford: Oxford University Press.

Huang, J., Gamble, D., Sarnlertsophon, K., Wang, X., and Hsiao, S. (2012). Feeling music: Integration of auditory and tactile inputs in musical meter. *PLoS ONE*, 7: e48496. DOI = 10.1371/journal.pone.0048496.

Huddleston, W. E., Lewis, J. W., Phinney, R. E., and DeYoe, E. A. (2008). Auditory and visual attention-based apparent motion share functional parallels. *Perception and Psychophysics*, 70: 1207–16.

Jackson, F. (1982). Epiphenomenal qualia. *The Philosophical Quarterly*, 32: 127–36.

Jiang, Y. and Chen, L. (2013). Mutual influences of intermodal visual/tactile apparent motion and auditory motion with uncrossed and crossed arms. *Multisensory Research*, 26: 19–51.

Johnston, M. (2006). Better than mere knowledge? The function of sensory awareness. In Gendler and Hawthorne (2006), pp. 260–90.

Jordan, K. E., Clark, K., and Mitroff, S. R. (2010). See an object, hear an object file: Object correspondence transcends sensory modality. *Visual Cognition*, 18: 492–503.

Jousmäki, V. and Hari, R. (1998). Parchment-skin illusion: sound-biased touch. *Current Biology*, 8: R190.

Kahneman, D. and Treisman, A. (1984). Changing views of attention and automaticity. In R. Parasuraman and D. R. Davies (eds.), *Varieties of Attention*, pp. 29–61. Orlando: Academic Press.

Kahneman, D., Treisman, A., and Gibbs, B. J. (1992). The reviewing of object files: Object-specific integration of information. *Cognitive Psychology*, 24: 175–219.

Kamke, M. R., Vieth, H. E., Cottrell, D., and Mattingley, J. B. (2012). Parietal disruption alters audiovisual binding in the sound-induced flash illusion. *Neuro-Image*, 62: 1334–41.

Keeley, B. L. (2002). Making sense of the senses: Individuating modalities in humans and other animals. *Journal of Philosophy*, 99: 5–28.

Keetels, M. and Vroomen, J. (2012). Perception of synchrony between the senses. In M. M. Murray and M. T. Wallace (eds.), *The Neural Bases of Multisensory Processes*, pp. 147–77. Boca Raton, FL: CRC Press.

King, A. J. (2004). The superior colliculus. *Current Biology*, 14: R335–8.

King, A. J. (2014). What happens to your hearing if you are born blind? *Brain*, 137: 6–8.

Kriegel, U. (2015). *The Varieties of Consciousness*. Oxford: Oxford University Press.

Krubitzer, L. (2009). In search of a unifying theory of complex brain evolution. *The Year in Cognitive Neuroscience 2009*, 1156: 44–67.

Krystallidou, D. and Thompson, P. (2016). Cross-modal transfer of the tilt aftereffect from vision to touch. *i-Perception*, 7: 1–10.

Kubovy, M. and Schutz, M. (2010). Audio-visual objects. *Review of Philosophy and Psychology*, 1: 41–61.

Landy, M. S., Banks, M. S., and Knill, D. C. (2011). Ideal-observer models of cue integration. In J. Trommershäuser, K. Kording, and M. S. Landy (eds.), *Sensory Cue Integration*, pp. 5–29. New York: Oxford University Press.

Levine, J. (1983). Materialism and qualia: The explanatory gap. *Pacific Philosophical Quarterly*, 64: 354–61.

Lewis, D. (1980). Veridical hallucination and prosthetic vision. *The Australasian Journal of Philosophy*, 58: 239–49.

Lewis, D. (1983). *Philosophical Papers, Volume I*. Oxford: Oxford University Press.

Lewis, D. (1988). What experience teaches. *Proceedings of the Russellian Society*, 13: 29–57.

Liberman, A. M. (1996). *Speech: A Special Code*. Cambridge, MA: MIT Press.

Liberman, A. M., Cooper, F. S., Shankweiler, D. P., and Studdert-Kennedy, M. (1967). Perception of the speech code. *Psychological Review*, 74: 431–61.

Loar, B. (2003). Phenomenal intentionality as the basis of mental content. In M. Hahn and B. Ramberg (eds.), *Reflections and Replies: Essays on the Philosophy of Tyler Burge*, pp. 229–58. Cambridge, MA: MIT Press.

Lopes, D. M. M. (2000). What is it like to see with your ears? The representational theory of mind. *Philosophy and Phenomenological Research*, 60: 439–53.

Lycan, W. (1996). *Consciousness and Experience*. Cambridge, MA: MIT Press.

Lycan, W. (2000). The slighting of smell. In N. Bhushan and S. Rosenfeld (eds.), *Of Minds and Molecules: New Philosophical Perspectives on Chemistry*, pp. 273–89. New York: Oxford University Press.

Machamer, P., Darden, L., and Craver, C. F. (2000). Thinking about mechanisms. *Philosophy of Science*, 67: 1–25.

Machery, E. and Doris, J. M. (2017). An open letter to our students: Doing interdisciplinary moral psychology. In B. G. Voyer and T. Tarantola (eds.), *Moral Psychology: A Multidisciplinary Guide*, pp. 119–43. Cham: Springer.

Mack, A. and Rock, I. (1998). *Inattentional Blindness*. Cambridge, MA: MIT Press.

Macpherson, F. (2011). Taxonomising the senses. *Philosophical Studies*, 153: 123–42.

Maloney, L. T. and Wandell, B. A. (1986). Color constancy: a method for recovering surface spectral reflectance. *Journal of the Optical Society of America A*, 3: 29–33.

Mamassian, P., Landy, M., and Maloney, L. T. (2002). In R. Rao, M. Lewicki, and B. Olshausen (eds.), *Bayesian Modelling of Visual Perception*, pp. 13–36. Cambridge, MA: MIT Press.

Marr, D. (1982). *Vision*. San Francisco, CA: W. H. Freeman.

Martin, M. (1992). Sight and touch. In Crane (1992), pp. 196–215.

Matthen, M. (2005). *Seeing, Doing, and Knowing: A Philosophical Theory of Sense Perception*. Oxford: Oxford University Press.

Matthen, M. (2014). How to be sure: sensory exploration and empirical certainty. *Philosophy and Phenomenological Research*, 88: 38–69.

Matthen, M. (2015a). Active perception and the representation of space. In Stokes, Matthen, and Biggs (2015), pp. 44–72.

Matthen, M. (2015b). The individuation of the senses. In Matthen (2015c), pp. 567–86.

Matthen, M. (ed.) (2015c). *The Oxford Handbook of Philosophy of Perception*. Oxford: Oxford University Press.

McDowell, J. (1994). *Mind and World*. Cambridge, MA: Harvard University Press.

McGurk, H. and MacDonald, J. (1976). Hearing lips and seeing voices. *Nature*, 264: 746–48.

Merleau-Ponty, M. (1945/2012). *Phenomenology of Perception*. London: Routledge.

Meyerhoff, H. S. and Scholl, B. J. (2018). Auditory-induced bouncing is a perceptual (rather than a cognitive) phenomenon: Evidence from illusory crescents. *Cognition*, 170: 88–94.

Millikan, R. G. (1989). In defense of proper functions. *Philosophy of Science*, 56: 288–302.

Milner, A. D. and Goodale, M. A. (1995). *The Visual Brain in Action*. Oxford: Oxford University Press.

Miracchi, L. (2017). Perception first. *The Journal of Philosophy*, 114: 629–77.

Mitroff, S. R., Scholl, B. J., and Wynn, K. (2005). The relationship between object files and conscious perception. *Cognition*, 96: 67–92.

Mole, C. (2011). *Attention is Cognitive Unison: An Essay in Philosophical Psychology*. New York: Oxford University Press.

Mongillo, E. A., Irwin, J. R., Whalen, D. H., Klaiman, C., Carter, A. S., and Schultz, R. T. (2008). Audiovisual processing in children with and without autism spectrum disorders. *Journal of Autism and Developmental Disorders*, 38: 1349–58.

Müller, K., Aschersleben, G., Schmitz, F., Schnitzler, A., Freund, H.-J., and Prinz, W. (2008). Inter- versus intramodal integration in sensorimotor synchronization: A combined behavioral and magnetoencephalographic study. *Experimental Brain Research*, 185: 309–18.

Nagel, T. (1974). What is it like to be a bat? *The Philosophical Review*, 83: 435–50.

Nanay, B. (2010). A modal theory of function. *The Journal of Philosophy*, 107: 412–31.

Nanay, B. (2012). The multimodal experience of art. *The British Journal of Aesthetics*, 52: 353–63.

Nanay, B. (2013). *Between Perception and Action*. Oxford: Oxford University Press.

Nath, A. R. and Beauchamp, M. S. (2012). A neural basis for interindividual differences in the McGurk effect, a multisensory speech illusion. *Neuroimage*, 59: 781–7.

Neander, K. (1991). Functions as selected effects: The conceptual analyst's defense. *Philosophy of Science*, 58: 168–84.

Noë, A. (2004). *Action in Perception*. Cambridge, MA: MIT Press.

Nudds, M. (2001). Experiencing the production of sounds. *European Journal of Philosophy*, 9: 210–29.

Nudds, M. (2003). The significance of the senses. *Proceedings of the Aristotelian Society*, 104: 31–51.

Nudds, M. and O'Callaghan, C. (eds.) (2009). *Sounds and Perception: New Philosophical Essays*. Oxford: Oxford University Press.

O'Callaghan, C. (2007). *Sounds: A Philosophical Theory*. Oxford: Oxford University Press.

O'Callaghan, C. (2008). Seeing what you hear: Cross-modal illusions and perception. *Philosophical Issues*, 18: 316–38.

O'Callaghan, C. (2011). Against hearing meanings. *Philosophical Quarterly*, 61: 783–807.

O'Callaghan, C. (2015). The multisensory character of perception. *The Journal of Philosophy*, 112: 551–69.

O'Callaghan, C. (2017). Grades of multisensory awareness. *Mind & Language*, 32: 155–81.

O'Callaghan, C. (2020). Perceptual capacities, success, and content. *Philosophy and Phenomenological Research*, 100: 738–43.

Open Science Collaboration (2015). Estimating the reproducibility of psychological science. *Science*, 349: aac4716-1–8.

O'Regan, J. K. and Noë, A. (2001). A sensorimotor account of vision and visual consciousness. *Behavioral and Brain Sciences*, 24: 939–1031.

Orlandi, N. (2014). *The Innocent Eye: Why Vision Is Not a Cognitive Process*. New York: Oxford University Press.

Palmer, S. E. (1999). *Vision Science: Photons to Phenomenology*. Cambridge, MA: MIT Press.

Panagiotidi, M., Overton, P. G., and Stafford, T. (2017). Multisensory integration and ADHD-like traits: Evidence for abnormal temporal integration window in ADHD. *Acta Psychologica*, 181: 10–17.

Parise, C. V. and Ernst, M. O. (2016). Correlation detection as a general mechanism for multisensory integration. *Nature Communications*, 7: 1–23.

Pasalar, S., Ro, T., and Beauchamp, M. S. (2010). TMS of posterior parietal cortex disrupts visual tactile multisensory integration. *European Journal of Neuroscience*, 31: 1783–90.

Peacocke, C. (1983). *Sense and Content*. Oxford: Clarendon Press.

Perkins, M. (1983). *Sensing the World*. Indianapolis, IN: Hackett.

Phillips, I. (2018). Unconscious perception reconsidered. *Analytic Philosophy*, 59: 471–514.

Piccinini, G. and Craver, C. (2011). Integrating psychology and neuroscience: Functional analyses as mechanism sketches. *Synthese*, 183: 283–311.

Pick, H. L., Warren, D. H., and Hay, J. C. (1969). Sensory conflict in judgments of spatial direction. *Perception and Psychophysics*, 6: 203–5.

Posner, M. I. (1980). Orienting of attention. *Quarterly Journal of Experimental Psychology*, 32: 3–25.

Pryor, J. (2000). The skeptic and the dogmatist. *Noûs*, 34: 517–49.

Pylyshyn, Z. W. (1999). Is vision continuous with cognition? The case for cognitive impenetrability of visual perception. *Behavioral and Brain Sciences*, 22: 341–423.

Pylyshyn, Z. W. (2007). *Things and Places: How the Mind Connects With the World*. Cambridge, MA: MIT Press.

Ramachandran, V. S. and Hubbard, E. M. (2001). Synaesthesia—a window into perception, thought and language. *Journal of Consciousness Studies*, 8: 3–34.

Rescorla, M. (2015). Bayesian perceptual psychology. In Matthen (2015c), pp. 694–716.

Rescorla, M. (2018). Perceptual co-reference. *Review of Philosophy and Psychology*. DOI = 10.1007/s13164-018-0411-6

Richard, A. M., Lee, H., and Vecera, S. P. (2008). Attentional spreading in object-based attention. *Journal of Experimental Psychology: Human Perception and Performance*, 34: 842–53.

Richardson, L. (2013). Sniffing and smelling. *Philosophical Studies*, 162: 401–19.

Robbins, P. and Jack, A. I. (2006). The phenomenal stance. *Philosophical Studies*, 127: 59–85.

Rock, I. (1983). *The Logic of Perception*. Cambridge, MA: MIT Press.

Rock, I. (ed.) (1997). *Indirect Perception*. Cambridge, MA: MIT Press.

Rock, I. and Victor, J. (1964). Vision and touch: An experimentally created conflict between the two senses. *Science*, 143: 594–6.

Rosenthal, D. (2015). Quality spaces and sensory modalities. In P. Coates and S. Coleman (eds.), *Phenomenal Qualities: Sense, Perception, and Consciousness*, pp. 33–65. Oxford: Oxford University Press.

Schellenberg, S. (2014). The epistemic force of perceptual experience. *Philosophical Studies*, 170: 87–100.

Schellenberg, S. (2016). Phenomenal evidence and factive evidence. *Philosophical Studies*, 173: 875–96.

Schellenberg, S. (2018). *The Unity of Perception*. Oxford: Oxford University Press.

Scholl, B. and Nakayama, K. (2004). Illusory causal crescents: Misperceived spatial relations due to perceived causality. *Perception*, 33: 455–69.

Schwitzgebel, E. (2008). The unreliability of naive introspection. *The Philosophical Review*, 117: 245–73.

Sekuler, R., Sekuler, A. B., and Lau, R. (1997). Sound alters visual motion perception. *Nature*, 385: 308.

Shams, L. and Beierholm, U. R. (2010). Causal inference in perception. *Trends in Cognitive Sciences*, 14: 425–32.

Shams, L., Kamitani, Y., and Shimojo, S. (2000). What you see is what you hear. *Nature*, 408: 788.

Shams, L., Kamitani, Y., and Shimojo, S. (2002). Visual illusion induced by sound. *Cognitive Brain Research*, 14: 147–52.

Shams, L. and Kim, R. (2010). Crossmodal influences on visual perception. *Physics of Life Reviews*, 7: 269–84.

Shams, L., Ma, W. J., and Beierholm, U. (2005). Sound-induced flash illusion as an optimal percept. *NeuroReport*, 16: 1923–7.

Shams, L., Wozny, D. R., Kim, R. S., and Seitz, A. (2011). Influences of multisensory experience on subsequent unisensory processing. *Frontiers in Psychology*, 2: 1–9.

Shimojo, S. and Shams, L. (2001). Sensory modalities are not separate modalities: plasticity and interactions. *Current Opinion in Neurobiology*, 11: 505–9.

Siegel, S. (2006a). Subject and object in the contents of visual experience. *The Philosophical Review*, 115: 355–88.

Siegel, S. (2006b). Which properties are represented in perception? In Gendler and Hawthorne (2006), pp. 481–503.

Siegel, S. (2009). The visual experience of causation. *Philosophical Quarterly*, 59: 519–40.

Siegel, S. (2010). *The Contents of Visual Experience*. New York: Oxford University Press.

Siegel, S. (2012). Cognitive penetrability and perceptual justification. *Noûs*, 46: 201–22.

Siegel, S. (2017). *The Rationality of Perception*. Oxford: Oxford University Press.

Siewert, C. (1998). *The Significance of Consciousness*. Princeton: Princeton University Press.

Simner, J., Mulvenna, C., Sagiv, N., Tsakanikos, E., Witherby, S. A., Fraser, C., Scott, K., and Ward, J. (2006). Synaesthesia: The prevalence of atypical cross-modal experiences. *Perception*, 35: 1024–33.

Simon, S. A., de Araujo, I. E., Stapleton, J. R., and Nicolelis, M. A. L. (2008). Multisensory processing of gustatory stimuli. *Chemosensory Perception*, 1: 95–102.

Small, D. M., Gerber, J. C., Mak, Y. E., and Hummel, T. (2005). Differential neural responses evoked by orthonasal versus retronasal odorant perception in humans. *Neuron*, 47: 593–605.

Smith, B. C. (2015). The chemical senses. In Matthen (2015c), pp. 314–52.

Snowdon, P. (1981). Perception, vision and causation. *Proceedings of the Aristotelian Society*, 81: 175–92.

Speaks, J. (2015). *The Phenomenal and the Representational*. Oxford: Oxford University Press.

Spelke, E. S. (1990). Principles of object perception. *Cognitive Science*, 14: 29–56.

Spence, C. and Bayne, T. (2015). Is consciousness multisensory? In Stokes, Matthen, and Biggs (2015), pp. 95–132.

Spence, C. and Driver, J. (eds.) (2004). *Crossmodal Space and Crossmodal Attention*. Oxford: Oxford University Press.

Spence, C. and Squire, S. (2003). Multisensory integration: Maintaining the perception of synchrony. *Current Biology*, 13: R519–21.

Stein, B. E. (2012). *The New Handbook of Multisensory Processing*. Cambridge, MA: MIT Press.

Stein, B. E., Burr, D., Constantinidis, C., Laurienti, P. J., Alex Meredith, M., Perrault, T. J., Ramachandran, R., Röder, B., Rowland, B. A., Sathian, K., et al. (2010). Semantic confusion regarding the development of multisensory integration: A practical solution. *European Journal of Neuroscience*, 31: 1713–20.

Stein, B. E. and Meredith, M. A. (1993). *The Merging of the Senses*. Cambridge, MA: MIT Press.

Stiles, N. R. B., Li, M., Levitan, C. A., Kamitani, Y., and Shimojo, S. (2018). What you saw is what you will hear: Two new illusions with audiovisual postdictive effects. *PLOS ONE*, 13: 1–22.

Stokes, D. and Biggs, S. (2015). The dominance of the visual. In Stokes, Matthen, and Biggs (2015), pp. 350–78.

Stokes, D., Matthen, M., and Biggs, S. (eds.) (2015). *Perception and Its Modalities*. New York: Oxford University Press.

Stone, J. V., Hunkin, N. M., Porrill, J., Wood, R., Keeler, V., Beanland, M., Port, M., and Porter, N. R. (2001). When is now? Perception of simultaneity. *Proceedings of the Royal Society of London. Series B: Biological Sciences*, 268: 31–8.

Strawson, G. (2010). *Mental Reality*, 2nd edition. Cambridge, MA: MIT Press.

Strawson, P. F. (1959). *Individuals*. London: Methuen.

Talsma, D., Senkowski, D., Soto-Faraco, S., and Woldorff, M. G. (2010). The multi-faceted interplay between attention and multisensory integration. *Trends in Cognitive Sciences*, 14: 400–10.

Thaler, L. and Goodale, M. A. (2016). Echolocation in humans: an overview. *WIREs Cognitive Science*, 7: 382–93.

Travis, C. (2004). The silence of the senses. *Mind*, 113: 57–94.

Treisman, A. (1988). Features and objects. *The Quarterly Journal of Experimental Psychology*, 40A: 201–37.

Treisman, A. (1996). The binding problem. *Current Opinion in Neurobiology*, 6: 171–8.

Treisman, A. (2003). Consciousness and perceptual binding. In A. Cleeremans (2003), pp. 95–113.

Treisman, A. and Gelade, G. (1980). A feature-integration theory of attention. *Cognitive Psychology*, 12: 97–136.

Treisman, A. and Schmidt, H. (1982). Illusory conjunctions in the perception of objects. *Cognitive Psychology*, 14: 107–41.

Tye, M. (2000). *Consciousness, Color, and Content*. Cambridge, MA: MIT Press.

Tye, M. (2003). *Consciousness and Persons: Unity and Identity*. Cambridge, MA: MIT Press.

Valberg, J. J. (1992). *The Puzzle of Experience*. Oxford: Clarendon Press.

Vatakis, A. and Spence, C. (2007). Crossmodal binding: Evaluating the "unity assumption" using audiovisual speech stimuli. *Perception and Psychophysics*, 69: 744–56.

Violentyev, A., Shimojo, S., and Shams, L. (2005). Touch-induced visual illusion. *Neuroreport*, 16: 1107–10.

Vroomen, J. and de Gelder, B. (2000). Sound enhances visual perception: Cross-modal effects of auditory organization on vision. *Journal of Experimental Psychology: Human Perception and Performance*, 26: 1583–90.

Watkins, S., Shams, L., Tanaka, S., Haynes, J. D., and Rees, G. (2006). Sound alters activity in human V1 in association with illusory visual perception. *NeuroImage*, 31: 1247–56.

Watson, R., Latinus, M., Noguchi, T., Garrod, O., Crabbe, F., and Belin, P. (2014). Crossmodal adaptation in right posterior superior temporal sulcus during face–voice emotional integration. *Journal of Neuroscience*, 34: 6813–21.

Welch, R. B. and Warren, D. H. (1980). Immediate perceptual response to inter-sensory discrepancy. *Psychological Bulletin*, 88: 638–67.

Williamson, T. (1990). *Identity and Discrimination*. Oxford: Blackwell.

Witthoft, N. and Winawer, J. (2013). Learning, memory, and synesthesia. *Psychological Science*, 24: 258–65.

Wong, H. Y. (2017). In and out of balance. In F. de Vignemont and A. J. T. Alsmith (eds.), *The Subject's Matter: Self-Consciousness and the Body*, pp. 311–33. Cambridge, MA: MIT Press.

Wright, L. (1973). Functions. *The Philosophical Review*, 82: 139–68.

Wu, W. (2014). *Attention*. New York: Routledge.

Zampini, M. and Spence, C. (2004). The role of auditory cues in modulating the perceived crispness and staleness of potato chips. *Journal of Sensory Studies*, 19: 347–63.

Zhou, W., Jiang, Y., He, S., and Chen, D. (2010). Olfaction modulates visual perception in binocular rivalry. *Current Biology*, 20: 1356–8.

Zhou, W., Zhang, X., Chen, J., Wang, L., and Chen, D. (2012). Nostril-specific olfactory modulation of visual perception in binocular rivalry. *The Journal of Neuroscience*, 32: 17225–9.

Zmigrod, S. and Hommel, B. (2011). The relationship between feature binding and consciousness: Evidence from asynchronous multi-modal stimuli. *Consciousness and Cognition*, 20: 586–93.

Zmigrod, S., Spapé, M., and Hommel, B. (2009). Intermodal event files: Integrating features across vision, audition, taction, and action. *Psychological Research*, 73: 674–84.

Zmigrod, S. and Zmigrod, L. (2015). Zapping the gap: Reducing the multisensory temporal binding window by means of transcranial direct current stimulation (tDCS). *Consciousness and Cognition*, 35: 143–9.

Index

For the benefit of digital users, indexed terms that span two pages (e.g., 52–53) may, on occasion, appear on only one of those pages.